When East Meets West

When East Meets West
Media Research and Practice in US and China

Edited by

Fran C. Blumberg

CAMBRIDGE SCHOLARS PUBLISHING

When East Meets West: Media Research and Practice in US and China, edited by Fran Blumberg

This book first published 2007 by

Cambridge Scholars Publishing

15 Angerton Gardens, Newcastle, NE5 2JA, UK

British Library Cataloguing in Publication Data
A catalogue record for this book is available from the British Library

TABLE OF CONTENTS

Part II: Media Research

Part III: Media Education

LIST OF ILLUSTRATIONS

LIST OF TABLES

INTRODUCTION

FRAN C. BLUMBERG & MIN-KYUNG PARK, FORDHAM UNIVERSITY

The impetus for this book was a series of guest lectures for the "Issues in Applied Cognition" Institute sponsored by Fordham University's Graduate School of Education May 26-27, 2005 and convened at Fordham University in New York City and May 30-June 7, 2005 at The Beijing Center for Language and Culture in Beijing. The institute was a graduate level seminar in which the guest speakers represented leading researchers and practitioners in media research and production, media psychology, and journalism from two vital media capitals, New York City and Beijing.

The book that has since emerged is designed to serve as a reference that brings together theoretical perspectives, research findings, and cultural practice in the examination of media from a primarily Sino-American vantage point, as commented upon by Chinese, US, and U.K. researchers and practitioners. The need for such a reference is prompted by China's status as a nascent superpower and the ramifications of that emerging status for collaborative ventures and exchange of information with the US One flourishing context in which to engage in "sharing" is media. Such an example was demonstrated in The China's People's Daily Online (Harry Potter's "Goblet", 2005) reporting the remarkable success of Hollywood's newest Harry Potter film, that earned nearly 66.6 million yuan (8.2 million USD) in only 10 days. The National Committee on United States-China Relations (2006) also recently reported on an exchange program among Chinese journalists and US media and communication specialists to promote the media's role in informing the public about and preventing HIV/AIDS.

More ominous ramifications of the cultural exchange facilitated by the mass media are also in evidence. For example, Barboza (2005) reported for the *New York Times* on the market for professional gamers in China to play for Western patrons. One 23-year-old gamer is quoted as characterizing his work as highly lucrative,

> I make $250 a month, which is pretty good compared with the other jobs I've had. And I can play games all day.

The West also has capitalized on the Chinese interest in gambling as Las Vegas, the US gambling capital, packages Chinese New Year as a major holiday event. According to Friess (2007),

> The importance of Chinese New Year to the casino industry is clear by the lengths to which properties [in Las Vegas] go to court Asian gamblers during the holiday (p. A14).

Collectively, these examples highlight the reciprocal transmission of cultural content between the West, as exemplified here by the US, to the East, as exemplified by China; two countries with highly divergent societal norms, values, and history. However, as China continues to develop as a superpower, greater reciprocity will be apparent. The goal of this volume is to provide the basis for consideration of the theoretical and practical issues that both China and the US media will encounter as they move toward greater economic and political interdependence. This discussion will be approached through the lens of media practice, research, and education.

The practice section is dedicated to the voices of practitioners in media: media market researchers, journalists and editors, and developers of children's educational programs. The section opens with Yao's overview of the differing segments of China's current media industry, which has made rapid strides toward revenue generation since China joined the World Trade Organization in 2001. As Yao indicates, China's growing media industry has necessitated new policies governing the type of relationships permissible with internally and globally-based media organizations, and the accompanying need for greater numbers of media research professionals. How these policies will impact and be impacted by an industry whose sectors continue to grow at ever-faster rates both within and outside China will remain interesting "viewing" for years to come.

Tarnowsky's chapter (Chapter 2) provides a compelling survey of how photographs have been used to express and suppress political views within the US media. Drawing from his extensive experience working for one of the premier US news magazines, *Newsweek*, Tarnowsky illustrates how photographic images long have been used to manipulate public sentiment within the US and promulgate foreign policy in the world. The gravity of this influence has spawned myriad standards for how and in which media venue a given image should be used, or perhaps altered.

Nice's chapter (Chapter 3) elaborates on a particular photographic image, that of the magazine cover. According to Nice, covers telegraph to potential readers what content to expect and to what audience that content is directed. The intricacies of delivering this message to readers is discussed based on Nice's experience as a magazine editor and that of fellow editors of women's and girls' magazines.

A demonstration of the limitations of journalistic freedom is presented by former *South China Morning Post* reporter, Nailene Chou Wiest in Chapter 4. Wiest provides a historical context in which to understand the moral and professional issues that Chinese journalists must confront when reporting news in newspapers that are government controlled. Wiest presents examples of how current and former journalists have juggled what to present as truth, and the painful consequences that often accompany the decisions they make.

Shalom Fisch illustrates an example of how West meets East in the case of the vastly popular US educational television series, *Sagwa, the Chinese Siamese Cat*. This show is notable for its packaging of Chinese values and history for consumption by young US children. Fisch walks the reader through the extensive process whereby Chinese traditions are translated and made understandable for young viewers, while maintaining the integrity of these customs.

In the second section, discussions of empirical and qualitative research on media messages and media tools in both the US and China are presented. Shi's chapter (Chapter 6) opens the section with consideration of how the Chinese audience, the largest in the world, is responding to the new onslaught of global media, particularly films and television programs from the West. Shi illustrates how Chinese audiences' responses to what Shi calls "Hollywoodization," and "Disneyfication," have reflected a tempered enthusiasm; that is, Chinese viewers appreciate the opportunity to join a more global community via media but still show strong preferences for media reflective of their voice and their voice within the world.

Blades and Oates (Chapter 7) compare China and the West with reference to advertising that is directed toward children. Drawing on their expertise in the study of children's comprehension of and responses to advertisements, they demonstrate developmental universals in children' understanding of advertisers' intent to persuade.

Zhou et al., (Chapter 8) also examines the impact of advertisements on adults' consumer behavior in China and the US and find more differences than similarities. The authors specifically examine how the cultural congruency of visual elements of TV commercials might influence viewers' evaluation of and intention to purchase the advertised product. Their findings demonstrate the need to be mindful of cultural preferences when versioning advertisements for countries with differing cultural values.

Denk (Chapter 9) revisits issues of journalistic freedom in China in his qualitative study of media coverage of religion, which remains largely in the background of Chinese society and is interpreted as an expression of Chinese history and culture. In contrast, religion in the US often frames political issues. As part of his analysis, he compares media coverage of religious practices in

China from the Chinese media vantage point and that of media in other countries. He also contrasts how a major religious event, the election of a new pope, is interpreted in US, U.K., and Chinese media.

Zhang et al., (Chapter 10) present a brief report of research from their laboratory concerning effective designs for mobile cell phones used by Chinese consumers. As part of their investigation, they consider the impact of factors such as font and background colors and the scrolling style of text on users' comprehension of text-based messages. The importance of their work is underscored by the fact that China is currently home to the largest cell-phone market in the world.

The book concludes with a final section on media education. Craven and Hogan, as science educators, consider international efforts such as those underway in China and the US, to promote and assess science knowledge among their nation's pre-baccalaureate students (see Chapter 11). The authors also discuss efforts to promote understanding of science content presented via the media.

Blumberg, et al., (Chapter 12) consider how differences in the prominence of the three major media forms common to the US and China, namely newspapers, television, and the internet, have implications for the development of media literacy instruction among children and adolescents. This concern is pressing as both countries continue movement toward greater diversification of media and greater access by young users.

Clearly, the chapters within this volume offer a select set of snapshots of how media in China and the US look at one point in time. This moment is one that includes China preparing for the Beijing 2008 Olympics and the US grappling with its involvement in an unpopular war. However, as Tarnowsky indicates in his chapter on photojournalism, these visual images may capture a "decisive moment" in the fledgling media interdependency between the US and China.

References

Barboza, D. (2005) Ogre to slay? Outsource it to Chinese. *New York Times* (9, December).

Friess, S. (2007). Las Vegas adapts to reap Chinese New Year bounty. *New York Times* (21, February), A14.

Harry Potter's "Goblet" conjures up 66.56 million yuan in China (2005, November, 30). *People's Daily Online.* Retrieved December 12, 2005 from http://english.people.com.cn/205511/30/eng20051130_224505.html

National Committee on United States-China Relations (2006). HIV/AIDS and the media. *The National Committee on United States-China Relations Notes, 34*, pp. 11-13, & 27.

PART I: MEDIA PRACTICE

CHAPTER ONE

AN INSIGHT INTO MEDIA RESEARCH IN CHINA

YICHEN YAO, MILLWARD BROWN

At present, the China media industry includes 2,119 newspapers, 9,074 magazines, 570 publishing houses, 282 broadcast stations, 314 television (TV) stations, including 60 educational TV stations, 320 publishers of audio-visual products, 121 publishers of electronic publications, and 668,900 websites (Cui, 2005).

In November, 2005, China's largest media organization, China Central Television Station (CCTV), launched its annual auction for prime time advertisements for 2006. This event attested to the rapid growth of the media industry, which over the past three years has yielded an average growth rate of 27% for auction income. In fact, the income for 2005 reached 5.9 billion yuan (USD 0.7 billion), surpassing 2004's income of 5.2 billion yuan (USD 0.65 billion), 3.3 billion yuan (USD 0.4 billion) in 2003, and 2.6 billion yuan (USD 0.3 billion) in 2002 (Center for Media Operation & Management, 2005). Despite this rapid growth, the media industry remains under strict governmental control and does not accept investments from overseas investments.

How this industry will be transformed as China moves toward greater interdependence with other nations, particularly Western nations, remains an interesting question that first warrants an understanding of the historical and current basis for the China media industry as presented below.

The growth of the media industry in China

In both developed and developing countries, the media industry is generally comprised of TV, radio, newspapers, and magazines. These four traditional types are vital to the Chinese media industry, and in 2004 earned 120 billion yuan (USD 14.12 billion). These earnings also accounted for half of the income derived from all advertisement-based revenue in China (Cui, 2005a & b). The Chinese media market, however, encompasses more than traditional media. For example, according to a 2005 report by the Center for Media Operation and

Management, the media industry could be divided into 14 segments whose total output in 2005 exceeded 327 billion yuan (USD 39.64 billion). These 14 segments included book publications, box-office values of film, internet and cable TV fees, TV, internet games, and newspaper, TV, journal, and radio advertisements (See Fig. 1-1). The top five revenue producing segments were book publications (USD 14 billion), journal issues (USD 3.7 billion), and advertisements from advertisement agencies (USD 6.4 billion), TV (USD 3.9 billion), and newpapers (USD 3.3 billion) (See Fig. 1-2).

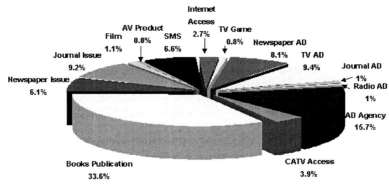

Fig. 1-1: Media industry segments in China (2004)
Data Source: Report on Development of China's Media Industry (2004–2005) (Cui, 2005a)

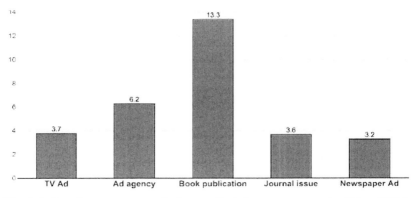

Fig. 1-2: Top five revenue producing media industry segments in China (2004) (Cui, 2005a)
Unit: billion USD Data Source: Report on Development of China's Media Industry (2004 - 2005)

Presented below are brief "snapshots" of these major segments of the industry as they stood in 2003 and 2004 for which comprehensive reports are available.

The press and publication industry (2004)

According to the Planning and Financial Department of the Press and Publication Administration of China, at the end of 2003, there were 570 publishing houses in the country responsible for the production of books, magazines, and newspapers. In that year alone, 190,391 book titles were published, an increase of 11.4% as compared to 2002. A remarkable 9,074 periodicals were published in 2003, with the average impression per issue reaching 20,000 copies. As compared with 2002, the number of periodicals increased by 0.5% as the average impression per issue decreased by 2.44%. Findings for 2003 also indicated that 2,119 different newspapers were published with the average impression per type reaching over 19,000 copies. This figure reflected a decrease by 0.84% in number while the average impression per issue increased by 1.88%.

Except for book publications, the growth rates for magazines and newspapers were relatively low, which could have reflected that media reform began in paper media, leading to more severe competition. Thus, some magazines and newspapers, especially international magazines such as Chinese versions of *Cosmopolitan, Elle*, and *Fortune,* attracted more readers while other magazines struggled. Simlarly, magazines such as *Readers* and *Zhiyin* that focused on national issues were more likely to attract a readership that those that concentrated on regional issues only.

In the case of newspapers, however, regional newspapers were more popular than national ones. This situation reflected the advertisement income in central cities in which regional newspapers were published such as Beijing (e.g. *Beijing Youth Daily, Beijing Daily*), Shanghai (e.g. *Xinming Daily*), and Guangzhou (e.g. *Guangzhou Daily*) which accounted for roughly 25% of the newspaper advertisement revenue in China in 2004 (Lin, 2005a).

The radio and TV industry

According to the Statistical Flash-report issued by the National Radio, Film and TV Administration in 2004, the coverage rate of national radio and TV continuously increased on a small scale as compared to the advertisement income and audience fees from the radio and TV industry throughout the country.

For example, the coverage rates of national radio and TV were 94% and 95% respectively, with an increase of 0.3% compared with the figures from the previous year, allowing 95% of areas in China to receive a TV signal (Cui, 2005a). The number of Cable Assist Television (CATV) users reached 114.7 million, reflecting an increase of 8.53 million compared to the previous year. Digital TV, which had been promoted in 2002, yielded 257,000 subscribers.

In 2004, the gross income of the national radio and TV industry was 76.5 billion yuan (USD 9.27 billion), and 5.97 billion yuan (USD 0.72 billion) respectively. These figures demonstrated the consistent expansion of the radio and TV industries within China. However, provinces and municipalities in Eastern China developed much faster than those in Western China, in accordance with the development status of the regional economy. In fact, Shanghai, Guangdong, Beijing, Jiangsu, and Shandong, all located in Eastern China were among the top five markets in gross income for the radio and TV industries.

Status of the advertising industry in China

According to statistics from the State Administration for Industry and Commerce of the People's Republic of China (PRC), by the end of 2003, there were 101,800 advertisement companies operating in China, reflecting an increase of 12,200 over that of 2002. The advertisement turnover amounted to 107.87 billion yuan (USD 13.1 billion), reflecting an increase of 17.6 billion yuan (USD 2.13 billion), or 19.44% compared with that of 2002, and accounted for 0.92% of the GNP (Yao, 2005). Fig. 1-3 shows that the revenue of the entire advertisement industry rapidly increased, especially in the periodical, radio, and TV advertisement sectors.

The sharp growth in the periodical sector may reflect that it is the most international media venue in China and a relatively inexpensive venue in which to advertise (Lin, 2005b). Except for magazines with largely political content, many world-famous fashion magazines (e.g. *Cosmopolitan* and *Elle*), and business magazines (e.g. *Fortune* and *Business Week*), all offer a simplified-characters Chinese version for readers in China. (Chinese can be written in two ways: simplified and traditional, although the pronunciation is very similar. Regions such as mainland China and Singapore currently use the simplified Chinese. Regions such as Hong Kong and Taiwan still use traditional Chinese.) As these magazines are aimed at people from middle-class and professional backgrounds, the advertising potential of these periodicals is greater than most other magazines.

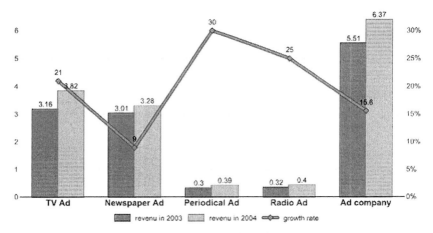

Fig. 1-3: Status of the advertisement industry in China (2003-2004)
Unit: Billion USD
Data Source: Report on Development of China's Media Industry (2004 - 2005)
(Cui, 2005a)

In 2004, the top 5 types of magazines that attracted the greatest number of advertisements were fashion (e.g. *Elle, Cosmopolitan, Ray*), business (e.g. *Fortune, Harvard Business Review*), computer (e.g. *Micro Computer, Internet Weekly*), city life (e.g. *Readers, City*) and vehicles. These different types of magazines accounted for roughly 75% of magazine advertisement in China in 2004 (Liang, 2005).

Rapid growth in the radio sector may be attributed to the increases in wealth in large cities such as Beijing and Shanghai where many individuals can now afford a car. As the car has become a normative mode of transportation for many citizens, radio advertising also has become increasingly popular, as car owners tend to listen to the radio while driving. The case of *Beijing Traffic Radio* provides a vivid example of the growth in the radio sector. This station mainly broadcasts traffic information to drivers in the city and its net advertisement revenue in 2004 exceeded 170 million yuan (USD 21.3 million), whereas the revenue in 1996 was only 1 million yuan (USD 0.13 million) (Liang, 2005).

Rapid growth in the TV sector may be attributed to its status as the most popular media venue with the greatest influence on consumers. For example, according to the *2004–2005 Behavior and Life Style Year Book* (2004), an annual national wide consumer study conducted by CTR (one of the largest marketing research company in China) with the Communication University of

China, roughly 92% of China's citizens in the 10 biggest cities (Beijing, Shanghai, Guangzhou, Shenzhen, Chengdu, Chongqing, Wuhan, Xian, Shenyang and Nanjing) watched TV every day, followed by newspapers (which, on average, are read daily by 60% of citizens), and radio (which, on average, is listened to daily by 20% of citizens). Thus, the vast popularity of TV among the Chinese public accounted for its popularity as a venue for advertisers, and consequently, the most expensive medium in which to advertise.

Advertisements are often seen as a reflection of the health of a country's economy and of the most successful industries within it. In 2003, the top five advertisement sectors in China were based in real estate, pharmaceuticals, food, electronic appliances, and cosmetics. Each of these sectors has at least doubled their spending on advertisements compared to 2002 as shown in Fig. 1-4. The estimated gross expenditure on advertisements was roughly 12.5 billion yuan (USD 1.6 billion) in 2004, with a growth rate of 15% as compared to 2003 (Cui, 2005).

Category	Amount of Spending (Unit: Billion USD)	Compared with 2002	Compared with total
Real estate	1.85	156.97%	14.75%
Medicines	1.55	134.16%	11.82%
Food	1.21	108.45%	9.30%
Electronic appliance	1.07	111.76%	8.16%
Cosmetic	0.88	110.27%	6.77%

Fig. 1-4: Status of top five Chinese advertisement sectors (2003)
Data Source: State Administration for Industry and Commerce

Comparison of major media companies in China and the US

As compared with the major media companies in the US, the companies in China are relatively small albeit with much potential for growth. CCTV, the largest media company in China, as of 2004, had revenue of about 8 billion yuan (USD 1 billion) (Sun & Liu, 2005), with the net revenue estimated at around 16 million yuan (USD 2 million). When compared with leading US companies such as *Time Warner Inc.* and *Disney*, the gap between their sizes is significant. In 2004, for example, the total revenue of *Time Warner Inc.* was 42 times that of CCTV (See Fig. 1-5) (Yahoo.com, 2005) The gap between media corporations in China and the US is also apparent in the internet sector. Specifically, internet companies in China have developed very quickly in the last few years, and some of them, such as Sohu and Sina (the top two Chinese internet sites with largest number of daily viewers), are listed in NASDAQ. However, their size remains very modest compared to the larger internet companies in the US (see Fig. 1-6).

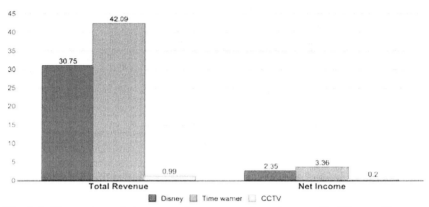

Fig. 1-5: Comparisons between total revenue and net income for Disney, Time Warner, and CCTV (2004); Unit: Billion USD
Data source: Yahoo Financial (Disney, Time Warner)

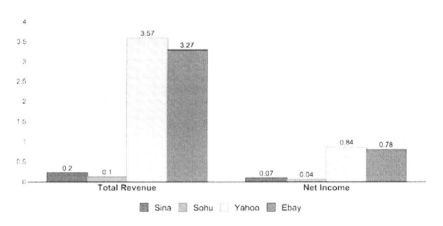

Fig. 1-6: Comparisons between total revenue and net income for Sina, Sohu, Yahoo, and Ebay (2004); Unit: Billion USD
Data source: Yahoo Financial (Disney, Time Warner)

Media policies

Changes in China's media policies have been influenced by entering the World Trade Organization (WTO) in 2001 and through new regulations and market openings, which have, in turn, had an impact on who can own a media business in China. For example, as compared to many other industries, the opening of the media industry has been slow, and until 2004, foreign investors could not establish businesses freely in the Chinese media market. In its report, *Temporary Regulation on Joint Venture Program Producing Company*, issued by the Ministry of Commerce and National Bureau of Radio, Film and TV in November, 2004, foreign companies were cited as not allowed to establish a production company without a partner from China. Even after having met this condition, the foreign company was limited to a 49% maximum stock share (Sun & Liu, 2005).

By the year 2004, most media companies were government-owned, and traditional media including TV and radio stations, continued to be state-owned. In the internet sector, however, a significant number of sites were privately owned. Specifically, all TV and, radio stations, and most newspapers and magazines were government-owned (called Party newspapers), whereas a small percentage of newspapers and magazines were owned and controlled by the Communist Party. Most websites, however, were owned by private companies or investors; some of which were listed on US stock exchanges, and in other countries.

According to Cui (2005a), most traditional media organizations in China are institutions, oriented more toward the government than the market, and are not bona-fide enterprises despite industrial characteristics such as company management and marketing strategies. For example, China's media industry is still highly monitored and controlled. In December 2004, 6 private TV stations were closed in Anhui province, and numerous county TV stations, that did not follow national broadcasting regulations, were severely punished (Sun & Liu, 2005). However, the continuing development of the economy has prompted the loosening of media regulations as well as the appearance of greater numbers of joint venture media companies.

It is widely understood that the media industry needs more investment and competition to develop. Thus, a media revolution has begun that will accelerate as an increasing number of regulations aimed at opening of the industry are introduced. When China signed the treaty to enter the WTO, the government agreed to open up the media industry in advertising, distribution of books, newspapers, and periodicals, audio and video products, cinema services, and importation of movies. However, China did not agree to open up the TV and radio industries, to allow foreign companies to establish their own TV or radio stations, or to participate in the sector through joint-venture companies. The negotiation of this situation was handled through a series of regulations. For example, one regulation applied to advertising agencies as ordered by the Ministry of Commerce in March, 2004, specified that the maximum amount of foreign investment in a cooperative advertising agency could amount to 70% of the total allocation. Solo foreign investment advertising agencies were allowed to form by December, 2005 (Cui, 2005b).

Despite regulations limiting foreign involvement in the Chinese media industry, foreign investors have managed to establish media-based businesses in China. For example, the News Corporation, was allowed to locate SKY TV in Guangdong province in March, 2002. (SKY TV is an entertainment channel focusing on TV drama, fashion, and music to the exclusion of programming on political, economic, and ethnicity issues.) One year later, it was allowed to locate in other provinces on a limited basis. The Dow-Jones AD (Shanghai) Co, Ltd., an advertisement corporation owned solely by foreign investment, was founded in China during August, 2004. Similarly, the first Sino-foreign film joint venture (Zhongying-Warner-Hengdian Film and Television Co, Ltd), established in October 2003, involved Zhongying, the largest film-maker in China; Hengdian, a Zhejiang-based TV drama and film company; and the Time Warner group based in the US (Cui, 2005a).

Clearly, the media industry in China has great potential as the last largely unopened industry to foreign investment. However, foreign investors also need to be mindful that the industry is still easily influenced by government policies, and still carries significant risks. In fact, there are some contradictory reactions to media change outside China. For example, some scholars believe that the media industry in China is becoming more open. According to Kalathil Shanthi, an associate at the Carnegie Endowment for International Peace in Washington D.C., the Chinese media no longer serves as a primarily a voice for the Party and the government. Less optimistic about the openness of the Chinese media is The Committee to Protect Journalists (CPJ), an independent organization based in New York, that continues to publish an annual report, *Attacks on the Press* (Wright, 2004), highlighting what it sees as the lack of progress in China's media industry. The report indicated that "it was a disappointing year for those who hoped that President Hu Jintao would allow a greater degree of freedom for China's increasingly market-oriented press" (Wright, 2004, p.7). The report also indicated that being a journalist was the third most dangerous career in China, after policeman and mineworker.

Clearly, the media environment in China is changing, but as compared with the amazing growth of the economy, the rate of change is relatively slow. The different voices from overseas observers show that the changes in China's media sector have been noticed, but still deviate from Western media operation standards.

Snapshot of the media research industry in China and its tools

The media research industry is a relatively small branch of the media industry overall and is designed to provide rating data and audience research reports to media operators. The first nationwide audience research study, *Sample Analysis on TV Audience in 28 Cities*, was conducted in 1986 by CCTV, and was subsequently seen as the benchmark for the media research industry in China. Although CCTV and other large TV stations initiated their own media research, soon thereafter they realized the need for help from professional media research companies. This need partially reflected the demand for adequate resources to collect the data and for professional researchers with the requisite skills to analyze and make sense of the data collected. Accordingly, professional services firms expanded to provide important research services to media organizations, advertisement agencies, and multinational companies.

The availability of media research service in China since the late 1980s is recent compared to developed countries such as the US, whose media research industry was established in the late 1920s. The impetus for the emergence of an independent market research industry was the industry reform that resulted from China's opening-up policy. Specifically, as the government began to cut state subsidies to media operators during the late 1990s, these operators, in turn, sought increased income from advertising. This shift formed part of the broader transition from solo state-owned to state-owned and market-oriented organizations as companies realized the need to better know their customers. This need was reflected in the establishment of professional media research firms.

Media research firms also developed as a result of growing competition in the rapidly expanding media market that began in the late 1990s. Given the pressure from foreign investors and new media such as the internet and cell phones, the traditional media operators also contributed to the general desire to better understand the audience so as to attract greater revenue. Similarly, the foreign companies that were establishing ventures in China, especially multinational companies, needed to know the potential effects of their actions before making investment and advertising decisions.

China's media research business is international partly because the industry is relatively new and partly because it serves a largely foreign clientele. Media research in China, as in the US, focuses on different forms such as TV, newspapers, and radio. The measurement of TV audience size is of greatest concern and Chinese media research companies currently follow global practices and regulations and use state-of-the art techniques to measure it. *The Global Guidelines for Television Audience Measurement*, co-published by the Europe Broadcasting Union, the US Advertisement Research Foundation, and the European Society for Opinion and Marketing Research in 1999, specifies basic regulations for Chinese companies that wish to measure Chinese television audiences. These regulations include how to identify the audience and how they should be treated during the course of collecting information about their viewing patterns. These regulations are widely adhered to by many top media agencies, such as AGB Nielsen Media Research. (See Shi, this volume, for greater consideration of the preferences of the Chinese audience.)

The primary methods used to measure audience in China are the diary card, the people meter, and the telephone interview, consistent with methodology used in the US and other countries. The diary card is perhaps the simplest way to collect data and entails having respondents complete information on all channels and programs they watch daily over the course of a week. The cards are then collected for analysis by the research companies. The people meter is a specially designed machine that is connected to a respondent's TV and records all programs watched during the survey period. The diary card and people meter are often used for long term monitoring of TV programs watched while random telephone interviews made to members of a target audience are usually used for evaluating a special TV event or to examine short-term viewing patterns.

The two major data suppliers in mainland China are CSM Media Research and AGB Nielsen Media Research. The former was founded in 1996 as a joint venture between CTR Market Research and the TNS Group from France. CSM Media Research is based in mainland China, and recently extended its business to Hong Kong. CSM Media Research operates both people meters and diary panels for most of the largest Chinese TV stations such as CCTV and Liaoning TV.

AGB Nielsen Media Research is a joint venture formed by the VNU Group (the world's largest research group, based in the Netherlands) and Kantar Group (the world's fourth largest research group, based in the UK) that provides TV audience research in 30 countries including China. AGB Nielsen Media Research started business in China in 1996 and now operates people meters in 12 cities and has panels in 11,600 households covering 72 Chinese cities. CSM and AGB Nielsen are the two major data suppliers in mainland China, and collectively occupy at least 90% of the TV audience measurement market (AGB Nielsen Media Research-China, 2005).

Notably, foreign companies such as P&G are much more likely to trust the data provided by AGB Nielsen, as the service they provide follows international standards and because the level of evaluation is comparable to   services available in other countries. Many advertising agencies, especially 4A

(American Association of Advertising Agencies) advertising agencies, are AGB Nielsen's clients. In fact, to attract more foreign companies, large TV stations in China such as Anhnui TV buy rating data from both CSM and AGB Nielsen. Normally, data provided by CSM will be highly regarded by local China companies; data from AGB Nielsen will be a selling point for multinational companies.

Other media research companies specialize in radio audience measurement or research on readers, such as the SMR Group based in Guangzhou. SMR conducts both media and marketing research and is responsible for the development of the SMR broadcast program evaluation and advertisement value analysis system and for annual publication of the *China Radio Market Research Report*. This report provides the most respected overview of the Chinese radio audience. For example, the 2005 report interviewed 9,000 people across 30 cities in China. The content of the report ranges from basic radio station preference in different markets to radio station marketing strategies.

Another company that is a leading brand in print media research is Sino Monitor International. This company was established in Beijing in 1998, and is responsible for publishing the annual *China Market and Media Study*, which is one of the largest continuous media consumption studies to be conducted in China. The study has covered 70,000 respondents across 30 cities in China every year since 1998 and is conducted in conjunction with the British Marketing Research Bureau (BMRB), and now represents China in the Target Group Index (TGI). TGI is a global network of single-source market research surveys that examine consumer and media consumption habits in over 50 countries and is used to help identify target markets and to aid in marketing and advertising decisions (TGI, 2005).

Increasing numbers of Chinese universities also have been implementing active media research and the establishment of academic institutes, three of which have strong national reputations in the media research field. One institute is the Survey and Statistic Institute (SSI) located at the Communication University of China that focuses on diverse kinds of media research including journalism, advertising, media management, program editing, and photography. The SSI, which was founded in 1992, enjoys a prestigious clientele including CCTV, the International Olympic Committee, and the People's Bank of China.

The Public Opinion Research Center (PORC) is affiliated with Renmin University of China. Since its start in 1986, the PORC has provided consultant services to many media organizations such as People Daily, CCTV, and Beijing TV Station. One of the newest centers, founded in 2003, is the Center for Media Operation and Management at Tsinghua University. In 2005, it published *Media Blue Book—Report on the Development of Media Industry of China (2004-2005)*, which was the first report to describe the media market in China and was recommended by The State Council Information Office to foreign investors during the Fortune Forum in Beijing, May 2005.

How are ratings used in China

Because TV is the most popular media venue in China, with an advertising income of around USD 3.7 billion in 2005, TV audience measurement is the largest market in media research. Rating analysis, which includes a series of indexes such as Gross Rating Point (GRP), shows how many people watched a given program, and program market share, which is used to understand competition status during a particular time period, is the main product from media research and is designed to elucidate characteristics of the Chinese audience. This information, in turn, has implications for decisions about program positioning, adjustment of program content, program scheduling or line-ups, and program cancellations.

As in other countries, TV station operators, independent producers, advertisement agencies, and advertisers are the main users for these ratings although each venue may require different indexes. For example, TV station operators require reports examining market share, audience impressions, and competition status to help them produce better programs to attract more viewers. Advertisers may require advertisement cost information or a target consumers analysis to help their client market to certain audiences and develop media plans to approach them. Independent producers need rating information to sell their program to TV stations and advertisers.

Access to rating data is often limited as only the largest TV stations can afford to purchase it. Among 314 TV stations in China, at most one third of them have bought rating data, and TV stations in small or middle-sized cities are unable to do so. However, an increasing number of smaller media research companies such as China Television Communication (CTC) have been established to provide services for smaller stations. Since 2004, CTC has provided rating information to TV stations like Tangshan and Handan (both which are middle size cities in Hebei province). In 2005, service to other small TV stations in Henan province was initiated.

When considering TV rating data in China, the political orientation of a program also is considered in conjunction with measures such as return on investment (ROI). However, more objective measures of program appeal are typically given greater weight when evaluating programs that should be retained or potentially cancelled. Efforts are underway by TV stations such as CCTV and the China Radio and TV Society to develop rating systems that take into account political orientation, media pundits, ROI, and audience appeal. In fact, CCTV launched its own rating system in 2003. This system, however, continues to evolve.

Understanding the Chinese audience through ratings

Ratings, particularly those for TV, are ultimately used to understand the Chinese audience with respect to who they are, what they like to watch, and when they watch. For example, findings from the *China TV Report 2002—2003*, co-published by CSM and the Communication University of China, indicate that, like other countries, 7:00 pm—10:00 pm is prime time for China's audience. TV also is watched most around the Spring Festival, the lunar New Year, which typically falls between late January and early February. Compared with audiences in South China, those in North China are more likely to watch TV. Overall, females are more likely to watch than males. The three favorite program genres are TV drama, news, and documentaries. The primary audiences for these shows are students, workers, and government officials.

According to a survey conducted in 2005 by Eurodata TV Worldwide, a European media research company (Liu, 2005), Chinese audiences spend only 150 minutes per day watching TV while the global average is 180 minutes. For example, the Japanese average is 301 minutes (number 1 globally) and the US average is 248 minutes (number 2 globally). One proposed reason for China's low average is that people are able to purchase DVDs of favored programs at very low prices, which diverts them, particularly the young, from broadcast programs.

What is next for the media research industry?

In 2004, the media industry of China accounted only for 2.3% of the GDP. In developed countries, such as the US and Great Britain, the media industry usually accounts for approximately 5% of the GDP. The Chinese journal *Securities Daily*, however, predicts that the media industry will become a backbone of the Chinese national economy by 2008 (Cui, 2005b).

The advertising industry, as linked with the media in China, also is expected to blossom. For example, the CEO of multinational media giant WPP group, Martin Sorrell, predicts that China will be the second largest advertising market in the world by the end of 2008 (See People's Daily Online, August 27, 2005). The advent of the 2008 Olympic Games and the continued development of the Chinese economy also insure that the media industry will attain status as a vital industry.

Author's note

Special thanks are extended to Dr. Ron. J. Anton, director of The Beijing Center for Chinese Studies, and to Leon Li for their helpful comments on this chapter.

References

AGB Nielsen Media Research. (2005). *Network coverage.* Retrieved from http://www.agbnielsenmediaresearch.com/whereweare/countries/china/china .asp?lang=english.

Center for Media Operation and Management. (2005). *The report on China's mass media industry: 2004-2005. China New Opportunity—Media.* The State Council Information Office, People's Republic of China.

China Advertising Association. (2004). *China advertising yearbook—2004.*

CSM. (2005). *CSM wins Hong Kong TV research contract.* Retrieved from http://www.csm.com.cn/en/news/050706.html

CSM. (2005). *Network coverage.* Retrieved from: http://www.csm.com.cn/en/network/ index.html

CSM & Communication University of China. (2003). *China TV report 2002— 2003.*

Cui, B. (2005a). *Report on the development of China media industry (2004 - 2005),* China: Science Academic Press.

—. (2005b). Structural reform and transition: 2005 general report of development of China's media industry. *China New Opportunity—Media.*

Liang, W. (2005). *Advertising strategies of Beijing traffic radio.* China: The Social Science Academic Press.

Lin, Y. (2005a). *China's newspaper advertising market: 2004 analysis.* China: The Social Science Academic Press.

—. (2005b). *China's periodical advertising market: 2004 analysis.* China: The Social Science Academic Press.

Liu, Z. (2005). Survey on TV consuming world wide. *The Beijing News.* Retrieved from http://ent.sina.com.cn/x/2005-04-15/1042703275.

Ministry of Commerce of the People's Republic of China. (2004). *Rules for foreign enterprises investing to ad enterprises.* Retrieved from http://www.hebgs.gov.cn/yw/yp/ygs_bszn_content.asp?articleid=769

Murdoch, R. (2004, September 24). *The value of culture industry.* Retrieved from http://www.china.org.cn/chinese/zhuanti/qkjc/667274.htm

People's Daily Online (2005, May 27). *China's mass media industry claims 30 million Yuan market scales in 2004.* Retrieved from: http://english.people.com.cn/200505/27/eng20050527_187162.html

Phoenix TV. (2003, June 20). *China's ad market will rank 2nd by the end of 2010.*

Retrieved from:
http://www.phoenixtv.com/home/finance/cjxw/200306/20/76719.html
Shanthi, K. (2002, Winter). Chinese media and the information revolution. *Harvard Asia Quarterly*. Retrieved from:
http://www.carnegieendowment.org/publications/index.cfm?fa=view&id=92
4
SMR. (2005). SMR Group official website. Retrieved from:
http://www.smr.com.cn/
Sun & Liu (1995). *Report on Development of China's Media Industry (2004-2005)*. China: The Social Science Academic Press.
TGI. (2005). TGI International website. Retrieved from:
http://www.tgisurveys.com
The State Administration of Radio Film and Television (2004). *Opinions on promoting the development of radio, film and television industry*. Retrieved from http://www.sarft.gov.cn/manage/publishfile/21/1568.html
—. (2004). *Temporary rules for managing Sino-foreign joint ventures and cooperative enterprises producing and operating radio and television program*. Retrieved from:
http://www.sarft.gov.cn/manage/publishfile/21/3289.html
WPP predicts China's ad market will grow to be world's NO. 2(2005, August, 27). *People's Daily China Online* (English). Retrieved from:
http://english.people.com.cn/200508/27/eng20050827_204913.html
Wright, A. (2004). *Attacks on the press 2004*. Retrieved from www.cpj.org
Yahoo.com. (2005). *Time Warner Inc: Income statement*. Retrieved from:
http://cn.finance.yahoo.com/q/uis?s=TWX&annual
Zheng L. (2005). Survey on TV consuming world wide. *The Beijing New*. Retrieved from http://ent.sina.com.cn/x/2005-04-15/1042703275.html

CHAPTER TWO

UNDERSTANDING PUBLISHED PHOTOGRAPHIC IMAGES IN CONTEXT

TOM TARNOWSKY

Interpretation of perceived stimuli is subjective. We all use our previously gained knowledge in efforts to understand the accumulated fragments of experiences from our daily lives. To interpret the meaning of visual images seen every day, the same skills are employed as those used for the written word, music, or any sensory experience. The present is informed by the past.

We are constantly bombarded by the ubiquitous media of the 21st century. For example, we now have the internet and its attendant tools and services in portable laptop computers, PDA devices, and increasingly sophisticated cell phones capable of making and emailing photos and videos as well as receiving news reports and entertainment. Local and international libraries, universities, and archives of all types are making public their increasingly digitized collections, including photographs and graphics of all kinds. The amount of available information seems almost unlimited, even to practiced researchers. With the efforts of search engine companies such as Google, the amount of available information will grow far beyond what is now accessible.

The speed at which images appear and disappear in modern media, and the virtually unlimited number of images available in all media, can make any single image seem less important. For many readers who engage in frequent multitasking, quick glances and instantaneous judgments are made while attention is divided among various interests. One might be captured by an image long enough to think about it in a conscious way. Often, we see images only fleetingly while flipping through pages of print or electronic editorial and commercial content. The reader's judgment is used, not necessarily consciously, each time an image flickers briefly on a screen. A viewer's interest may or may not be captured. There is intense competition among print and online publishers vying for a few seconds of the reader's attention. Glance at the offerings of any newsstand to see which cover art jumps out at you, becoming successful for that instant in winning your eye and perhaps your purchase. The reader is referred to Nice, this volume, for greater consideration of this issue.

In 2005 alone, according to the Magazine Publishers of America (MPA), 350 new magazines were launched on the American market. In 2006, 101 magazines were started in the first three months of the year. The MPA counted 1,400 consumer magazine titles among its members in 2006 (MPA, n.d.). The American Society of Magazine Editors (ASME) lists over 19,000 titles (MPA, n.d.). Add to this, local, regional, and national newspapers, the web versions of most print media, various internet portals to a seemingly unlimited variety of websites, and proliferating media via broadcast, cable, satellite, and cell phone. Almost all media depend heavily on graphic images as an integral part of the mix of information offered. It is within this burgeoning multimedia framework that we will attempt to understand photo images and the thousand words a good picture is said to be worth.

Musicians often refer to someone who listens to a wide variety of music as someone who has big ears. In the same way, a reader who pays attention to a wide range of media might be said to have big eyes. The best way towards a good understanding of the visual media is to absorb as many sources as possible, no easy task in the rich soup of old fashioned print and modern electronics. In addition, many readers/viewers pay attention only to sources that reinforce their existing social, political, or aesthetic prejudices or to only a narrow range of media of personal interest. Many media consumers now receive most of their information from television or internet sites, rarely casting a glance at a printed newspaper. Ideally, a media consumer would sample a wide range of sources for information and opinion. But the day has only 24 hours and one needs one's sleep.

Photographs as communicators of ideas: A brief history

One media venue that has a longstanding history of attracting the viewer's eye is that of photography. Daguerreotype photography was introduced in 1839 in France. Each image was one of a kind. Many technical advances followed, but it was not until improvements in printing press technology that precise and realistic halftone photographs could be published on the printed page. During the American Civil War of the 1860s, viewable news photos of battlefields were displayed in galleries owned by Matthew Brady and other photography pioneers, necessarily limiting access to those realistic images. After the turn of the 20th century, the strong impact of realistic photo imagery quickly made it an intrinsic part of the newspaper publishing formula. The first box cameras and glass negatives used by photojournalists often required tripods to hold the heavy equipment steady. Only a few photos of an event could be produced with this cumbersome paraphernalia. As lighter sheet and roll film was developed and film speed increased as camera size decreased, photographers became better able to record many aspects of an event. The advent of the 35 millimeter film camera allowed photographers greater flexibility and ease of movement, and ushered in the beginning of modern photojournalism as we know it today. News photography is still evolving as it takes advantage of the rapid advance of digital technologies.

At its extremes, photography can be employed in the service of the highest human aspirations or it can pander to base instincts and to ignorance, fear, and hatred. Among the many uses of photography to which the medium can be employed, the unadorned reality of news photos should rank high. A free press is a basic tenet of American law and culture, codified in the First Amendment to the US Constitution. Visual images are an integral part of that free press. The citizens of most Western cultures would agree that shining a bright light on a festering problem goes a long way towards curing it, but each country has its own values and traditions affecting the production of news. Stability is often valued more highly than the risk of upheaval from the widespread exposure of troublesome realities. Countries have laws concerning press freedom, privacy, libel and public safety, as well as varying definitions of each. All affect the ultimate use of news photos. Other applications for photography are used in commerce, art, politics, science and technical specialties, and the study of history. In fact, it is sometimes difficult to determine the influences of news, art, or commerce in a single photograph. For purposes of this article we will consider primarily still photographic images in the context of print media and the internet as they are used for photojournalism.

News and photojournalism

News photography can be defined as the unembellished documentary recording of current events as they happen, using a range of photographic styles in an attempt to tell the truth. A wide range of events fit this definition, from a simple "man in the street" interview, to a war photographer covering battlefield action. Although conflict is not a necessary element of photojournalism, it often offers the strongest images. One view, popularized during the 1960s, an era of American and European student activism, maintained that the mere presence of a photographer altered the behavior of those photographed. For example, demonstrators have been known to perform for the camera to gain more attention for their cause. A practiced photographer will often try to be as unobtrusive as possible to avoid upsetting the natural progress of an event, but it is not always possible to be a "fly on the wall" in the middle of a riot. Modern demonstrators in countries outside the United States often carry signs bearing their messages in English, knowing they will get more recognition in American media. "Death to America" is a strong message only if Americans can read and understand it.

The "decisive moment", as described by photographer Henri Cartier-Bresson (1952), is the ideal many photographers seek. It is that frozen moment that can sum up an entire event, an idea, or reveal the character of a personality in one telling image when the picture becomes a good composition, rising to a level of artistic expression from that of the straightforward transmission of information. The image can record a quiet pastoral moment, a tragic event, or anything in between. It can become the photo that tells a story.

News photographers, like many journalists, are often committed idealists, many with strong social and political views, driven by conscience to be the documentary witnesses of great events. They are intent on showing the truth as they see it through their sometimes risky assignments in countries embroiled in turmoil. Even as they attempt to adopt an attitude of professional detachment, photographers are rarely seen as neutral observers of events by the participants in a conflict. Readers are often unaware of the human costs paid by journalists in pursuit of a story. Despite the danger, many photographers are drawn to areas of conflict because the stark images at hand are much more likely to offer the opportunity for a clear view of the elemental forces driving current events. Conflict has often produced the strongest news photos.

In fact, the Committee to Protect Journalists, a professional advocacy group, reported 47 journalists confirmed killed worldwide in 2005 and 85 killed in Iraq alone since 2003, in addition to 35 translators, drivers, and guards working for them in the dangerous environment of an unstable country. These numbers do not count the wounded and some whose deaths cannot be confirmed. Classic American images of conflict are numerous from the era of civil rights demonstrations and the Vietnam War. Prize winning photos include the African-American civil rights marcher in Boston beaten with his own American flag standard by a counter-demonstrator as well as one of the student killed by National Guard rifle fire at Kent State University in Ohio in 1970 during an anti-war demonstration. The brutality of war was illustrated in the streets of Saigon in the image of the summary execution of a suspected guerilla at the moment of his death. The horrors of war visited on civilian populations is remembered in the image of a young naked Vietnamese girl running towards the camera, her clothes having been burned off by a napalm fire bomb attack during military action.

Most photo assignments, however, are not dangerous. Sometimes a photo capturing a standard event can crystallize the opposing views in a public debate of an important issue. One such event occurred in 1994 when the top executives of seven major tobacco companies were sworn in as a group before a US House of Representatives Subcommittee on Health and Environment. Each executive testified under oath that he believed nicotine was not addictive. The image of the seven hands raised in unison is a classic photo in the debate over the health effects of cigarettes. Years after the event, the image is often used to illustrate the continuing debate. The photo tells a large part of the "story" as any good photo will. Even photos of the most common triumphs and tragedies such as fatal car crashes, house fires, sporting contests, family events, and school graduation ceremonies can tell a detailed story if a good photographer captures the elusive decisive moment.

Photo essays: Are ten photos better than one?

When space and budget allow, publishers will sometimes devote more space for additional photos on a single story. When given the opportunity, many photojournalists and their editors try to document an important story or theme over an extended period of time to gather views of a particular world unavailable to most people. The resulting photo essays are often striking for their intimate detail and artistic dimensions usually beyond the possibilities of a daily news assignment. The themes are often social, political, or anthropological in nature, but can range across a wide array of subject matter. The variety of photos gives the reader a wider look at human and geographic details, forming a more complete picture of the issue or event. Recent examples of this type of story would be the extended coverage in 2005 of Hurricane Katrina in New Orleans, the Pacific tsunami, the refugee crisis in Darfur, Sudan, and the conflicts in Iraq and Afghanistan. A classic photo series by W. Eugene Smith documents the tragic health consequences of industrial mercury poisoning, known as Minimata Disease, in a fishing village in Japan after World War II. Smith's photo essay is a standard point of reference for any photojournalist.

The results of these long term photo essay efforts can be found in *National Geographic* magazine or newspapers and other news and feature magazines and photo industry magazines such as Photo District News (PDN) that covers the photo business in general, across a wide range of specialties, from news to art and fashion.

Photojournalism in context

Each publication, of any type, has its own standards and reputation for accuracy and fairness, ranging from "bible of the industry" to "tabloid trash" and "partisan propaganda." Many publications are seen by critics as too far to the left or to the right in the political spectrum, pro- or anti-business, and slanted one way or the other in their editorial coverage. The preferences of their readers as reflected in circulation numbers determines the success of a publication, since most are dependent on advertising revenue for profits and advertising rates are, in turn, dependent on readership circulation numbers. One million readers of every issue published can be a powerful endorsement of editorial policies, whatever they may be.

In the quest for understanding, awareness of the context in which a photo appears can be as important as the image itself. The same photo can be used by two different publishers for opposite reasons; one laudatory, one critical. The editorial slant of the publication should be taken into account when evaluating a photo. The local business journal likely has a different point of view than the local alternative lifestyle paper reporting the same story. Even publications of almost equal status can produce the same story with very different editorial results. One need only compare the *Time* and *Newsweek* issues of June 27, 1994 in which the cover picture of O.J. Simpson, a US former sports hero accused and eventually acquitted of murdering his wife and her friend, was retouched by *Time* magazine to make him look more sinister. *Newsweek* used the same photo un-retouched (see Fig. 2-1).

Fig. 2-1: *Newsweek* cover picture of O.J. Simpson, US former sports hero, acquitted of murdering his wife and her friend, on the left and retouched photo used by *Time* on the right.

US publications clearly cover a wide range of editorial values. A reader of
any of them should be aware of the biases they are widely thought to exhibit so
as to be able to interpret their choices of published stories and photos. For
example, The *New York Times*, *Washington Post*, *Time* magazine, *Newsweek*,
and *The New Yorker* magazine are seen as serious national publications, often
pejoratively referred to as the "liberal media" by conservatives, but seen as
mainstream by those who read them. *National Review* magazine and the *Weekly
Standard* are criticized as "conservative mouthpieces" by those of more liberal
opinions. The *Wall Street Journal* is seen as a dependably friendly paper to big
business interests. *USA Today* is a daily news digest meant to appeal to the
widest possible national audience.

Tabloid style local newspapers such as the *New York Post* and the *New York
Daily News*, featuring bold headlines, detailed sports coverage, local politics,
crime reporting, gossip pages and scandals have a more populist orientation,
appealing primarily to the working class audience who are often skeptical of
getting a fair shake from the higher powers. Their editorial slant ranges from
left to right, depending on the issue.

Most of the publications listed above are referred to as "corporate media" by
smaller, left-leaning, independently owned publications such as local
alternative lifestyle papers. It might help a reader to know who the corporate
parent is of any publication to gauge the editorial independence of the
newspaper or magazine in question. Indeed, large corporations and billionaires
do own a large number of publications. Depending on their aims and ethics,
they can be very good publications, supported by the deep pockets of their
owners. Reporting and photography assignments are expensive, custom made
efforts, often requiring extensive resources and manpower to produce only a
few columns of copy and one accompanying photo.

In many countries censorship is seen as necessary to protect the state. Photos
of labor strife, insurrection, catastrophic accidents, famine or other upheavals
are not likely to be exposed in the media. The stark imagery would be seen as
an embarrassment and a threat to the governing hierarchy. Writers, artists and
photographers are sometimes banished, imprisoned, or forbidden to work in
their chosen field if they are considered a threat to the status quo. (See Chou-
Wiest, this volume, for discussion of media censorship in China.)

To get a sense of how much effort can go into producing fair and balanced
coverage of a big story at a reputable newspaper, read the Sept. 10, 2006
"Public Editor" column by Byron Calame of The *New York Times* on the
subject of military action between Israel and Hezbollah in Lebanon. Internal
discussions over the use of news photography at the newspaper are revealed by
the *New York Times*' own in-house critic to explain the resulting coverage of
the story. The very fact that a "public editor" exists might reassure readers that

editors are trying to be fair in their coverage. Also, see an additional Public Editor column by the same author in the October 22, 2006 *New York Times* on the topic of protecting the quality of "hard news" production values by subsidizing them with the advertising revenues from the "soft news" sections of the paper. The column addresses the economic pressures the old print media are under and how those pressures might affect the quality of the reporting.

In all cases, consideration of the source is of paramount importance. The choice of photos used in a particular publication might reflect a prevailing bias. One newspaper might use a photo of an individual in a pose of authority to present him in the best possible light. Another publication might use a photo of the same person making him look less heroic, or even untrustworthy if the subject is less revered. US President Richard Nixon offered photo opportunities for both types of treatment. Much was made of his five o'clock shadow of a beard and his sometime awkward posture by those who wanted to accentuate his negative attributes. Clearly, the reader must decide whether a publication is being fair in the treatment of a public issue or of an individual subject.

Editorial standards in photojournalism: Hard or soft?

Editorial standards can vary widely, even at different departments of the same publication. The "hard news" local, national, international, and business sections of a newspaper probably have different rules and editing standards than the Arts and Leisure or other "soft news" sections. News events happen, are witnessed and captured by photographers, but are not overtly influenced by their actions. The "soft news" or "feature" stories are often engineered to a high degree by editors producing images in a photo studio and by celebrities and their agents trying to create a positive impression. Demands are often made by photo subjects for their own choice of photographer and makeup artists in return for their cooperation. Aesthetic qualities dominate production of such articles. It is a case where art direction trumps news in the production of a photo.

News is a serious attempt to inform the public of important events and trends. Photos accompanying news stories are likely to be factual representations and specific to the attached story. They are usually fresh photos, produced within the current news cycle, but can also be relatively recent "stock" photos from a news photo archive.

Soft news or service feature articles might have a serious intent in the form of "news you can use" such as advice and information on available financial, medical, or educational options. Just as often, they are meant to entertain and the accompanying service article photo may be a more generic illustration in the form of a stock photo from a commercial archive. For instance, a business article about the proliferating uses for office work done on desktop computers could be illustrated with a pre-existing photo of an office worker with one or more computers mounted on her desk. Such photos often come from a "stock" archive of photos on a wide range of general subjects. They are not necessarily produced for the story to which they are attached. Art production departments of publications are also very good at quickly producing photo illustrations from available stock materials. Movie still photos used in a review of a new film come from the movie production company, usually through a publicists' office. They are "publicity" photos, a form of advertising. Pictures in a food magazine can be from a commercial archive offering a wide range of basic food images that have been photographed from every possible angle with many variations of lighting and special effects. There are usually thousands of images available from various sources on any general subject. An experienced researcher can find hundreds to choose from within a short period of time. Almost all modern commercial photo archives make their digitized photo collections available from websites to clients with a password.

Whether the story is hard news or a soft feature, events can be manipulated by public relations specialists, business interests, politicians, and other interested parties for their own purposes. We have all seen press conferences at which a spokesperson tries to put a particular spin on events in the public eye. How many times have you seen a criminal defense lawyer describe his client as an honor student or the victim of a political witch hunt? A US congressman, Tom DeLay of Texas, indicted for violating campaign finance laws, made sure to smile for his police mugshot, making it look more like a high school graduation picture than the standard glum expression of a police booking photo.

In the field of still photography, "Photo Ops" are what politicians and others offer in a graphically rich setting, meant to refer to the point of view they are promoting and to build their public images. Consider all the interested parties pointing fingers of blame after Hurricane Katrina in New Orleans in 2005. Consider the pictures of sympathetic politicians commiserating with victims in the rubble of any earthquake, tsunami or typhoon. Advance teams are often sent to manufacture a tableau on site, so that a visiting dignitary can simply walk into the picture and pose for a few minutes while being generously covered by the press corp, armed with cameras and microphones for the picturesque imagery and sound bite to be broadcast on the television evening news and displayed on tomorrow's front page. Political election campaigns are especially likely to try to engineer events for their candidates. These types of events often make good pictures and they must be covered as news events by a responsible press, but a discerning reader should be able to read between the lines of the images and accompanying stories. Clearly, it is not always easy to tell the genuine from the manufactured event. Political and commercial entities with the ability to manipulate the press often attempt to do so for their own ends.

Sometimes it is the pictures you do not see that convey meaning. Censorship by government or self censorship by the media can affect the reader's exposure to reality. Press access to multiple flag draped coffins of American war dead arriving at a US military base from Iraq was abruptly ended. The issue of respect for the dead and their grieving families was raised by government spokespersons. Members of the media argued that the government was trying to hide the growing human cost of the war. Both arguments have merit, depending on ones beliefs, but it often said that "truth is the first casualty of war."

Photoillustrations

Photoillustrations, generated by multi-talented photographers and illustrators, have become a very popular hybrid of photographs and illustrations, even in serious news coverage. The boundary between photography and artist-generated illustrations can blur almost imperceptibly when advanced art and production techniques are combined. Generally, they show an abstract concept using whole or partial photos in a form combined with elements of illustration. They are imaginative, often humorous attempts, to show a complex idea in the form of a simple visual conceit. The results often synthesize an idea difficult to portray adequately with a simple news photo of a person or event. For example, to illustrate a stock market crash in an original way, photographs of rodeo bulls, representing the bulls of Wall Street, were used in a magazine illustration during the high tech stock collapse in 2001, showing the bulls leaping from a cliff. The clichéd alternative would have been to use a trading floor picture of stockbrokers, an image seen dozens of times by any reader of the financial pages. A photo of a politician in legal trouble might be shown on the deck of a sinking ship. Workers racing to save enough for their retirement years have been photographically portrayed as track and field athletes leaping over hurdles toward their financial finish line.

Almost all this work involves using electronic image scanners or computer illustration software to manipulate the various photo elements of the composition into a new piece of art. The photo editor or art director usually discusses visual concepts with an illustrator/photographer until a good idea is agreed upon, to the benefit of the reader who can, with the addition of a skillfully written headline, usually recognize the general theme of the story with a casual glance at the newly created photoillustration. Ethical considerations are usually taken into account when the line between photo and art is blurred. The "credit line" accompanying such art should be prominently displayed and read, "Photoillustration by..." to help the observant reader recognize the difference between a real and a manipulated photo. It is not always easy to tell the difference.

An issue related to photo illustration is the surreptitious manipulation of news photos. Sophisticated computer retouching tools are widely available and sometimes employed beyond merely sharpening a slightly blurry photo, correcting the color balance, or cropping to eliminate distracting elements. Many photographers and photo editors have been criticized or lost their jobs over unethical manipulation of images. Although efforts to manipulate photographic images extends back to the early years of photography, current techniques can produce undetectable changes that add or eliminate important elements of a picture, changing the "reality" of the information contained in favor of a better composition or a more convenient "truth" fitting editorial or artistic demands. In the early days of photography, before ethical photojournalism practices were seriously considered, American Civil War photographers were known to move the bodies of battlefield casualties into more aesthetically pleasing positions to compose a better photo. Today, although extensive retouching and manipulation of the subject is an exception rather than the norm at publications with ethical guidelines, it does occasionally happen. High ethical standards for the realistic portrayal of news events are not universally followed.

Manipulations of photos raise the question of how much truth and reality one image can transmit. Since most news photos are taken with camera shutter speeds measured in hundredths of a second, one could argue that any single photo is no more than a momentary reality. One's perception of an event or a personality can be manipulated by a poor or biased choice of photographs. In most cases, the larger context of the still news photo can only be inferred from other knowledge we have of current events and history. To put it another way, nothing stands alone. Everything is connected.

Photography other than photojournalism

Commercial Photography

Most publications and many websites cannot exist without advertising, the major source of revenue and profits. Magazines have advertising pages and most websites have popup ads and commercial links to grab readers' attention with expensively produced high quality graphics. For many years, alcoholic beverages, cigarettes and automobiles, known as "booze, butts, and buggies" were a primary source of advertising revenue. It should be no surprise that editorial coverage of these areas was often covered more gently than other news stories, damping criticism of their products and practices.

There is a very wide range of specialties in commercial photography. Indeed, almost all other areas of photography are utilized by commercial interests to sell products or services, relying heavily on art, fashion and special illustrative effects to appeal to customers. It is sometimes difficult to tell where editorial ends and advertising begins within a publication or website, especially in feature publications such as "shelter" magazines whose articles often utilize furniture, fixtures, and appliance products advertised in the same issue. Lifestyle publications, travel, car, and entertainment publications, for example, all have advertising tailored to appeal to their respective audiences.

Art photography

Photo galleries and aesthetically oriented magazines such as the *New Yorker* and other fashion, design, travel and leisure, and lifestyle magazines use a wide variety of art photography for their editorial and advertising pages, ranging from stark black and white portraiture to abstract designs.

History

Picture archives provide a way to keep in touch with and learn from the past. Historic photos provide visual samples of what the world was like before our own lives. Horse drawn trollies, sailing ships, coal stoves, derby hats, and starched collars no longer exist, but even inconsequential images from past eras show us how much material change has taken place during a century of industrial and political revolutions.

Recent technological changes in photojournalism

Rapid technological changes have affected how photos are taken, edited, and stored. With the recent advent of digital cameras, more possibilities for editing and manipulation are available to the photographer on assignment and for the editor in the office. Photographers now have the ability to regularly see their work and pre-edit it, if permitted by their editors, before transmitting photos electronically to the main office. Digital darkroom software allows the photographer to optimize the quality of the pictures very quickly. Some publications allow pre-editing by the working photographer and some frown on it as a matter of editorial control. Previously, most rolls of exposed but unprocessed film were quickly sent to the office on tight deadlines, sometimes thousands of miles by courier, especially for color film, which is not easily developed on the fly. In most cases the photographer would see his own work published days or weeks later, and might never see the entire assignment of numerous rolls shot on assignment until months later, if ever. Now, standard photo equipment includes a laptop computer with a built-in modem over which the images can be edited and sent instantaneously from almost anywhere in the world.

Exceptions during the days of film technology were in sports photography or other daily deadline news work shot at a distance from the home office. A photographer or an assistant often set up a temporary darkroom in a stadium, broom closet, or hotel bathroom so that the film could be "souped" on the spot and the best photos "wired" on bulkier pre-computer analog versions of electronic scanners and transmitters. The rolls of film shot led to voluminous files of "outtakes," most stored in file "morgues," rarely viewed again, but occasionally providing an important photo not recognized at the original event. One recent example is the "ropeline" photo of President Bill Clinton greeting the then unknown Monica Lewinsky, a relationship that led to the impeachment of a US president. The new digital memory cards on which photos are stored are often erased quickly after editing for reuse, so that outtakes are becoming a thing of the past. The use of film cameras, although not obsolete, is fading fast in the news business.

Editorial decisions about what is published

The judgment of photo editors and other decision makers at a publication is influenced by their own needs and perceptions, including editorial prejudices, budget constraints, critical feedback from readers, and business concerns of publishers. No editor wants to be blamed for the loss of paid advertising revenue due to an offended advertiser who pulls his advertisements from the publication. The independence of the editorial production side as opposed to the business needs of a news publication is always a goal, known as "separation of church and state," but editors must balance how aggressive they will be on a long term basis. They will sometimes tone down or eliminate a story and its accompanying photo if they think it might limit their freedom to make editorial decisions in the future. The traditions and cultures of publications play a large part in what is ultimately published. The press censors itself to a degree, based on prevailing conditions and an understanding of its core audience. Most US publications shy away from showing the most gruesome photos of war or accidents, believing their readers would be offended by such things. If a few readers cancel subscriptions in protest of coverage of a particular story, it is noticed by executives at the publication.

Thus, the news image we ultimately see in print can be affected by the filtering process of publishers, senior editors, company lawyers, reporters, art directors, photographers, and photo editors and researchers. The aforementioned "decisive moment" can appear very differently to one editor to another. Only at the point of publication does the reader finally have the chance to interpret a photo in the context of the printed page or computer screen.

The process is complicated and the value of the final image for the reader depends on how much faith and trust one can have in a specific publication. There is a good reason daily and weekly press coverage is often referred to as "the first rough draft of history." It is produced under tight deadlines, without the luxury of time to consider the story within the larger context that only future events can provide. New facts often emerge after publication; sources for information are sometimes unreliable and often have their own political, social or personal agendas. The images and stories one reads in a publication should never be considered as the last word, but only the latest chapter in a continually unfolding story.

Meaning can change over time. For example, the photograph you see today may have more or less significance in the future. Some critical events occupying our attention today will fade in significance over time. Pictures of famous or infamous people who had strong effects on their world 100 years ago might mean very little to modern readers, fame and infamy being fleeting. Who will recognize American businesswoman and publisher Martha Stewart in the year 2075? She may be a household name today because of her business success and marketing skills, but will her home furnishings enterprise and reputation outlast her? Other photos will gain in significance for reasons we might not yet understand. Standard scenic post card pictures of the World Trade Center towers in New York, known primarily as a symbol of American financial strength, a tourist attraction, and mostly unloved as architecture, have acquired a much more complex meaning since September 11, 2001. The towers have attained that rare iconic status in a history still unfolding.

Photo icons represent a type of shorthand or summary of much bigger themes and ideas. These photos have the power to generate strong reactions decades after their production because of the gateway they open to shared cultural memories and the significance of the historical events they illustrate. Some photos, especially historical ones, symbolize national self image, sum up a historical era, perpetuate a national myth, or symbolize an entire culture. They become the icons of a culture and touchstones for themes of national and personal identity. They are often tied to momentous events in a nation's history, but they can be popular cultural images too. Examples of US iconic images are shown in Figs. 2-2 through 2-7 below.

Fig. 2-2: The first powered airplane flight of the Wright Brothers. 1903. Credit: Library of Congress

Fig. 2-3: 1930's depression era poor mother with children by Dorothea Lange.
Credit: Library of Congress

Fig. 2-4: US astronaut Buzz Aldrin walks on moon, 1969. Credit: NASA

Fig. 2-5: US astronaut Bruce McCandless performs untethered space walk, 1984.
Credit: NASA

Fig. 2-6: World Trade Center Towers, weighted with new meaning since September 11, 2001.

Fig. 2-7: Tortured Iraqi prisoner at Abu Ghraib prison, as made available to the public in 2004.

Overall, a reader can only understand and interpret a news photo based on his own body of knowledge gained from paying attention over a period of time. Uninformed looking is not the same as seeing and comprehending. The critical abilities needed to understand the meaning of a photo and the intent of the media source in which it appears can be gained by keeping an open mind, being aware of the global framework in which events occur, reading widely, constantly, and with a dose of skepticism. As stated earlier, nothing stands alone. The long and twisting road of history is what makes a news photo possible. The present can only be understood in the light of historical events and trends of decades and centuries. With a sufficient understanding of the past the reader can better understand the present, making each picture worth the thousand or ten thousand words it is said to be.

Suggested websites to visit for further information

For greater consideration of some of the issues considered above, the reader is encouraged to take advantage of the following online collections.

For discussions about the impact of still photographs, visit :
www.pbs.org/ktca/americanphotography/filmandmore/transcript3.html

For discussion of use and censorship of gruesome war pictures presented by the American Journalism Review, visit www.ajr.org/article.asp?id=2989

To view a continually updated collection of manipulated news photos, visit: www.cs.dartmouth.edu/farid/research/digitaltampering/

To view how history has been captured via photos, look for the prints and photographs in the Bain collection at the US Library of Congress, available via www.loc.gov. Also visit the collection of the New York Public Library at www.nypl.org and the George Eastman House at www.geh.org.

References

American Society of Magazine Editors (n.d.) Finance & Operation Fact Sheets. Retrieved from: http://www.magazine.org/finance_and_operations/finance_operations_trends _and_magazine_handbook/20922.cfm

Cartier-Bresson, H. (1952). *The Decisive Moment.* Retrieved from http://e-photobooks.com/cartier-bresson/decisive-moment.html

Magazine Publishers of America (n.d.) About the MPA. Retrieved from www.magazine.org.

CHAPTER THREE

MAGAZINE JOURNALISM: TARGETING PRINT PUBLICATIONS TO REFLECT A DESIRED AUDIENCE

LIZ NICE, UNIVERSITY OF SHEFFIELD

Introduction: The battle for the reader

The legendary press magnate William Randolph Hearst once said: "All you need is a pretty girl and a doe-eyed dog to sell a magazine" (as cited in Crowley, 2003; p. 7), but magazines have changed somewhat since the 1930s. Pretty girls still proliferate on magazine covers but magazine editors and publishers have been finding for several years now that a girl alone—even a very famous one— isn't nearly enough to persuade readers to buy their product. There's also not much call for dogs these days, doe-eyed or otherwise.

The magazine industry, despite predictions of a collapse during the dot.com boom of the mid-1990s, continues to thrive and new magazine launches are multiplying from New York to Beijing. Established publishers, including Hearst Magazines, are expanding into new markets such as Eastern Europe and India, while the rapidly expanding Chinese market, which had only about 1000 magazines 30 years ago, had 9,000 officially licensed periodicals by 2005 (FIPP, 2005). Meanwhile, the total amount that companies are spending on magazine advertising in China is expected to top an unprecedented $1 billion by 2005 (Magazine Publishers of America online, 2005a).

However, intense growth brings intense competition and personal interviews with a selection of past and present magazine editors conducted between August, 2005 and January, 2006 suggest that the battle for the reader is the hottest contest of all. According to Sarah Pyper, former special projects editor of *Us Weekly* and executive editor of *In Touch*:

> The reader is everything and the magazines that do best are the ones that know their readers as intimately as the staff know their friends. You can have all the marketing in the world but unless you offer the reader something she wants to buy, you have nothing.

The concept of "targeting" the reader, a term borrowed from contemporary marketing, whereby potential consumers are identified and wooed by producers, is not new. In fact, periodicals have been targeting readers to sell themselves and other commodities, through advertising, from at least the beginning of the 19th century (Beetham & Boardman, 2001). In the early 21st century, however, attempts by magazine editors to reflect the needs, desires, and lifestyles of their chosen audience—the feverish pursuit of what "the reader really wants"—grow ever more desperate.

In much of Europe, magazine editors have become enslaved by what Marie O'Riordan, the editor of *Marie Claire* (UK) has called "the crack addiction of covermounts" whereby covermount refers to the industry term for free gifts that now accompany increasing numbers of magazines as an inducement to purchase. This tactic began as a failsafe way of instigating a rapid sales hike for a particular issue but has now become so ingrained in some markets that many publishers are afraid to "go naked"—the term publishers generally use to describe the rarity of an issue that offers no complementary gift. Since the mid-1990s in the UK, men's and women's lifestyle and teen magazines have been wilting under the weight of gifts such as free sunglasses, chocolate bars, CDs, bikinis, lip glosses, bags, and sarongs. The process has become similarly ingrained in Italy where the publisher Mondadori has offered readers the choice between lower-priced magazines or more expensive versions with gifts, while in Poland, Hungary, and the Czech Republic, readers have accepted price hikes on some magazines in return for better covermounts (FIPP, 2003).

The US has largely resisted the "gifting" trend, although the introduction of stickers, nail art, and Valentine's cards to some teen magazines and software trials on some computer titles may indicate a diminution of resolve. If so, European editors would doubtless urge them to desist. As well as the rather dubious morality of the practice—most covermounts are produced in the developing world for around 50 cents or less per gift (Rowan, 2001). Many editors feel that far from increasing brand loyalty, what started as a cost effective way of attracting new readers has simply escalated reader promiscuity, leaving once loyal devotees happy to ditch their old brands to shop around for whichever magazine offers the better gift.

The practice of gifting may also discourage advertisers, who question how much readers really engage with editorial—and consequently, with their advertising—when they have bought a magazine purely for its free gift. Editors, meanwhile, are left wondering why they bother spending hours perfecting their stories and layouts if readers are only really looking at the freebie, which tends to be arranged, rather discouragingly, by the non–journalistic marketing department, although editors are usually consulted. In some markets, "gift wars" have gotten so out of hand that magazines have been outdoing each other with quite extraordinary proliferations—the UK teen title *Bliss* recently went on sale promising *eight* free gifts.

However, while the European practice of gifting now seems somewhat naïve, it was born out of the same impulse which drives *all* magazine editors - the desire to please their reader, win their loyalty and so retain and augment sales. Editors are under constant pressure to please their advertisers. Unlike in Europe, where copy sales tend to account for the larger proportion of magazine income, (McKay, 2000) and China, where magazine revenues are still predominantly circulation based (FIPP, 2005), latest figures show that US advertising revenues make up 54% of revenue compared to 46% from circulation (Magazine Publishers Association, 2005b). However, increasing sales remain the editors' preoccupation, because, as indicated in a discussion with Margi Conklin, former editor of *New Woman* (UK) and deputy editor of *Elle* and *In Style:*

> If you're attracting readers, advertisers will come. But if sales drop, advertisers lose faith and you lose from both sides. So, as an editor, you focus on sales first.

The bulk of US magazine circulation revenue (70%) is subscription-based with 30% of revenue coming from single copy sales at the newsstand (Magazine Publishers of America, 2005b). The editor's job, then, entails a delicate balancing act between keeping existing readers happy, while striving to attract new ones, who might ultimately become new subscribers or at the very least buoy up the more lucrative newsstand sales. "You've got to make the reader your focus entirely," according to Margi Conklin:

> It's hard because you're being pressed in different directions. Every advertiser wants you to look like *Vogue* but that's not necessarily what the reader wants. Ultimately though, the reader must come first.

Maintaining this stance may be easier said than done, particularly in a country as culturally diverse as the US.

> In the UK, there are shared references; everyone watches the same TV programs and there are more shared sensibilities and attitudes but there is a world of difference between your reader in New York and LA and your reader in Montana and Virginia

says Sarah Pyper.

> So, you have to be clever about how you define the reader and she becomes more about broad concepts than a particular persona. It's about being fun and glamorous, feisty and sociable, feeling bad for Jennifer Aniston when Brad Pitt leaves her, yet still yearning to know every detail about Brad's new love. You're

basically adopting an *attitude* in the hope that, wherever your reader lives, she will buy into that.

Targeting readers entails more than simply "adopting an attitude" however. Many magazines have global editions; FHM has 30 editions worldwide, *Marie Claire* has 24 (IPC Media, 2006), and *Cosmopolitan,* the largest magazine franchise in the world, is published in 36 languages and sold in more than 100 countries (Hearst Corporation, 2006) This situation has created a homogeny of newsstands that can be disconcerting. However, while the brand values of a *Cosmopolitan* or a *Marie Claire* may be relatively consistent across all its editions, no magazine can merely reproduce identical material from the home publication without at least some nod to the local audience.

This situation may not always have been the case. In China, for example, which had 50 foreign magazines as of mid-2005, (FIPP, 2005), an initial fascination with Western life allowed some tolerance for translated articles. However, a magazine such as *FHM China*, for example, now produces 30% of its articles locally and covers local issues—such as the best bars in Beijing. Imported material must also be relevant to the Chinese audience, including features on extreme sports, sex, and digital cameras (Glossy Magazine, 2004). The choice of *FHM China's* first two cover girls is evocative: their first was the Chinese actress Zhao Wei; their second, Britney Spears.

"Whether you're publishing in Portland or Poland you've got to relate to the reader," as indicated in a recent discussion with Betsy Fast, editor of *Twist* magazine which publishes editions in Poland, the Czech Republic, and the US.

Our Polish editions take some of our editorial but also have a very strong, local stamp on their articles and advertisements—for instance, Polish *Twist* is full of advertisements for cell phone ringtones which we scarcely carry here [US] at all. Whatever country you're in, you've got to target the reader you have. You've got to make every story relevant to that reader's life or they won't want to know.

This fervent belief has all magazine editors obsessing conscientiously about who "the reader" is and what they want. According to McRobbie (1999), however, whether the reader should be given such a potentially tyrannical hold over a publication, bearing in mind that the reader is often a more nebulous concept than concrete consumer, remains a question. Similar queries concern how editors actually set about putting their reader first and the tangible benefits of doing so. Also, might editors be paying lip service to an ideal without much thought for what the reader *really* wants and needs?

Why the reader comes first

Advertisers certainly believe that magazines are experts in targeting the needs of a desired audience because of the "halo effect" (Johnson & Prijatel, 1999); the ingrained belief that because magazines and audiences have such a strong relationship, the moment an advertiser appears in a magazine, it basks in that glow, and consequently benefits from product endorsement on a par with a recommendation from a friend. Some critics find this relationship alarming. According to Morrish (2003):

> There is no more vexed issue than the relationship between the editor and the advertising department... A certain distance is desirable if the independence and integrity of the editorial department is to be maintained (p. 103).

Meanwhile Gloria Steinem (1994), the editor of *Ms* who ultimately banished advertising from her pages, wrote angrily of the pressure she endured to provide a "supportive editorial atmosphere or complimentary copy" (p. 131) for advertisers.

Editorial resistance aside, studies cited by the Magazine Publishers of America (2005a) have shown that the faith advertisers place in magazine advertising is not misplaced. Consumers *are* more likely to find magazine advertising more acceptable and enjoyable than the advertising in any other media, as they find it less interruptive, more engaging, and more credible than the advertising in other media. For those who advertise in magazines, more than half of readers have been found to take action on magazine advertisements, or were at minimum, left with a more favorable opinion of the advertiser than they had had before it was featured in their magazine. Admittedly, the 'Magazine,' as the magazine industry's chief mouthpiece, have a vested interest in perpetuating the belief that magazine advertising touches the parts the more ubiquitous TV advertising cannot reach.

However, it does not take an expert to know that constant interruptions of one's favourite television programs are far more irritating than a pretty Chanel advertisement appearing opposite enjoyable editorial in one's favorite magazine. Thus, magazine editors raving about their amazing relationships with their readers may not reflect an entirely philanthropic desire to please those who write in to them each week. Indeed, the editor is keenly aware that the more they emphasise their "great relationship," the more of an enticement to the advertising dollar they become. Specifically:

> publishers ... juggle their desire to "speak to readers" with their imperative for advertising revenues...thus, the lifestyle rhetorics that women's magazines (adopt are) ...not simply innovative ways of "speaking" to women, but ways of addressing women without estranging advertisers (Gough-Yates, 2003, p. 154).

The great relationship can be a source of stress for editors. For example, Gough-Yates (2003) talks of publishers' anxieties about how to target young middle class women and editors are keenly aware of the importance of sustaining reader loyalty by convincing readers that *their* magazine, above all, is the one that understands them best. Ruth Whitney, the celebrated editor of *Glamour* from 1967–1998 might have believed that: "If six months go by and you have offended neither your readers nor your advertisers, chances are you're not doing your job as editor" (Whitney, 1993 as cited in Johnson & Prijatel, 1999, p. 93). However, today most editors will tend to follow Norman Cousins (1971), editor of the *Saturday Review* from 1940-1971, "Readers must feel respected and valued; they must feel that they are not just keys on a cash register but partners in an ongoing venture" (as cited in Johnson & Prijatel, 1999, p. 188). As Morrish (2003) adds, "Readers want you to know them and like them well enough to give them things they haven't asked for" (p. 29).

Editors of women's lifestyle titles often talk of holding up a "mirror" to their reader. For some, that mirror is reasonably accurate—reinforcing the reader's sense of their identity and place in the world and reassuring them that they are where they are supposed to be (e.g. *Jane*). For others, the mirror image may be more distorted, offering the reader a better or best version of herself (e.g. Cosmopolitan, Glamour*). For others still, that version may even be a complete fantasy—an editorial *Picture of Dorian Gray* as it were. (e.g. *Vogue, Elle*), The mirror image analogy doesn't fit with all types of magazines. For example, specialist titles (e.g. *Autoweek, National Geographic*) and celebrity titles (e.g. *US Weekly, Entertainment Weekly*) may focus more on the reader's interests than their emotions or demographic. Still, for all editors, the starting point is the reader, whose lives, personalities, and enthusiasms will be varyingly reflected back at themselves in the pages of the magazine from front to back. Usually a blend of editorial instinct, advertising pressure, and market research determine how deeply the mirror is cracked.

Questions remain concerning how editors set about putting their reader first and the techniques they use to achieve this goal.

How the reader comes first

Magazines have a long history of developing commercial, rhetorical, and structural strategies to involve the reader. In fact, methods used by Victorian women's magazines to get to know the reader better and make her feel more involved with her magazine, such as inviting her to write in with problems, stories, and comments or offering her competitions, special offers, and incentives to buy (Beetham & Boardman, 2001) are still commonly used.

The process has become slightly more scientific however, and despite Morrish's (2003) warning, "A magazine designed solely to meet research criteria will have no center, no identity and no soul" (p. 37), market research has become increasingly prevalent. Some editors refer to readership surveys, such as the Mediamark Research Inc (MRI) bi-annual reports on magazine readers (which list the age, income, time spent reading magazines, occupation and opinions of magazine readers from thousands of interviews) and the annual Study of Media and Markets by Simmons Market Research Bureau which profiles readers' demography and purchase behavior through personal interviews (Johnson & Prijatel, 1999). Editors also attend focus groups, sometimes observing readers through one-way-glass panels as they discuss their magazines. At other times, editors more informally, join reader discussions themselves. They hold reader days, organize reader panels and events such as roadshows, "meet the editor days," and competitions. They devour readers' letters. Editors whose readers are far removed from them in age—such as teen magazine editors—might visit schools or even plague neighbors with teenage children in their quest to better understand their reader. Some editors have even been known to telephone subscribers to chat about the latest issue; indeed, as Gough-Yates (2002) observed of the women's magazine industry, there has been

… a much greater emphasis on 'understanding' the lifestyles, lives and aspirations of some groups of women than previous media scholars have acknowledged (p. 155).

"We want to know everything," says Kristin McKeon Nieto, deputy editor of *J14*, former managing editor of *New Jersey Monthly* and associate editor of *Family Circle* in a personal interview. "We want their hopes and dreams, their fantasies, their desires, and expectations. We want it all." Occasionally, editors admit they aren't the least bit interested in who their reader *really* is. "It was like that at *Penthouse*," says a former associate editor.

We knew who our reader was but we pretty much tried not to! I'm afraid the idea of the reality was a little too scary so there was definitely a bit of writing not for the reader we really had, but for the reader we wanted it to be!

However, with most editors, the drive for ever greater reader intimacy is all-consuming. For example, Margi Conklin indicated, "We should probably get to know the reader even more than we do. It's one of the things that gets put off because there never seems to be enough time or money."
However, meeting the actual reader, as opposed to the ideal reader of the editor's imagination may not always be as palatable as an editor might like. As McRobbie (1999) puts it, the reader can become a space of "projection" for

magazine professionals but editors frequently despair of focus groups where readers seem to delight in providing inarticulate information such as: "You should do more articles about shoes" a week after your "shoe issue" was your lowest selling issue of the year. Another irritation is that publishers will frequently tell editors in one breath to "take focus groups with a pinch of salt" while indirectly pressurising the editor to act on their findings at the same time. Particularly on a struggling title, publishers are always looking for the elusive "answer" to poor sales, so naturally can not help pushing editors to follow the one source—the reader focus group—that is always happy to provide one. Focus groups can also be instructive. "We were so bored of (the actor) Chad Michael Murray and convinced ourselves that our readers must be sick of him too, especially since he had gotten married and become strictly 'unavailable'," said Kara Higgins Wahlgren, deputy editor of *Twist* in a recent personal interview.

> But the focus groups showed that he was as popular as ever—far more than we had realized—so it made sense to include him in our next issue when we wouldn't have done otherwise.

Another way of getting close to the reader represents perhaps the most significant change in the magazine industry in the last ten years—the increased closeness magazine editors have obtained with their readers via the internet. According to Higgins Wahlgren, "It takes a real effort to sit down and write a letter to a magazine. But sending an email is so much easier so the feedback we receive has magnified." Email has also revolutionized magazines' relationships with their readers while many magazines are also setting up blogs, such a National Magazine Exchange's MySpace edition, where editors can spend hours talking to readers one to one. "Instead of having a vague image of a remote teen in Virginia, it's like having the person you're writing for in the next room," said Kristin McKeon Nieto while *Twist's* Betsy Fast added, "It's hard to imagine how we ever managed without [the internet]."

In the same way, editors can now access reader opinion instantaneously via reader polls. According to Wahlgren, "We can poll 600 readers in two days. It's unscientific, but it's also a whole lot better than we had before." These polls are then included within the editorial, giving readers instant access to what *they* think. Readers are even being asked to vote online to choose editorial content—helping editors to decide on everything from whether to do a feature on internet dating to which celebrity should grace the cover. "We gave readers a list of five celebrities and were shocked that Kate Moss ran out the overwhelming winner, even beating J-Lo," said Margi Conklin of her time at *New Woman*.

We'd imagined that Kate was too cool for our readers but we listened to what they said and used her in our January issue, meeting our sales target in the process.

The burgeoning role of the reader in magazine editorial provides an interesting area for further academic study. Specifically, is the reader really leading the way along the editorial path—or are editors kidding themselves that they are reader-led when really their concept of the reader is capricious at best? Caroline Oates, in a study of UK women's weeklies (1999), highlighted the use of ostensibly reader-generated material such as readers' letters, photographs, problems, and real life stories to create what she called an illusion of reader participation in magazines. Illusion may be too strong. Writers and editors do inevitably tweak reader contributions to fit house style but readers' letters aren't generally fabricated and their photographs can't be. However, the extent to which magazine producers inflect the reader contribution process with their own discursive practices clearly warrants further research. Thus, Gough-Yates' (2002) plea for more appreciation of the significance of magazine producers' own cultural lives and experiences is long overdue. Certainly, the producers of magazines are at the heart of the search for who the reader is. McRobbie (1999) has highlighted the possibility of a shared world view between employees and readers of women's magazines, arguing that women's magazine employees and contributors are often well educated, self-proclaimed feminists—and readers of magazines themselves—a fact often forgotten by many feminist critics of women's magazines (e.g. Ferguson, 1983; McCracken, 1993; Ballaster et al., 1991; Jackson, 1996; McKay, 1999) who have tended to depict them simply as purveyors of patriarchal oppression with purely commercial motives. Perhaps instead, women's magazines are run by women who are searching for answers to the same questions as their readers and it is this quest that dominates their editorial approaches more than anything else. At the very least, as Gauntlett (2002) suggests, to categorize them as evil writers and victim readers is far too simplistic.

The extent to which an editor's understanding of the reader is often based on little more than intuition may also surprise some. Unlike advertisers, who exhaustively study reader demographics and psychographics, (Johnson & Prijatel, 1999) editors tend to be rather less scientific. "So you're writing for *Trail* magazine," said Matt Swaine, lecturer in magazine journalism at Cardiff University in a recent interview.

Start picturing him. He might live in the city but he likes to go climbing in the Peak District every now and then. He dreams of climbing every peak in the UK. Once you've got him in your head, and you can visualize his hopes and dreams, that's where your ideas come from. That's how you know what the reader really wants.

Many magazines hold conferences in which staff leave the office to get closer to the reader although actual meetings with readers are rare. Instead, staff will contrive to create one, using a mixture of data, past experience and gut feelings to settle on everything from what car the reader drives to what supermarket they use. According to a recent interview with Marina Gask, former editor of teen titles *Sugar* and *More!*

Some of it is from using data provided by our marketing and advertising teams but a lot of it is part of a creative process of putting yourself in the reader's place. Sometimes we'll even give the reader a name. She becomes a clearly defined individual, a recognizable person, and every decision you take is with "Doris" or whoever in mind.

McRobbie (1999), who found that magazine employees would engage with the reader in an emotional, intimate way, rather like a friend, noted another rather unempirical method for connecting with the reader, which entailed employing staff because they appeared to embody the imagined reader's qualities. "You've always got to have at least one member of staff who, for you, embodies the reader," agreed Margi Conklin. "It may turn out that she's a bit better educated than the reader really is but you need that touchstone; in fact, you rely on it." Other magazine producers use relatives: "I rely on my six teenage nieces,' said *Twist's* Kara Higgins Wahlgren. In teen magazines, a similar process can be also observed through the use of interns who are frequently used as reader representatives and often find themselves directly shaping editorial policy. One teen magazine editor justified including diets in her magazine—something which had long been a taboo in the teen market— because of an experience with an intern.

She had "fat" written on her right fist and when we asked why, she said it was to stop her every time she reached for cake. She was this tiny little thing and we couldn't believe it. Our features meeting immediately turned into a counselling session and we realized that we had to start including diet information because our readers were doing it anyway, only they were doing it all wrong. (Lisa Smosarski, editor, *Bliss,* personal interview, August 2005).

The reader can be "a composite of people you know" according to Conklin, "a mixture of all the girls I've seen in focus groups" according to Fast, or even "me at that age" according to McKeon Nieto, but he or she is always, at least in part, a construct of the editor's imagination.

Gough-Yates (2002) has theorized that changes in publishers' perceptions of readers of women's magazines have changed over the past 50 years, culminating, from the mid-1980s onwards, in a desire within the industry to understand cultures of femininity 'on the ground.' Publishers then produced new forms of knowledge about women consumers and attempted to theorize the links between women's individuality and patterns of lifestyle and consumption (p. 153).

Market researchers have further participated in this process by helping to define reader profiles for advertisers. No analysis of the ways in which editors target their readers, however, is complete without acknowledging the predominantly creative, instinctive, and occasionally irrational process that editors seeking readers actually employ. According to Sarah Pyper,

> You get your data on your reader's average age and salary and you do your online surveys into what they like, but at the end of the day, it comes down to instinct.

Conklin added,

> It's hardly an exact science which is what makes it so exciting journalistically—as well as incredibly frustrating.

Clearly, issues arise as to what "inexact" techniques editors use to appeal to their readers and whether they actually work.

Techniques for targeting readers—how do editors draw readers in?

The cover

The battle for the reader begins with the cover which is the first thing the reader sees on the newsstand and gives an editor about five seconds to yell, as loudly as they possibly can, "Pick me!" Regular readers will recognize their favorite title from the logo and typefaces which are used every issue to ensure continuity and easy recognition while cheerful, vibrant colors, and layout surprises such as starbursts, flashes, and "belly bands"—thick bands across the center of the magazine to flag up a great offer or big story—are used to attract attention. However, a balance is involved in the luring of new readers and ensuring that regular readers don't look at the cover and become instantly put off, bearing in mind Morrish's (2003) axiom, "Old readers are better than no readers" (p. 45).

This balance relies on the cover image and the coverlines, which are the lines of text used to sell the delights within. When the American Society of Magazine Editors (ASME) voted for its top 40 covers in 2005, a plethora of images including John Lennon curled naked around Yoko Ono on the day he

died (*Rolling Stone,* January 22, 1981), a small dog (*National Lampoon's* iconic
If You Don't Buy This Magazine We'll Kill This Dog, January, 1973) a black on
black image of the burning Twin Towers, (*Time,* September 24th, 2001) and
National Geographic's 12 year old Afghan refugee (June, 1985) were billed by
ASME Executive Director, Marlene Kahan as "an evocative snapshot of our
nation and its preoccupation throughout the past four decades." Of the winning
covers, 32 were photographs and seven were illustrations. Only two displayed
typeface exclusively; *Esquire's* Vietnam-era "Oh my God—we hit a little girl"
cover (October, 1966) and *Time* magazine's October 8, 1966 cover: "Is God
Dead?" Images then, and the words that accompany them, make the first
connection between reader and editor and by far the most important one, not
least because, in the US, 80% of consumer magazine newsstand sales are
determined by what is on the cover (Johnson & Prijatel, 1999). (See Tarnowsky,
this volume for further consideration of photojournalism.) When a cover star is
used, eye contact is crucial. "With the model's gaze on 'you', the magazine
invites 'you' into its world" (Winship, 1987, p. 12). The attitude of the cover
star must also be consistent with the personality of the magazine. According to
Gask,

> If your magazine is about fun and having a good time, the cover star will reflect
> that. If it's celebrity gossip and the story's about Jennifer Aniston's heartbreak
> then you want a picture of her looking heartbroken because you know that's
> what the reader wants to see. And if you're a men's magazine, the girl on the
> cover will naturally look like she's up for a good time—though never, of course,
> in a threatening way.

Celebrity covers have become increasingly ubiquitous and editors spend
days agonizing over which cover star to use. *Twist's* Betsy Fast noted,

> The reader is with me the whole time. I'm thinking: will she like *him*? Does she
> still like *her*? How will she react to this person or that one? I carry my image of
> the reader around with me everywhere—she never leaves me—and she is the
> inspiration behind every decision I take.

When a cover star is used in lifestyle magazines, it's about the reader's
aspirations. "It...offers hope—of sorts: she is successful; why not you? It is a
seductive appeal" (Winship, 1987, p.12). Sometimes the cover star will be a
celebrity—Cameron Diaz will grace the cover of *Cosmopolitan* because she
epitomizes the fun, fearless female that the *Cosmopolitan* brand evokes.
Sometimes the star will be a model—the way the cover of *Woman's World*
might show a slim, middle-aged woman brandishing the amazing cake she just
baked. According to Gask, former editor of teen titles *Sugar* and More!,

It's all about promises. This is what we will give you if you come and join our magazine club. And the coverlines will reinforce that. Get More Sex! Look Great Naked! Have More Fun! Lose More Weight! The cover sets out what the editor believes the reader wants. Every decision is designed to lure the reader in, to welcome her into the magazine's world.

The technique for enticing readers varies with different magazines. For instance, *National Geographic's* Afghan refugee girl targets the reader in a different way—not with "This is you," or "This is what you could be," but "This is what you care about," or perhaps, in an even more sophisticated way, "This is what you like to *tell* yourself you care about." Whether a cover uses a celebrity, a model or no cover star at all, the reader remains the force behind every cover decision. Editors must consider what readers will buy into, what will they buy, and most of all, how we can give them what they want. The danger though is surely in the assumption that all readers want the same things; the inevitable consequence of a process of deciding on a reader and aiming everything at them. As indicated by Margi Conklin,

> It's not always just about one reader. If you're on a women's magazine, some readers might be single, some married, some with kids, some not wanting kids and it can be difficult. So, sometimes it is about defining a lifestyle you hope the reader will identify with or choosing topics that you think "readers" generally will be interested in. But let's face it, having "a reader" in mind is the most practical journalistic device.

As Marina Gask added,

> You have to have someone to aim at, but you must always be prepared to change your mind about them—readers change, and you need to constantly update your information. One focus group a year doesn't even begin to cover it—there has to be an ongoing dialogue.

Magazine critics, such as Duke who wrote of American teen magazines "lagging behind girls desires to see new, more inclusive images of femininity" (Duke, 2000, p. 386) have argued that the reader is too narrowly defined by magazine editors who fixate on an homogenous being of a particular race or class, leaving no room for ethnic, body, or sexual diversity. Magazine editors tend to accept this criticism, but, like McRobbie (1999), who challenged critics of women's magazines to outline what exactly they did want, they also question how, practically and realistically, they could be expected to do anything else. As Conklin noted,

> In women's magazines, there are the five pillars that sell: dieting, dating, cheap fashion, celebrity gossip, and hair. All the glossies are the same and every month you'll see at least one coverline devoted to each. That's the irony. You expend

all this energy defining your reader and exploring what makes your editorial proposition unique but then on the cover it has to be the same five pillars that everyone else is doing! I think that's where we really underestimate women—it's always about the lowest common denominator, whatever you can do to chase sales. The attitude is: it's worked for the last 15 years. And because you're under so much pressure to sell more copies, there's never any room to take risks.

Coverlines, while luring the reader in with their promises, also work on building the reader's trust. Winship (1987) remarked on the technique of using the word "you" to address the reader as in

> The dress that's perfect for *you.* There is the suggestion that the relationship being struck up is an intimate one between the magazine and "you"–just one reader…it heightens the sense of, on the one hand, the magazine speaking to the "lonely woman" and, on the other, the strength of the support the magazine provides for its readers (p. 12).

This tactic is not consistent across all magazines. Sarah Pyper said that

> celebrity magazines tended to steer clear of you as rather patronizing, preferring to allow readers the space to relate to stories about celebrities without insulting their intelligence by trying to imply that incredibly wealthy stars with their chauffeurs, masseuses and personal trainers were really just like them. Readers aren't stupid and it's important to remember that.

She also noted the value of news in coverlines. One reason celebrity magazines have become so successful in recent years has been that, with the rising cult of celebrity, celebrity gossip has become an important currency in the battle for readers, given its appeal across demographics. "We may not know what shoes our reader would buy or what breakfast cereal she eats but we certainly know which celebrities she's interested in," said Pyper, who adds that celebrity magazines' most lethal weapon is the "office gossip" it provides. "You just know the second she's finished reading her magazine, she's in her office saying, 'You'll never guess what I just heard…'"

The degree of news that magazines can offer varies. Monthlies, for instance, often have up to 10 week lead times so getting genuine exclusives can be tough. One technique common to all magazine covers, however, is the device of asking questions that tap into the reader's basic needs and then promising that the answers lie inside.

> "Always tired?" "Fed up of being taken for granted?" "Trying to lose weight?" Covers also show readers working together to help the magazine and each other: "What you told us about sex this month."

They can show an understanding of reader constraints: "101 great new looks at prices you can afford" and they can celebrate the reader: "10 things guys secretly love about you." (The) relationship with magazines (is) like an unconditional friendship. The magazine would always be there when (the reader) had a moment, to talk to them for as long as they could spare. Similarly, just as one enjoys oneself when in the company of a human friend because that friend reflects and brings out one's own personality, so it is with a favorite magazine. The magazine reinforces the reader's identity; the magazine plays back to the reader the values with which he or she identifies (PPA Marketing, n.d.). Such hardcore targeting can be very seductive.

Other techniques

Covers are only the first strand of the invisible umbilical cord that magazine editors use to attach themselves to readers. Once inside the magazine, every element, from the editor's letter onward, is scrupulously targeted for maximum reader impact. As Marina Gask indicated,

> It starts with the editor's letter, which says "come into our world. It's safe and friendly and full of people like you." Then you have the letters page, which says, this is *your* magazine. It cares about what *you* think. It knows what *you* are all about.

Letters and problem pages help define the reader with laser-like precision. A letter that begins "I can't get a boyfriend" immediately targets a teen reader as precisely as "My son wants me to change my will" instantly relates to the reader of *Woman's World*. Letters will always show readers' names, ages, and states, reflecting exactly the reader demographic the editor aims to reach and leaving all readers in no doubt that a given magazine is meant for them. Readers will also be defined by the celebrities featured—*Cosmopolitan* names Patrick Dempsey 'Fun, Fearless Male' of the year because *Cosmopolitan* readers are expected to find him very attractive, just as *FHM's* reader is defined by his attraction to Brooke Burke. The *way* celebrities are featured is also significant: *Faith Hill, Her powerful Katrina Rescue Story plus details on how you can help* (*Marie Claire*, Jan 2006) could only be a *Marie Claire* story, defining the reader as someone who wants to know about celebrities as much as any *US Weekly* reader, but who also appreciates a worthy cause element and an opportunity to personally contribute to something worthwhile.

"Every headline must also relate to the reader and offer them something they want," says Kristin McKeon Nieto,

> whether it's information, entertainment, gossip or just a sense of wellbeing. Then you use hyperbole to make it sound more attractive: The Juiciest Scandals of

2005, The Hottest Love Secrets of the Stars. And you're constantly looking to give the reader added value with headlines that promise extras—Win a date with Chad Michael Murray! Win a backstage pass! Free stickers for your cell!

The language and tone magazines use is another crucial way in which magazine editors target their readers. Jackson, Stevenson, and Brooks (2001) noted the way men's magazines use a "friendly, ironic, laddish" tone, showing an understanding that their reader would not respond well to any suggestion of patronization. Similarly, editors argue that the use of irony makes it more acceptable for men to accept advice without feeling inadequate, and unites them in a conspiracy with the magazine against those who don't get the joke, (principally women), further cementing the reader/magazine bond. McRobbie (1999) commented too on the use of irony in women's magazines which allowed readers to

> participate in conventional gender stereotypical rituals of femininity without finding themselves trapped into traditional gender-subordinate positions (p. 53).

According to Kristin McKeon Nieto,

> Getting the tone right is something we pay a great deal of attention to. On a teenage magazine, it's got to be very conversational, not too formal, not too cutesy, just the kind of language the reader would use when speaking to a friend. But on *New Jersey Monthly,* where you're writing for a professional reader in their 40s and 50s, it's all about giving them information, what restaurants to go to, what their house is worth, so the tone needs to be far more authoritative for it to work.

Simplicity of design and layout is another factor cited by editors as a way of targeting readers. Sarah Pyper noted,

> "You've got to make every story look inviting. There's a two second rule—can the reader tell in the first two seconds what the story is about and learn enough to make a decision as to whether to read it or not."

Ways of adhering to this rule include using bright colors, "pull quotes" (larger quotes which flag up the best elements of the story), sidebars (shorter copy boxes at the side of the story which break up the article and make it less of a "heavy read") and many pictures and captions. Critics who complain about facile magazines may want to bear the "two second" rule in mind.

Giving the reader something to take away, what editorial teams call the "service element" is also vital. Critics complain that magazines help to "reinforce an underlying value that the road to happiness is attracting males for a successful heterosexual life by way of physical beautification" (Evans et al.,

1991, p. 110) and see a sinister consumerist conspiracy—offering readers the remedy to all their problems through consumption (McCracken, 1993). However, editors see the situation differently. Specifically, they see readers who want information, advice on what to buy, what clothes and make-up products to wear, what the gossip is, what's coming out at the movies, and on TV—and so, to successfully target their reader, they feel compelled to provide this kind of material. Indeed, on a day to day basis, "giving the reader what he or she wants" obsesses most editors far more than sales or ideological considerations such as whether an article on "How to Get Your Man" may be a bit anti-feminist.

"Every story has to give the reader something they can get out of it," said Kara Higgins Wahlgren.

> If you do a feature on celebrities and how they shop, you will have to do a quiz sidebar: What's your shopping style? Or a box out: What does your favorite shop say about your personality? And every sensational headline should have a service element. *How Mariah Carey beat the haters—and how you can too!* You've got to relate it back to the reader every time.

The most obvious way of relating back to the reader is through the use of real life articles. In these stories, editors carefully choose subjects that readers can relate to, told through the eyes of people like them. Glossy women's magazines tend to specify that only attractive women of the reader demographic can be used with the intention of reflecting the reader back at herself, but in a positive light. For example, Margi Conklin contended that,

> You've got to put up a mirror to the reader and say this is who you are. That's why the subjects of real life stories have to be same age, the same social background, and have the same cultural references—so we drop in in-jokes and references to things like Ipods that are part of their world. It's all about giving the reader a point of reference that she can then reflect back on the things that are happening in her own life.

Techniques vary across magazines for this relating back, but editors view the distinctions between the toolkit for life that *their* magazine offers, as opposed to that provided by others, as the key to winning the battle for more readers. Differences of tone, personality, and the way a story is covered may seem almost imperceptible to the casual observer but there is a carefully contrived reason why the editor of *People* might cover a celebrity break up story as *How Jen's Coping* while the *National Enquirer* or *Star* would be more likely to focus on the fights and alleged infidelities that have led to the break up of a marriage.

> It is the subtle, between-title variations of character which make the relationship between the reader and the chosen magazine such a strong, personalized bond...The range of different psychological worlds offered by different

magazines means that readers can select ones which are exactly "me" (PPA Marketing, n.d.).

Are readers at risk from targeting?

The idea of editors targeting and defining a reader so precisely has been seen as sinister by some critics (e.g. Friedan, 1963; McRobbie, 1978; Ferguson, 1983; Ballaster et al., 1991; Evans et al., 1991; McCracken, 1993; Jackson, 1996) who have been suspicious of the techniques used by magazine journalists to lure readers. Clearly, there exists a fundamental incompatibility between creating magazines for mainstream markets, which aspire to appeal to as many readers as possible, and academic views about the undesirability of magazines producing homogenous blueprints for men and women which leave no room for racial or sexual diversity or indeed for any aspiration beyond "finding a man, losing weight, looking one's best, and learning to cook" (McRobbie, 1978, p.3).

Men's magazines, more accurately, the sub-category identified as 'LadMags,' have been criticized for their one-dimensional texts which override feminism, treat women as sex objects, and reinforce gender polarities (Gauntlett, 2002). Women's and teen titles, by comparison, have been seen as "dangerous" (Duffy & Gotcher, 1996) because they encourage and exploit female insecurities, offer limited options (i.e., heterosexuality is always seen as normative), reinforce sexual stereotypes, and suggest that the only remedy for life's ills is through buying more make-up and clothes. Postmodern scholarship (e.g. Frazer, 1987; Hermes, 1995; McRobbie, 1999; Duke, 2000) has largely rescued readers from fears of "corruption by magazine," painting them more as "producers of meaning rather than the cultural dupes of media institutions" (Hermes, 1995, p. 5) and focusing on the reader's ability to interpret magazine messages in their own way and not necessarily to their detriment. Ballaster et al. (1991), lament editors' lack of embarrassment at the contradictory messages they project at readers but do acknowledge that these contradictions, "as femininity itself is contradictory," (p. 7) may lie at the heart of the magazines' success. McRobbie (1999), in a reversal of her earlier stance (1978) has ostensibly turned feminist criticism on its head, suggesting that perhaps a new form of feminism exists in some women's magazines that sexualizes young women and encourages brazen conduct, even if this form of feminism is one that many may not accept.

While women's magazines continue to preach "be yourself" next to photographs of stick-thin models and articles about how to create "a whole new you," a truly comfortable marriage between critics and magazine editors still seems distant. However, there may yet be common ground. For example, most editors admit that at times they do underestimate readers, which is viewed as regrettable and unintentional, rather than a coherent plan. Indeed, many say they feel compelled, by sales pressure, to suppress an urge not to overestimate readers.

"We'd love to write more in depth articles but in focus groups readers tell us they just want to look at the pictures," said Kristin McKeon Nieto, while Betsy Fast added,

> I like to think that my reader is serious about her future but I also have to accept that she doesn't read *Twist* because she's that kind of person, and she doesn't want 20 top tips from me on how to get a cool job. She reads *Twist* because she wants a half hour to relax and have fun. She wants escapism—and to expect more from a magazine, which is essentially a piece of entertainment, doesn't make much sense.

Does the reader really come first?

Media consultant Lu Xiang, president of Zeno Management, says growing magazine markets such as China still have something to learn from foreign publishers, particularly in terms of promoting a stronger advertising to editorial ratio in a country where most magazines remain circulation led. For example, in 2004, gross advertising revenues of *Cosmpolitan, Elle, Ray-li* (from Japan), and *Esquire* comprised 25% of the entire magazine advertising market in China (FIPP, 2005).

The extent to which Chinese magazines might also profit from Western techniques for targeting readers requires further research but, considering how ingrained an almost obsessively reader-centric approach is in US and European publishing, it is important to consider the effectiveness or genuineness of the above methods for luring readers.

Clearly, Western editors go to great lengths to get to know their reader and strive to reflect him or her back at themselves through the pages of their magazine. As a result, whether a concept, a strategy, an idea of one person or a data-inspired demographic, the reader must be a vivid presence in the minds of all editorial staff who continually strive to uncover what has replaced 'pretty girls' and 'doe-eyed dogs' as the readers' obsession du jour.

Such practices, at their best, generate deep bonds between magazines and their readerships which feed long term brand loyalty and increase a magazine's attractiveness to advertisers at the same time. But this is the ideal. Meanwhile, in a magazine market increasingly turning to other inducements to purchase such as covermounts, reader targeting remains a shadowy art where the only certainty is that you can never be certain of the reader; that he or she is essentially "unknowable" (Gough-Yates, 2003).

Inevitably, some editors will abandon searching for the reader and offer a magazine that they like instead. This approach, however, is rarely successful. According to Gask,

> It often happens because the staff become more important than the reader. Maybe the staff don't want to be associated with 'uncool' music or want the fashion to be more the kind of thing they would wear, even if the reader would not. Sometimes you will see magazines resisting the mainstream because the staff do not want to be thought of as mainstream. But it's never as successful when magazine teams try to lead their readers. It's always got to be a case of them leading us.

Continually, Western editors argue that the reader leads them and not the other way around. But this always, to a greater or lesser extent, must be a delusion. The reader may be 'the most important person in the office' but it is always important to remember that they are also the only person in the office who isn't actually there.

References

Ballaster, R., Beetham, M., Frazer, E., &, Hebron, S. (1991). *Women's worlds: Ideology, femininity and the woman's magazine*. London: Macmillan.

Beetham, M. (1996). *A magazine of her own: Domesticity and desire in the woman's magazine*. London: Routledge.

Beetham, M., & Boardman, K. (2001). *Victorian women's magazines: An anthology*. Manchester, UK: Manchester University Press.

Crowley, D. (2003). *Magazine covers*. London: Mitchell Beazley/Octopus Publishing Group Ltd.

Duffy, M., & Gotcher, J. M. (1996). Crucial advice on how to get the guy: The rhetorical vision of power and seduction in the teen magazine *YM*. *Journal of Communication Inquiry, 20*(1), 32-48.

Duke, L. (2000). Black in a blonde world: Race and girls' interpretations of the feminine ideal in teen magazines. *Journalism and Mass Communication Quarterly, 77*, 367-392.

Evans, E.D., Rutberg, J., Sather, C., & Turner, C. (1991). Content analysis of contemporary teen magazines for adolescent females. *Youth and Society, 23*, 99-120.

Ferguson, M. (1983). *Forever feminine: Women's magazines and the cult of femininity*. London: Heinemann.

FIPP (2005). China, the story so far... *FIPP's Magazine World, 46*. Retrieved January 25, 2006, from http://www.fipp.com/Default.aspx?PageIndex=2002&ItemId=12707

—. (2003). Covermounts: At what cost? The implications surrounding burgeoning developments [Electronic Version]. (2003). *FIPP's Magazine World, 38.* Retrieved January 22, 2006, from: http://www.fipp.com/Default.aspx?PageIndex=2002&ItemId=12185

Frazer, E. (1987). Teenage girls reading Jackie. *Media, Culture and Society, 9,* 407-425.

Friedan, B. (1963). *The feminine mystique.* London: Gollancz.

Gauntlett, D. (2002). *Media, gender and identity: An introduction.* London: Routledge.

Glossy magazines seek to score with Chinese men. (2004, September 9). *China Today.* Retrieved from http://www.chinadaily.com.cn/english/doc/2004-09/09/content_373180.htm

Gough-Yates, A. (2002). *Understanding women's magazines: Publishing, markets and readerships.* London: Routledge.

Hearst Corporation (2006). *Cosmopolitan.* Retrieved from: http://www.hearstcorp.com/magazines/property/mag_prop_cosmo.html

Hermes, J. (1995). *Reading women's magazines: An analysis of everyday media use.* Cambridge, UK: Polity Press.

IPC Media (2006). *About IPC—Southbank.* Retrieved from: http://www.ipcmedia.com/about/southbank

Jackson, P., Stevenson, N., & Brooks, K. (2001). *Making sense of men's magazines,* Cambridge, UK: Polity Press.

Jackson, S. (1996). Ignorance is bliss when you're just seventeen. *Trouble and Strife, 33,* 50-60.

Johnson, S., & Prijatel, P. (1999). *The magazine from cover to cover: Inside a dynamic industry.* Lincolnwood, IL: NTC/Contemporary Publishing Group.

McCracken, E. (1993). *Decoding women's magazines: From "Mademoiselle" to "Ms".* Hampshire/London, UK: Macmillan Press.

McKay, J. (1999). Manuals for courtesans. *Critical Quarterly, 41*(1), 71-81.

—. (2000). *The magazines handbook.* London: Routledge.

McRobbie, A. (1978). *Jackie: An ideology of adolescent femininity (Stencilled Occasional Paper No. 53).* Birmingham, UK: Centre for Contemporary Cultural Studies, University of Birmingham.

—. (1999). *In the culture society: Art, fashion and popular music.* London: Routledge.

Magazine Publishers of America (2005a). *The magazine handbook: A comprehensive guide for advertisers, advertising agencies and consumer magazine marketers 2004/05.* Retrieved January 25, 2005, from www.magazine.org/content/files/mpa_handbook_04.pdf

—. (2005b). *China Publishing: 2005.* Retrieved January 25, 2006, from http://www.magazine.org/International/10407.cfm

—. (2005c). *American Society of Magazine Editors unveils top magazine covers of the last 40 years* (Press Release). Retrieved from http://www.magazine.org/Press_Room/13806.cfm

—. (2006). In an age of interruption, magazines engage. In *The magazine handbook: A comprehensive guide 2006/07* (pp. 24-38). Retrieved from http://www.magazine.org/content/Files/MPAHandbook06.pdf

Morrish, J. (2003). *Magazine editing: How to develop and manage a successful publication* (2nd ed.). London: Routledge.

Oates, C. (1999). *Designing women's magazines.* Paper presented at the Design Culture Conference, European Academy of Design, Sheffield, UK.

PPA Marketing. (n.d.). The personal character of individual title. Retrieved from http://www.ppamarketing.net/cgi-bin/wms.pl/626

Rowan, D. (2001, June 20). Magazine cover-mount wars. *Evening Standard.* Retrieved February 16, 2007, from: http://www.davidrowan.com/2001/06/evening-standard-magazine-cover-mount.html

Steinem, G. (1994). *Moving beyond words.* London: Bloomsbury.

Winship, J. (1987). *Inside women's magazines.* London: Pandora.

CHAPTER FOUR

AGENTS OF CHANGE:
CHINESE JOURNALISTS AND CENSORSHIP

NAILENE CHOU WIEST,
UNIVERSITY OF HONG KONG

The Chinese news media operate in an environment globally recognized as one of the most repressive. In 2006, Reporters Without Borders put China 163th out of 167 countries after having been rated 159th in 2005 (Reporters Without Borders, 2005). The institutionalized restrictions on media provide only one of the barriers that separate free speech and the intended audience. Like journalists in other parts of the world, Chinese journalists also contend with the mundane reality of newsroom politics, which often takes the form of a contest between ideas and interpretations of events and what becomes the news. Thus, reporters need to run a calculation of whether their work can get past the gatekeeper and who decides what information will or will not go forward (Shoemaker & Reese, 1995). This chapter takes a nuanced look at the multiple layers of constraints for Chinese journalists.

Many books and articles have described the bureaucratic suppression of the Chinese press (Lynch, 1999; He, 2004; Esarey, 2005). However, no matter how repressive the censorship may be, a journalist is not entirely without choice. The advance of technology and commercialization of the media have expanded the space for journalists to reach the readers. Through their tenacity, ingenuity, and political skills, some journalists now act as institutional entrepreneurs to introduce change that will shape the future landscape of the Chinese news media.

Following a brief discussion of the cultural roots of censorship, its present formal and informal bureaucratic structure, this article will consider censorship in various forms, and how journalists have availed themselves of loopholes in the system to make progressive changes or to undermine the system through unethical use of their privileges. These two journalistic approaches, while at the opposite ends of the spectrum, heighten an identity crisis of the profession.

Much of the content for the article relies on extensive interviews with fellow Chinese journalists.

Traditional culture and statecraft

Censorship in China, broadly defined as the official restriction of any expression believed to threaten the political, social or moral order, has strong cultural roots in China (See Denk, this volume). Censorship implies coercion. As in Chinese traditional psychological warfare, intimidation is both a strategy and a method: real force, however, is used sparingly. Assassinations and physical violence against working journalists are rare. The goal is to win without fighting or to win a big victory with only a little fighting. The censors are disposed to both soft and hard approaches, relying on cultural and cognitive measures to induce conformity.

An often quoted saying of Confucius is "The people may be made to follow a path of action, but they may not be made to understand it" (Waley, 1938/1989). In traditional Chinese statecraft, the ruling class used the knowledge it possessed to maintain its superiority. The masses accepted that the ruling class should enjoy certain privileges because of their role in governance, ostensibly based on their superior intelligence, which in turn, enabled all to live a happy life. In the present day, an authoritarian regime strengthens its rule by making policies to create and maintain that knowledge gap between the rulers and the ruled. The authorities must not be seen as ignorant or as making mistakes, lest their mandate be called into question. This culture explains both the instinct for cover-up and the need to maintain the informational asymmetry. Thus, criticizing the authority and harming the prestige of the Chinese communist party leadership remains a serious offense. Only the official Xinhua News and *People's Daily*, the official newspaper of the Communist Party Central Committee (Wu, 1994), are authorized to report about the leaders.

The ruling elite of the state needs reliable information to run the government. Both the communist party and the state are intertwined at almost every level, sometimes sharing the same personnel, or as the Chinese refer to it as "two name tags, one team" (In this chapter, the authorities are referred to as the state, which refers to both the party and the state.) In the hierarchical world of political powers, the higher the echelon, the more one has access to information. The function of the censors is to use the power of the state to remove from public access information they judge should be privileged to a few. The censored material may not be necessarily immoral, obscene, or harmful to national security. Often, the material is suppressed to keep people ignorant. An example of this form of censorship is reflected by the fact that the digest of foreign newspapers, *Reference News* (*Cankao Xiaoxi*), published by the Xinhua

News Agency, was once reserved for only the political elite in the Communist Party, who were required to destroy the copies after reading. While this publication is now sold to the public and enjoys the largest circulation in China, a more secretive digest of news reports and commentaries gleaned from the foreign press (*Cankao Ziliao* is nick-named "big reference" as opposed to "little reference" for *Cankao Xiaoxi*) still has a highly controlled circulation.

News media as extension of the state

In the early years of the People's Republic, Chinese journalists proudly wore the label "mouthpiece" of the state. However, younger journalists who have come of age in the last two decades are more ambivalent about their relationship with the state (de Burgh, 2003). Still, no one has openly challenged the role of mouthpiece, which for working journalists is regarded both as a thing of the past and as an ongoing reality because the news media is tightly controlled by the state.

In China, journalists sometimes collect information to serve the state alone rather than for public consumption. This intelligence gathering role has complicated the identity of Chinese journalists. Serving as eyes and ears of the authorities, they are seen as an extension of the state. Censorship within this framework then becomes a matter of internal bureaucratic measures.

Commercialization of the news media in the early 1980s has unleashed changes in the news media as state subsidies have been cut for most of the media organizations. Newspapers, magazines, and broadcast stations must make profits by increasing circulation to attract advertisers. These money-makers are usually metropolitan dailies produced by media groups controlled by the communist party. Their role as a profit center within the group buys them some autonomy from the censors by delving into social issues that concern the public.

Commercialization also has given journalists job mobility and reasons for divided loyalties—serving the traditional master of the state and serving the public,who in turn bring in advertisers. Many journalists have come to believe that their authority derives from public trust and see themselves as speaking for the public. When this trend shows the promise of an independent Fourth Estate, the state makes sure that the power is exercised only in the areas it condones (Zhao, 1998).

Some state leaders actively promote the idea of "supervision by public opinion," known in Chinese as *Yulun jiandu,* whereby journalists are expected to exercise oversight on behalf of the public to expose wrong doing and corruption of officials. They also are expected to bring to light social problems and the search for solutions. This idea gained currency in the 1990s. Premier Zhu Rongji personally endorsed the investigative program "Focus" on China

Central Television (CCTV) and People's Supreme Court justice Xiao Yang also echoed this view. Thus, on the surface, the journalists are acting like watchdogs for the public interest. In practice, however, the state keeps the watchdog on a tight leash and the power to determine what to investigate and how far the probe should go is kept in the hands of the state. The public's "right to know" is an idea that the state has no obligation to honor. Although all governments around the world, to some extent, use communication apparatuses to ensure consent and legitimacy, China's state propaganda machinery determines what questions can be posed; namely, those that are answerable as the rest are excluded.

Despite pervasive content regulation, some journalists test the limits at the risk of harsh punishments in a continuous cat-and-mouse game. The motives are complex. They may be guided by professional idealism to give voice to the voiceless; they may defy authorities to gain approval and recognition from their peers. There also have been cases whereby investigative reporting became a tool for showing off the power of the press to gain leverage in political wheeling and dealing.

The Central Propaganda Department

The Central Propaganda Department (CPD) is a staff office of the Central Committee of the Chinese Communist Party. Its function is to disseminate the party's message and to provide guidance to the formation of correct public opinion. This "thought police" is more resented than feared. The CPD has played the crucial role of mobilizing people in mass movements in the past and served as the battleground for top-level factional infighting. The news media have always been deployed as a powerful tool for the regime to win the revolution and to safeguard the regime. The "stick of a pen" (*biganzi*) and the "barrel of a gun" (*qiangganzi*) are the twin pillars for bolstering the regime. Subjecting the media and the army to tight discipline and surveillance dated back to before the communists came to power (Dai, n.d.).

The CPD has no counterpart in the state—The Propaganda Ministry is a mistranslation of the CPD—but through the enmeshed party/state structure and by wielding party discipline, it controls the General Administration of Press and Publication; the State Administration of Radio, and Television; the Ministry of Information Industry; and the Xinhua News Agency. It is a common saying among the journalists:

The press has freedom.
Propaganda has discipline.
Propaganda has priority over the press.

From the CPD down, each level of the party committee—provincial, city, county, even villages—has its propaganda unit. An informal estimate, by a media studies professor, put the number of the staff nationwide at well over four million. The censors for news content and for setting guidelines, however, are a much smaller group within the propaganda offices, as the task for the majority of the propaganda staff is overseeing various publicity campaigns to promote education and thought work.

Watchers of the watchdog

The CPD exerts its control of news content through post-publication sanctions (Liebman, 2005). Vetting news content of concern, the Coordinating Committee of Reading and Criticism (*yueping xietiao xiaozu*), an extra-bureaucratic unit within the department, serves as the de facto super censor. This unit came into being after the Tiananmen Incident in 1989, when the wayward press was blamed for inciting the upheaval. State newspapers and broadcast stations were required to appoint "readers," "viewers," and "listeners" to sniff out politically suspicious material to then report to the CPD (Jernow, 1993).

Industry sources say that initially the creation of this tier of media censors was not taken seriously, as it was meant to give another paycheck to retired cadres—publishers and chief editors—to supplement their rather meager pension by reading papers at home and sending in reports on a semi-regular basis. These retirees, still imbued with the sense of mission, filled their notebooks with detailed criticisms, which was a source of headaches and hamstrung the work of their successors. This form of "geriatric journalism" also stifled the more creative practice of journalism and bound young journalists to old propaganda practice.

The power of press critics has grown over time in recent years, largely due to the apparatchiks of the press groups, who link performance bonuses for the editorial staff to the approval of the press critics. News organizations vie for their favor with fancy feasts and lavish gifts thereby cultivating ties so that press critics will be lenient in their criticism. The reports made by press critics gradually become guidelines for operation. Citations in the Press Critics' so-called "honor roll" can pay off valuable political dividends for newspaper leaders in advancing their careers (Li, 2006).

Li Datong, editor of *Freezing Point* (*Bingdian*), has questioned the authority of the press critics whose reports, at most, should reflect only their opinion as individuals. Specifically, Li found in their reports nothing but rigid thoughts, attacks, and gross generalizations. Rank-and-file journalists were unable to refute or argue their cases with the press critics, whose opinion hung over them "like Damocles' sword." This inability to dispute the press critics was compounded by media managers who, despite have largely disagreeing with the press critics, rarely raised any objections.

In an open letter protesting the suspension of *Freezing Point*, 13 retired senior party members concentrated their firepower on the press critics for abusing their power. They warned that the repression was bound to generate backlash. No changes resulted from their efforts.

Weakening of thought control

The era of economic reform since 1978 has brought about radical changes to the Chinese society. The market economy and market liberalism have steadily eroded the communist ideology. Although the Chinese communist party reaffirmed the orthodoxy of Marxism-Leninism, its propaganda department mouthpiece could no longer muster the moral authority to call this philosophy the absolute truth.

The authorities have periodically cracked down on dissent under various pretexts such as the campaigns against "spiritual pollution" in 1983. There has been a determined effort to keep the free press from China's pursuit of a market economy. The relentless control of the press is one way to raise the cost of "political coordination" to prevent the rise of opposition and effectively enhance the chance of survival of an authoritarian regime as presented in China (Bueno de Mequista & Downs, 2005).

Although the Chinese constitution protects freedom of speech, laws and regulations explicitly prohibit people from exercising this right. The State Secret Law, the Criminal Law, and the Sedition Law are used to put reporters in jail. Reporters charged with a crime are convicted 90% of the time (Committee to Protect Journalists, 2005). Defamation litigation is often initiated to intimidate the news media (Liebman, 2005).

To compensate for the eroded moral high ground, the CPD employed legions of thought police and installed technically sophisticated monitoring systems to control access to information and content, which was buttressed by frequent injunctions to instill self-censorship and showcase punishments of infractions (He, 2004). These laws were not frequently resorted to, because journalists were conditioned to observe the boundaries of what was permissible regarding ideologically sensitive subject matters.

The weakening of ideology occurred over the 13 years during which Jiang Zemin served as General Secretary of the Chinese Communist Party and his close confidant, Ding Guangeng, was his propaganda chief. Jiang spoke more often than any of his predecessors on the power of media and the need for media control. An engineer by training, he emphasized methods including the adoption of western communication techniques to get the political messages across, but he made no concessions on granting the media more freedom. As party boss of Shanghai, Jiang handled ideological matters with care, as Shanghai, once the stronghold of the Gang of Four, tried to shed its ultra-leftist image. Jiang had initially tolerated the progressive *World Economic Herald*, but as storms were gathering on Tiananmen in 1989, he removed the outspoken editor Qin Benli and suspended the publication, which won him good grace, as he was later summoned to Beijing to become the Party's General Secretary.

In the early years of his tenure as the General Secretary, Jiang manifested the conservatism of the post-Tiananmen years by blaming the media for fomenting discontent around June 4th in 1989. The media was perceived to have come under the influence of "bourgeois journalism" and abandoned the belief that it should serve only the party as its mouthpiece (Xu, 2003). Ding, a dour bureaucrat who was better known as the bridge partner of the paramount leader Deng Xiaoping, kept the news media in the firm hands of the party. Economic liberalism—competition and minimal state intervention—became the dominant discourse in the media to promote a market economy; broadening access to information was essential. Over the years, media literacy expanded with more discriminating readers who demanded not to be treated as simpletons and openly derided clichés and complained about untrue reporting. Recognizing that a full scale return to the crude Maoist propaganda was no longer feasible, Ding managed censorship in more subtle and invisible ways.

Commercialization of the media also had an effect on the loyalty of journalists. The market, the readers, and the advertisers were the new masters in addition to the old master of the state. The loosening of restrictions on employment and job mobility spurred reporters to take greater risks to flout the rules. The news media became more vibrant despite periodic tightening of control. The *Southern Weekend*, for example, enjoyed a national readership with its investigative reporting and critical commentaries.

The censors retreated increasingly behind the scenes. While there were showcase arrests and imprisonment, dismissal from jobs and shutting down of publications, the authorities increasingly used "non-political" means to deal with the wayward press. The progressive *Southern Metropolitan Daily*—a sister publication of the *Southern Weekend*—suffered a blow in 2004 when a manager and a highly respected editor were indicted on embezzlement charges in what appeared to be retaliation against the aggressive reporting of police brutality.

A subtler inducement to conformity was tied to the structure of compensation. Reporters who are paid a small base salary plus a piece rate on articles published, are inclined to write stories that hew to their editors' views and cause the least amount of hassle. As a result, the stories published tend to be politically safe.

Censorship in the bureaucratic muddle

The propaganda system is enmeshed in the tug of war between the central and the local government. The provincial propaganda chief in the bureaucratic matrix obeys the provincial party secretary and keeps a functional reporting line to the CPD. In this loosely knit web, or matrix of vertical and horizontal ties, the authority in most instances is fragmented (Lieberthal, 2003). What is censored in one province can be reported in another province. The *Southern Weekend*, a Guangdong-based paper, routinely published investigative reports of official corruption in neighboring provinces. In spring 2005, this extra-territorial muck-raking was no longer tolerated.

On the surface, reporters working for the national-level media enjoy more latitude in their reporting, but the provinces have their channels to stop the press or take television programs off the air. In 1994, CCTV launched a daily prime time investigative program "Focus" to promote public opinion oversight. Another news magazine program "News Probe," which was modeled after "60 Minutes" also flourished. However, as the producer of the News Probe admitted, half the films were never aired because sensitive nerves were touched. Often before the film crew returned to Beijing, a damage-control team already worked its way to the CPD to stop the show. In those cases, no reason for this halt was needed.

Through trial and error, journalists learned to expand the boundaries of reporting and the fear of running up against censorship diminished with each attempt. Reporters say they are often prepared to write "self-criticism" while doing their cutting-edge reporting. These confessions, containing a first-person account on why the permissible boundaries were breached, are kept in on a reporter's personnel file. Many journalists consider writing self-criticism as a routine job hazard. According to an interview with the author, one editor indicated that he had printed a story about a student scuffle at a local university campus, cognizant that doing so could mean writing a self-criticism because the incident might hurt the city's image. The defiance has grown over the years. By 2005, the reorganization of the *Beijing News* (*Xinjingbao*) prompted an unprecedented one-day strike. A month later, the shutting down of *Freezing Point* at the *China Youth Daily* became a cause celebre, which eventually ended in a compromise; the supplement resumed publication but the editors were banished to a "research office" in the newspaper.

Meddlesome mothers-in-law

The bureaucratic muddle creates a number of bosses for a news media organization. These bosses are often referred to as "mothers-in-law." A great deal of give-and-take goes on in this subtle and complex system. A mother-in-law (*popo*) refers to the mother of the husband. Thus, the news media sees itself as the daughter-in-law at the bottom of a traditional patriarchal family. She has no voice of her own. Although the patriarch holds the most power, he is remote from her everyday life. Instead, the young wife must cater to the whims of the mother-in-law. The relationship varies with personality and the dynamics between the two women. In general, the more docile the young wife, the more likely she is to be taunted by the mother-in-law. An assertive and cunning young woman, however, often knows how to engage in self protection and keep the old woman at bay.

The mother-in-law knows how to wield her power and to establish her authority by intimidating the meekest of her daughters-in-law. Over time, the hapless young woman is conditioned into a zombie. A young wife can develop her personality in a healthy way under an enlightened loving mother-in-law, which explains why some progressive newspapers flourished in Guangdong in the 1990s, until less enlightened mothers-in-law moved in to put them in their places. The *Southern Weekend* was reduced to a pale shadow of its former self after a new provincial party secretary changed the editorial managers of the paper in 2003.

Some news media can be driven to desperation by endless harassment over matters large and small. However, the daughters-in-law are not always victims. The shrewd one can sometimes even make the old woman look bad. As womenfolk, they can also form a united front to deal with forces from outside their system. Negotiation constantly goes on between these women. In a system that is unique to China, editorial managers and the local propaganda chief share the same career path. An editor-in-chief of a local paper can move on to be the propaganda boss and vice versa. Li Yuanjiang, who made *Guangzhou Daily* one of the most profitable newspapers in China, came to head the editorial operation by way of the city's propaganda office. He Huazhang, editor-in-chief of *Chengdu Business News*, moved on to be Chengdu's propaganda chief and later rose to become the city's vice mayor. Most of the senior editors are risk-averse, unwilling to jeopardize their future career to step out of the bounds—at least not too frequently.

Voodoo Censors

Jiao Guobiao, a former journalist and professor in the Journalism Department of Peking University, is among those who want to see the CPD abolished. He asserts that the CPD's fearsome image, like superstition, is nurtured by timid souls. There is no rational basis for cowering before this evil mother-in-law. In early spring of 2004, teachers and students talked in private about what could happen to Professor Jiao, who had declared war on the CPD. This period was a time when the news media had lived through a year of contraction swinging from a brief period of unprecedented tolerance back to the tight control. The relaxation during the SARS crisis in 2003 was short-lived. When the epidemic spread in Beijing and over half a dozen provinces, the government initially tried to keep information about the event under wraps. As the news circulated through informal channels on the internet and in the foreign news media, the central government fired two ranking officials for cover-up and promoted transparency. When the crisis passed, restrictiveness returned with a vengeance. Jiao, impatient with this step backward, believed that the genie could not be put back into the bottle and that it was time to shake up the system. He wrote his indictment of the Propaganda Department and sent the electronic draft to a few friends, and it became widely circulated on the internet. Listing 14 reasons that the CPD was an anachronism and an abomination to the healthy development of the Chinese news media, he called for its abolition. According to Jiao, the CPD's sins started with its gross interference in people's lives and preyed on their irrational fear—akin to superstition. Jiao accused the CPD of shielding corrupt officials and whitewashing the country's darkest moments. Arbitrary censorship distorts the media's sense of justice and deprives the people of media which they could trust. Looking around the modern world, Jiao found only that the Nazis had a comparable propaganda apparatus for brainwashing people. Jiao's fiery rhetoric combined a biting criticism with mock seriousness. He assumed the bombastic official language of propaganda to highlight the absurdity of the subject matter.

Many people responded on the internet and in private that Jiao had spoken about what they had felt all along but did not dare to utter it. Jiao saw himself as an iconoclast and that the magic of the CPD was in the eyes of beholders only. "I merely poked a hole in the paper screen," he said in an interview. In China, people are thrown in jail for speaking their mind and Jiao wittingly put himself to an important test.

Was it all irrational fear to cower in front of the Propaganda Department as Jiao had predicted? The CPD was in a bind. Instead of silencing Jiao in public, it worked through his university to apply pressure on him. By doing so, however, Jiao's prediction that the power of the CPD was exaggerated was somehow vindicated thus breaking its spell on the press. To provide for a "soft-landing," the CPD deployed its newly recruited troop of internet commentators to smear Jiao in cyberspace. They attacked Jiao's pro-US stance during the war on Iraq. Earlier, Jiao, like many liberals, supported the war to rid the country of a tyrant and to spearhead the spread of democracy in the Middle East.

The tactic was to refute "incorrect viewpoints" such as Jiao's without open confrontation. Since Jiao's postings were banned on the internet, the public got only one side of the argument. The upshot of the Jiao affair during 2004-05 was that the CPD became more secretive and retreated deeper into the background. Jiao lost his teaching position in 2005 and became a freelance writer for overseas publications.

The question remains whether the CPD is really like the Wizard of Oz, who appeared as no more than a snake oil salesman after Jiao parted the curtain and broke its spell. The answer, journalists say, is the CPD's power over personnel decisions in major media organizations to appoint and remove key personnel. In December 2005, the CPD flexed its muscles to dismiss the editor-in-chief and three deputies of the *Beijing News* after repeated run-ins over news reports frowned upon by CPD. After the newsroom went on a one-day strike in protest of the decision, the CPD rescinded the dismissal of the three deputies, but replaced the editor-in-chief, Yang Bin, who has since moved to edit an online news portal.

Journalists as agents of change

The examination of China's news media has traditionally been framed as a brutally repressive party-state machinery manipulating its mouthpiece, which fits the general description of China as a totalitarian state. The continued monopoly by the communist party, along with institutional inertia, makes the rise of the news media as an independent Fourth Estate seemingly a distant possibility. However, journalists have proven to be highly capable of availing themselves of the gaps created by the fragmented structure and the knowledge that the CPD is not as omnipotent as it has led one to believe.

The tyranny of censorship has shown its limits. When the reaction has become too strong, the authorities have had to step back to diffuse tension and preserve morale. This situation explained what happened in *Beijing News* in December 2005. The new generation of journalists born in the 1980s is now better educated and carries less baggage than their elders. Although journalists are recruited to reproduce the institutional setting, by the nature of their work which emphasizes curiosity, skepticism, and perseverance, they can become instigators of change. Their experience of playing cat-and-mouse with the censors has helped them to set realistic goals.

Radical and courageous journalists also can inspire others to follow, but it is a small number of professionally capable people with political skills who have steadily pushed the boundaries. They usually take very seriously the institutional structure and resist the temptation to go too far in what they report. Cumulatively, however, they have steadily pushed the boundaries.

In the age of commercialization, moral vision and integrity have become scarce resources, which paradoxically commands a high premium among journalists. A survey of young journalists in the Shanghai area in 2000 showed that esteem from their peers was valued as much as, if not more than, the accolades from their superiors. (Lu & Pan, 2002). Many looked to journalists with a strong sense of social consciousness before 1949 as their models. Even in the Communist era, defiant spirit of journalists like Liu Binyan, who advocated loyalty to one's principles above obedience to the Communist Party (Liu died in exile in the US in 2005) have continued to inspire the young generation of his followers. They make daily compromises with the knowledge that they will break free one day, which explains why the US film, *The Shawshank Redemption,* resonates so strongly with many Chinese journalists.

Zhang Jie, producer of the News Probe program, likes to remind his fellow journalists with a favorite quote: "Giants are born in chains."

References

Bueno de Mesquita, B., & Downs, G. W. (2005). Development and democracy. *Foreign Affairs, 84*(5), 77-86.

Committee to Protect Journalists. (2005, October 21). China (including Hong Kong). Retrieved March 30, 2007 from http://www.cpj.org/regions07/asia07/asia 07.html#china.

Dai, Q. (n.d.). Yan'an zhengfeng yundong zhong de "jiefang ribao" gaiban— zhongguo dalu xinwen kong zhi zhi faduan [The redesign of *Liberation Daily* during the rectification campaign at Yan'an—the debut of media control in mainland China]. Retrieved from The Chinese University of Hong Kong Web site: http://www.usc.cuhk.edu.hk/wk_wzdetails.asp?id=1421

Datong, L. (2005). *"Bingdian" gushi* [The story of "Freezing Point"]. Guilin, China: Guangxi Shifan Daxue Chubanshe.

—. (2006). *Using news to influence today.* Hong Kong: TideTime Publishing Company.

de Burgh, H. (2003). What Chinese journalists believe about journalism. In G.D. Rawnsley & M.-Y.T. Rawnsley (Eds.), *Political communication in greater China: The construction and reflection of identity* (pp.83-100). London: Routledge Curzon.

Esarey, A. (2005). Cornering the market: State strategies for controlling China's commercial media. *Asian Perspective, 29*(4), 37-83.

—. (2006, February 9). Speak no evil: Mass media control in contemporary China (A Freedom House Special Report). Retrieved from http://www.freedomhouse.org/uploads/special_report/33.pdf

He, Q. (2004). Zhongguo zhengfu ruhe kongzhi meiti [How the Chinese government controls the media]. New York: Human Rights in China.

Jernow, A.L. (1993). *Don't force us to lie: The struggle of Chinese journalists in the reform era.* New York: Committee to Protect Journalists.

Lieberthal, K. (2003) *Governing China: From revolution to reform* (2nd ed.). New York: W. W. Norton. & Company.

Liebman, B.L. (2005). Watchdog or demagogue? The media in the Chinese legal system. *Columbia Law Review, 105,* 1-157.

—. (2006). Innovation through intimidation: An empirical account of defamation litigation in China. *Harvard International Law Journal, 47,* 33-109.

Lu, Y. & Pan, Z. (2002). Chengming de xiangxiang: shehui zhuanxing guocheng zhong xinwen congye zhe de zhuanye zhuyi huayu jiangou [Imagining professional fame: Constructing journalistic professionalism in social transformation]. Retrieved from: http://academic.mediachina.net/academic_zjlt_lw_view.jsp?id=3880&peple=36

Lynch, D. C. (1999). *After the propaganda state: Media, politics, and "thought work" in reformed China.* Stanford, CA: Stanford University Press.

Reporters Without Borders (2006, October 23). North Korea, Turkmenistan, Eritrea: The worst violators of press freedom. In *Worldwide Press Freedom Index 2006.* Retrieved November 4, 2006, from: www.rsf.org/IMG/pdf/cm2006_as-2.pdf

Reporters Without Borders (2004). East Asia and Middle East have worst press freedom records. In *Worldwide Press Freedom Index 2004.* Retrieved November 4, 2006 from www.rsf.org/article.php3?id_article=11715

Shoemaker, P., & Reese, S. (1995). *Mediating the message: Theories of influence on mass media content.* Reading, MA: Addison-Wesley.

Waley, A. (Ed. & Translator) (1938/1989). *The Analects of Confucius.* New York: Vintage Books.

Wu, G. (1994). Command communication: The politics of editorial formulation in the *People's Daily. The China Quarterly, 194,* 194-211.

Xu, G. (2003) Makesi zhuyi xinwen lilun de feng fu he fazhan—xuexi jiang zemin tong zhi yuanyu xinwen gongzuo de zhongyao lunshu [Enriching and Developing the theory of Marxist theory of journalism—studying important discourses on news media work of Comrade Jiang Zemin]

Zhao, Y. (1998*). Media, market and democracy in China: Between the party line and the bottom line.* Urbana, IL: University of Illinois Press.

CHAPTER FIVE

SAGWA, THE CHINESE SIAMESE CAT: BUILDING AN AMERICAN TELEVISION SERIES FROM A FOUNDATION OF CHINESE CULTURE

SHALOM M. FISCH, MEDIAKIDZ RESEARCH & CONSULTING

The increasing globalization of television has opened opportunities for broadening children's experiences beyond their neighborhoods. In some cases, international sales of television series expose children to programs that have been produced in other countries and reflect other cultures. In other cases, television formats or elements that prove effective in one culture may be applied in series that are produced locally in other countries.

Critics of globalized media have argued that, if imported television series displace indigenous programming, worldwide distribution of television represents a form of "cultural imperialism" that can stifle the expression of local culture (e.g., Hendershot, 1999). Conversely, others have countered that this situation can be averted if, rather than importing intact programs, indigenous and international producers work in partnership to create a culturally appropriate version of a successful television series from another country. Notably, several papers have described the process through which international co-productions of Sesame Street have been created in countries around the world (e.g., Cole, Richman, & McCann Brown, 2001; Gettas, 1990). These papers detailed the process by which elements of a US television series (and its underlying educational curriculum) were adapted to fit the cultural context of another country.

Under either perspective, many of these cross-cultural papers have focused on television series that originated in the US or other western countries and were distributed or adapted elsewhere. By contrast, the present chapter takes an almost inverse approach, through a case study of the process by which elements of traditional Chinese culture were adapted to provide the context for an

American-made educational television series that was aimed at a diverse audience of children in the US and Canada.

Based on a children's book by Chinese-American novelist Amy Tan (1994), *Sagwa, the Chinese Siamese Cat* was an animated PBS series about a family of cats living in the palace of a rural magistrate in nineteenth-century China. The series was produced by Sesame Workshop (a.k.a. Children's Television Workshop), via a model of television production that has come to be known as the *CTW Model* or *Sesame Workshop Model*. Under this model, television series are created through an ongoing collaboration among three groups. The production team (producers, writers, etc.) are responsible for the creative content of the series. Educational content specialists are responsible for identifying and implementing the curriculum that underlies the series. Researchers conduct empirical research with children and families, so that the series can be tailored to the needs, interests, and developmental level of the target audience (e.g., Fisch, 2004; Mielke, 1990).

Aimed at an audience of 6- to 8-year-old children, *Sagwa* was designed to address three educational goals:

1. To support the social and emotional development of 6- to 8-year-old children as they grow into new roles and interactions within their families and society.

2. To help children see that certain situations and emotions are common to children's lives across cultures, and to model age-appropriate strategies for dealing with them effectively.

3. To foster an appreciation of other cultures by exposing a broad audience of children to elements of traditional Chinese culture, language, music, and folklore, and by encouraging children to value and appreciate them.

Using traditional Chinese culture as the context for a prosocial television series presented unique opportunities because North American children (whether of Chinese descent or otherwise) rarely see representations of this culture on television. At the same time, however, it also presented unique challenges, because the values of traditional Chinese culture and modern American culture differ in several significant ways (e.g., perceptions of the elderly). Thus, the challenge was to find ways to convey social messages that would be relevant to and appropriate for modern North American audiences without misrepresenting traditional Chinese culture.

Attaining that balance required a number of efforts regarding educational content and formative research studies with children and parents, each of which is reviewed in turn.

Educational content

Because of *Sagwa's* dual focus on socio-emotional development and Chinese culture, the educational content team needed to support the production team in both of these areas.

The content team supported the socio-emotional aspect in several ways. Apart from developing the educational goals listed above, which formed the educational spine of the series, content specialists began their role in production by helping writers understand the target audience. During the kick-off meeting that initiated production, the leader of the content team led a discussion with the production team about the social, cognitive, and physical development of 6- to 8-year-olds. An in-house document summarizing this developmental information was distributed as well (Program Research Department, 2000a). Understanding this age group was helpful to the production team, both in devising creative approaches that would be appropriate to the target audience and in developing characters who would act in age-appropriate ways.

Subsequent content activities included generating lists of age-appropriate topics and social messages, such as setting appropriate goals and demonstrating persistence in pursuing those goals, showing respect and tolerance for others, and resisting peer pressure. The lists of topics helped writers generate springboards for stories. As these stories were developed into scripts, storyboards, and finished episodes, the content team continued to collaborate closely with the production team. By providing input on stories, scripts, and storyboards, content experts helped to ensure that the social messages were conveyed clearly in each episode of *Sagwa*.

More relevant to the focus of this paper, however, are the content team's efforts regarding Chinese culture. An educational advisory board of experts in Chinese history and culture was recruited to serve as a resource that would enrich the team's understanding of Chinese culture and ensure the authenticity of the series' portrayals and visuals. In addition, the content team compiled a "Chinese Culture Resource Guide" that presented information on traditional Chinese food, games, celebrations, folk tales, proverbs, holidays, and arts (Program Research Department, 2000b). With bulleted information for easy reference, the resource guide made it easier for the production team to insert culturally appropriate material into the episodes; for example, if a script called for the young characters to play a game, the writer could consult the guide to select a game that would be appropriate to the time and setting. In several cases, the impact of the resource guide extended even further, when entire episodes were built around folk tales or holiday celebrations that the guide described. Finally, on a more personal level, efforts were made to include Chinese-

Americans among the members of the production and content/research staff, so that they might bring their own personal knowledge and experiences to the mix.

Throughout the process, everyone involved was deeply mindful of the need for balance between social content that was appropriate to both the traditional setting and the modern audience. Often, the key was to find a nexus where both cultures shared similar values, such as the need for learning, honesty, or teamwork. Many episodes of *Sagwa* centered on these sorts of topics.

In some cases, however, compromises were necessary to find a middle ground between the two cultures. For example, for modern audiences in the US, it was important to model meaningful, two-way communication between parents and children to resolve disagreements, at points when the traditional Chinese value of filial piety might call for children to accede to their parents' wishes without such discussion. Given the developmental needs of the modern-day audience, such content was included in the series, but care was taken to ensure that the portrayals did not extend too far beyond the boundaries of what might be acceptable within Chinese culture. The team's goal was to ensure that, even if the content might not always reflect ancient China with one hundred percent accuracy, it would always be authentic to the culture.

Formative research

Together, the content activities described above laid the educational foundation for the series. However, the true test of its success would lie in the reactions of *Sagwa's* target audience—that is, the degree to which 6- to 8-year-old children would be attracted to the series and retain its educational messages. For that reason, production was informed, not only by the educational resources and advisors discussed earlier, but also by an active program of formative research. Formative research is empirical research conducted with target-age children (and, when appropriate, their families) during the course of production, to address issues related to the comprehensibility and/or appeal of the material, with an eye toward identifying strengths and weaknesses that can help guide subsequent production. In this way, formative research serves to bring the voice of the audience into the production process (e.g., Fisch & Bernstein, 2001; Flagg, 1990).

In the case of *Sagwa*, researchers were mindful of the dual nature of the series' potential audience. The characters and settings of *Sagwa* needed to ring true and present recognizable images with which Chinese-American viewers could identify, while simultaneously introducing these traditional concepts, practices, and images to children of other ethnicities, who were likely to be far less familiar with them. With this dual audience in mind, all formative research for *Sagwa* was conducted with two complementary samples, one primarily Chinese-American and one not.

To achieve its maximum impact on production, formative research had to be conducted as early in production as possible. Although *Sagwa* was an animated series, research could not be delayed until animated segments were available, because animation is a time-consuming process. By the time animated segments would be available, it would be too late for the results of the research to impact on the majority of the episodes.

Thus, for *Sagwa's* first formative study, the scripts and storyboards for two episodes were used to create animatics—videotaped series of still pictures, accompanied by a rough audio track. Researchers showed the two animatics to a total of nearly 100 first- through third-grade children, and then interviewed them to assess the appeal and comprehensibility of the programs. The results of this early research were quite promising. Both Chinese-American and non-Asian children enjoyed the episodes and their characters. Comprehension of the episodes and their social messages (one regarding overcoming prejudices and the other about changing foolish rules) also was strong. Indeed, children's strong comprehension of these relatively simple social messages encouraged the production and content teams to introduce somewhat more complex and sophisticated social messages in subsequent episodes, such as demonstrating respect for elders in ways that are different than respect for friends (Program Research Department, 2000c).

Consistent results were found in a later study that was conducted after the first several animated segments were available. In this study, two animated episodes were presented to nearly 150 children; for the sake of comparison, they were also shown an episode of another, existing television series that was highly popular among the same age group. Again, the *Sagwa* episodes proved to be appealing and comprehensible to both Chinese-American and non-Asian children. More than three-quarters of the children also recognized the settings and characters as Chinese or (at least) Asian, citing either the backgrounds, clothing, cultural elements, or the appearance of the characters as reasons for their opinions (Program Research Department, 2000d).

Both of these studies boded well for the chances of *Sagwa's* ultimate success among children. To complement these studies, a set of focus groups also was conducted with parents of target-age children, to see how parents would perceive the series and its portrayals of Chinese culture (Hypothesis, 2001). As in the research with children, the focus groups included both Chinese-American parents (most of whom were born in China and had emigrated to the United States) and non-Asian parents. Both groups of parents reacted positively to the episodes they watched, although they thought *Sagwa's* appeal would be greatest for children at the lower end of its target age range because it was an animated series. They appreciated both *Sagwa's* social messages (which they saw as the primary educational content of the series) and its portrayals of Chinese culture, which were consistent with their own perceptions and experiences of Chinese culture. For example, one Chinese-American mother commented,

> "This is attractive and interesting to watch together, and I can explain some of the Chinese things, the symbols,"

while an African-American mother said,

> "It's a good show with ethnicity, because it gives a whole picture of different people and cultures. In this day, kids need to know about all kinds of people."

Conclusion

As noted throughout this chapter, the production of *Sagwa, the Chinese Siamese Cat* presented unique challenges in marrying contemporary western social messages to the culture and setting of nineteenth-century China. All of these content and research activities were essential to finding ways in which the parameters of both cultures could be accommodated in a series that children would understand and enjoy, and that parents would see as valuable and culturally authentic.

Certainly, a socioemotional television series could deliver social messages about topics such as respect, honesty, and responsibility without adopting Chinese culture as a framing context (and, indeed, many prosocial television series do). However, *Sagwa*'s portrayal of traditional Chinese culture lent an added layer of value for Chinese-American and non-Chinese children alike. For children of other ethnicities, the series provided an introduction to a culture that they may have known little about. For Chinese-American children, it provided an all-too-rare opportunity to see their own culture represented in mass media.

This chapter began by noting that, from an educational perspective, one of the great strengths of television lies in its potential to broaden children's experience beyond their immediate surroundings. As the instance of *Sagwa* illustrates, great care is needed to implement such content effectively. However, when handled appropriately, the potential value of such portrayals can be equally great.

Author's Note

This chapter owes a tremendous debt to the *Sagwa* content/research and production teams, without whom none of the activities described in this chapter would have been possible. More important, their tireless efforts gave rise to a television series that has entertained and educated literally millions of children.

References

Cole, C.F., Richman, B.A., & McCann Brown, S.K. (2001). The world of *Sesame Street* research. In S.M. Fisch & R.T. Truglio (Eds.), *"G" is for "growing": Thirty years of research on children and Sesame Street* (pp. 147-179). Mahwah, NJ: Lawrence Erlbaum Associates.

Fisch, S.M. (2004). *Children's learning from educational television: Sesame Street and beyond.* Mahwah, NJ: Lawrence Erlbaum Associates.

Fisch, S.M., & Bernstein, L. (2001). Formative research revealed: Methodological and process issues in formative research. In S.M. Fisch & R.T. Truglio (Eds.), *"G" is for growing: Thirty years of research on children and Sesame Street* (pp. 39-60). Mahwah, NJ: Lawrence Erlbaum Associates.

Flagg, B.N. (1990). *Formative evaluation for educational technology.* Hillsdale, NJ: Lawrence Erlbaum Associates.

Gettas, G.J. (1990). The globalization of *Sesame Street*: A producer's perspective. *Educational Technology Research and Development, 38(4),* 55-63.

Hendershot, H. (1999). *Sesame Street*: Cognition and communications imperialism. In M. Kinder (Ed.), *Kids' media culture.* Durham, NC: Duke University Press.

Hypothesis. (2001). *Sagwa the Chinese Siamese Cat*: A qualitative exploration of Chinese- and non-Asian-American parents' reactions to and perceptions of two test episodes. Unpublished research report.

Mielke, K.W. (1990). Research and development at the Children's Television Workshop. *Educational Technology Research and Development, 38(4),* 7-16.

Program Research Department (2000a). Facts about 6- to 8-Year-Olds. Unpublished educational content document. New York: Sesame Workshop.

—. (2000b). *Sagwa, the Chinese Siamese Cat*: Chinese culture resource guide. Unpublished educational content document. New York: Sesame Workshop.

—. (2000c). *Sagwa* board-a-matic study. Unpublished formative research report. New York: Sesame Workshop.

—. (2000d). *Sagwa: The Chinese Siamese Cat* segment study. Unpublished formative research report. New York: Sesame Workshop.

Tan, A. (1994). *Sagwa, the Chinese Siamese cat.* New York: Simon and Schuster.

PART II: MEDIA RESEARCH

CHAPTER SIX

NEGOTIATING THE GLOBAL/LOCAL: THE CONFLICTING RESPONSES OF CHINESE AUDIENCE IN THE ERA OF GLOBAL COMMUNICATION

ANBIN SHI, TSINGHUA UNIVERSITY

Today, the Chinese audience undoubtedly constitutes the largest body of its kind in the world, thanks to the coming of the era of global communication. The crushing power of capitalist globalization has not only brought forth a sustained economic prosperity since the late 1970s, but also the vast expansion of the local media marketplace in this world's most populous nation. Over the past 25 years, the growth of Chinese mass media has been spectacular: the number of newspapers, periodicals, and radio sets per capita is getting close to US ratios, with the number of newspaper titles growing 15-fold and books titles 20-fold (Cui, 2005).

In terms of broadcast media, Chinese Central Television (CCTV) plus some 3,000 other regional stations, and their accompanying satellite and terrestrial networks, make up the largest television system in the world. Given the over one billion current daily viewers and the estimated 128 million subscribers to digital pay-TV, by 2010 China may claim the largest share of the global television market (CCTV, 2005).

The Chinese audience has never lagged behind the trend of emergent new media. The country has around 110 million "netizens," 64 million of them broadband users, giving internet access to over 500 million. This figure is expected to rise by 25% annually in the next decade (Jiao, 2006). As the second largest market next to the US, Chinese mobile phone owners seem to be the world's most enthusiastic users of the newly-rising Short Message Service (SMS), having sent 300 million greeting text messages during the Lunar New Year's Eve in 2005 (Cui, 2005).

The cosmic figures and skyrocketing ratings lead to the quick conclusion that the Chinese audience has become a conspicuous power in the marketplace of global media and communication. This chapter will concern the complexities of global/local encounters from the perspective of the conflicting audience responses in contemporary China. For example, Chinese audiences seem to embrace global media uncritically and employ them as the catalyst to press for immediate press or media reform, as is reflected in the proliferation of diversified media outlets in the recent decade. However, their increasing exposure to global media products cannot but consolidate their own nationhood and indigenous cultural identities. This situation lends support to the Party-state's tightened authoritarian control of the incoming media imperialism, which is imposed by such global media powerhouses as Rupert Murdoch's News Corporation.

Global communication and China

The notion of "global communication" has become one of the more common, rather overused buzzwords in the recent decade. All types of events, processes, products, and ideas, from political scandal to military conquest, to consumer products, to markets, to culture—both "high" and "popular"—are endowed with a global embrace and therefore encompassed into the problematic category of "global communication" (Gurevitch, 1991; Rantanen 2005). There seems to be no society in the world today that is completely untouched by global communication, which has materialized under the patronage of the all-mighty transnational media corporations (TMCs). As one of the few marketplaces untouched by TMCs, China's entry into the World Trade Organization (WTO) since 2001, along with the successful bids for the 2008 Olympiad in Beijing and 2010 World Expo in Shanghai, opens up new avenues for China's integration into the US-led system of globalization and the consequent press/media reform.

Arguably, such a press/media reform is attributed, at least partially, to TMCs' strategic penetration into the Chinese marketplace. In 1999, Rupert Murdoch's News Corporation established its branch office in Beijing, inaugurating TMCs' presence in the realm of Chinese mass media. Since then, twenty-plus overseas channels have been licensed for limited broadcasting in experimental regions (such as Guangdong province) and in privileged location (such as five-star hotels). More importantly, TMCs' investment has crept into Chinese media system in various forms. A typical yet less attended example is the US-based International Data Group (IDG), who has launched twelve niche journals for netizens in China and plans to accrue an investment of three billion US dollars in the next two decades (Shi, 2005).

Such a rosy description of the press/media reform is incomplete if one neglects the response from the media audience in contemporary China. In terms of capital and resource, TMCs are supposedly invincible and unchallenged in Chinese media marketplace, in contrast to the local media and cultural industry in its embryonic form. As one local commentator roughly estimates, the total investment of one Hollywood blockbuster such as *King Kong* would almost equate to the annual expenditure of the entire film industry in mainland China (Xiao, 2005). However, powerful as they appear, TMCs must still make every effort to insinuate themselves into the favor of the local audience. As the numerous box-office or rating fiascos prove, the Chinese audience has the power to turn a cold shoulder to such globally popular media products as the US-based *Star Wars* film trilogy and the TV miniseries *Band of Brothers*.

The power of the Chinese audience is thus conducive to such a Janus-faced effect, which is worthy of scholastic attention. In face of the challenges posed by the all-powerful TMCs, one can easily adopt the assumption that "communication is a good thing" to hail the coming of global communication, which will surely bring forth a more harmonious order to the world and in particular, press freedom and media democratization to China. On the other hand, one can also counter TMC's penetration by way of the "cultural imperialism" approach (Tomlinson, 1991), advocating the preservation of the political, economic, and ideological autonomy of Chinese mass media. In many ways, either the seemingly unstoppable globalism or the equally unbridled nationalism cannot fully account for the complexities and intricacies of the Chinese characteristics in particular and those of global communication in general.

Any serious scholar of China studies and international communication should, as US media critic Jay Blumler (as cited in Gurevitch, 1991) succinctly puts it, attempt to

> get a conceptual grip, beyond the language of gee-whizzery, on an escalating yet formless, sprawling and global-shaking process that may be impinging on people's sense of places in the world and on the power of regimes to effect their wills within it (p. 191).

In what follows, I will approach the TMCs' impact on the national media system through a microscopic analysis of audience response. The global/local encounters in the realm of mass media have to return to the fundamental question of audience research, namely, whether the Chinese audience is active, passive, or something in between in the face of global media and communication. My account below of the paradoxical status quo of the Chinese audience is by no means confined to indigenous temporalities and localities;

rather, it suggests the complexities of the overall contradictions in the ongoing media/cultural globalization under the crushing power of the TMCs.

Transforming the local with the global

One immediate outcome of media/cultural globalization in contemporary China is the increasing access to international news coverage and exposure to the TMCs' media products. However, the officially sanctioned "open-door" policy and the social ambience of "keeping track of the world" (read industrialized Euro-America and Japan) have galvanized the Chinese audience's craze for news and media products imported from the outside world. One survey shows that 72.3% of Chinese TV viewers prefer "international" to "domestic" news programming (Chen et al., 1999). Daily newspapers such as *Huanqiu Shibao* (Global Times), magazines like *Shijie Zhishi* (World Affairs), and radio and television programming such as *Guoji Shixun* (World Express), all of which are devoted exclusively to non-Chinese news reportage, can yield soaring circulation or ratings in the increasingly competitive Chinese media marketplace.

Yet, in the realm of media and cultural industry, the open-door policy as such has still made the Party line, the "bottom line" (Zhao, 1995). Since China's entry into the World Trade Organization in 2001, local authorities still restrict the TMCs' penetration into the Chinese marketplace. The Chinese audience is still denied any direct access to such TMCs as CNN or the News Corporation. Any foreign newspapers such as the *New York Times* or news magazines such as *Time* are not allowed to publish Chinese editions to compete with the long-standing partisan "throat and tongue" such as the *People's Daily*. This situation does not mean that the TMCs must be tamed to the Chinese censors' yardstick before they can reach the local audience. On the contrary, TMCs can still creep into the Chinese media sphere with the help of the "invisible hand;" namely, the global market.

By means of such marketing strategics as content/format licensing and trade partnership, TMCs can safely claim their presence in the media consumption of the Chinese audience under the patronage of local names, brands, and/or titles. For example, the content of the *Global Times* is as much as 60% adapted directly or even translated verbatim from their overseas sources. Thus, it is not too difficult for Chinese audience to read a feature written by a *New York Times* correspondent, or to watch a clip of newsreel shot by a CNN cameraman. For example, during the 2003 Iraq War, as much as 75% of video footage used in the television coverage on Chinese Central Television (CCTV) was purchased from such US media organizations as ABC and CNN (CCTV, 2005). This dominance of American voices and lack of Chinese perspective can be partially attributed to the fact that there was no single Chinese television professional present in Baghdad during the heyday of the War. On numerous occasions, one may have experienced confusion towards the resemblance of the Iraq war coverage on CCTV news channel to that of its American counterparts.

It is more interesting to trace the TMCs' creeping influence from the perspective of the audience response. In many ways, the TMCs' penetration into the Chinese media sphere has diversified the local media landscape, and managed to change the local audience's mindset of news and media culture. The increasing exposure to international news and media flow has significantly changed the Chinese audience's perception of such fundamental questions of journalism and media studies as "what is news." Specifically, can mass media be both informative and entertaining? Can the principle of commercialized news media (e.g., "to bleed to lead") be routinely practiced in the socialist mass media? Can the Chinese partisan press follow the professional ethics of western journalism? In other words, the TMCs have equipped Chinese audience with a yardstick of western journalism to rethink and re-evaluate Chinese news media.

One recent survey (Hu & Zheng, 2002) shows that the majority of the Chinese audience is not satisfied with the status quo of the Chinese news media, which, in their view, "lags far behind their western counterparts." Seventy-six percent of the interviewees thought that the western news media remained neutral in their coverage; 53% of the interviewees believed that their Chinese counterparts could not maintain the principle of neutrality. According to one interviewee, the reason for this situation was that western news media tended to use different voices in accordance with their different standpoints whereas Chinese news media appeared uniform in their coverage of major events. This survey was cross-referenced by an earlier study of the audience response to Chinese news media in which 62% of the respondents showed their dissatisfaction toward Chinese news media and urged for "a press/media reform oriented towards the needs of the audience." In fact, "right to know," "immediacy," and "neutrality" are among the top objectives of such press/media reform (Chen et al., 1997).

Aside from news media, the film industry is another illuminating sphere of how the global has transformed the local. Traditionally, the Chinese film audience would rate the quality of a film based on its story, characterization, and cinematography. It is noteworthy that the Chinese film audience and their US counterparts defined "blockbuster" differently as recently as the mid-1990s. For example, when the quota-based importation of Hollywood blockbusters was initially implemented in 1995, a small-budget, virtually obscure art romance, *The Bridges of Madison County*, that starred Clint Eastwood and Meryl Streep, could strike a chord among as many as 160 million Chinese cinema-goers. However, after ten years' Hollywoodization in China, one can safely conclude that the local taste has become more identical to that of their American counterparts. A recent audience survey in Beijing shows that 73% of the respondents chose "audiovisual effect" as the determining component of an excellent film "worthy of cinema going," in contrast to 30% of those who choose "plot" (Huang, Yu, & Han, 2005). Based on this film logic, it is not surprising that Beijing audience ranks their film-viewing preferences for films made in the US (59%); in Hong Kong (57%); in mainland China (34%); in Europe (27%); and in Korea, Japan, and Southeast Asia (20%) (Huang et al., 2005). One has to bear in mind that the Hong Kong film industry follows the Hollywood-styled technocratic logic of "audiovisual effect" and henceforth gains popularity comparable to Hollywood production around the globe. In a word, the Hollywood logic has completely transformed the mindset of the Chinese audience in terms of what constitutes a high-quality movie.

The changing audience response contributes to redefining and restructuring the local film industry. Today, the demise of the plot-oriented "realistic" film, let alone the experimental art cinema, has become an accepted reality in contemporary China. Local film gurus such as Zhang Yimou and Chen Kaige all adjured their originally experimental aesthetics and avowed to produce Hollywood-styled blockbusters. Zhang's *Yingxiong* (Hero) and *Shimian Maifu* (The House of Flying Daggers), and Chen's most recent *Wuji* (The Promise) are all but endeavors of the Hollywoodization of Chinese cinema, obviously sanctioned by the changing taste of the Chinese audience. These movies grossed a historical new high of over 100 million yuan (approximately 20 million USD) at the box-office. Interestingly enough, the Hollywoodization of Chinese cinema takes the similar route of the aforementioned westernization of Chinese journalism, which started with the changing audience response and further pressed for the transformation of media to keep in step with the western yardstick.

Generally speaking, the increasing exposure to global media has enriched the Chinese audience's vision of the outside world, and transformed their conception of what constitutes a professionalized and high-quality media product, in lieu of the orthodox partisan "throat and tongue." The audience response has therefore catalyzed the ongoing press/media reform in contemporary China. Despite some ebbs and flows, the recent decade has seen a gradual liberalization and mercerizing of the Chinese media sphere, which is best evinced by the booming of the more commercialized and neutralized "metropolitan" press as an alternative to the dominant partisan press. Increasingly more investigative journalism appears in Chinese news media under the patronage of the officially sanctioned "the surveillance of public opinion" *(yulun jiandu)*, which significantly contributes to the democratization of Chinese political system. If we admit that the global has posed significant challenges and henceforth transformed the local, the aforementioned case studies in China all point to the potency and relevance of audience power in this ongoing process of media/cultural globalization.

Resisting the global with the local

To draw a quick conclusion that the Chinese audience generally prefers global media to their local counterparts is merely to examine one side of the coin. Despite the crushing power of global media and communication, it is still too early to claim that the Chinese audience has been totally subjugated to "Hollywoodization," "Disneyfication," or more generally, homogenized as part and parcel of the "global audience." As elsewhere in the world, the Chinese audience also endeavors to resist the sweeping influence of globalization with increasing awareness of nationhood and indigenous cultural identities.

The studies cited above have shown that in the realm of news media and film, the Chinese audience maintains a positive response to the influence of global media, which further is conducive to a press/media reform in contemporary China. However, other studies might delineate a totally different picture from the rosy characterization of a "global-media-friendly" Chinese audience. Interestingly, in the same audience survey that acknowledges the Hollywood hegemony in Chinese film marketplace (Huang, et al. 2005), scholars also remind us of a contrasting domination of homemade television serials. According to the survey, the Chinese audience's preference for TV serials by place of origin ranks for those made in Hong Kong and Taiwan (55.1%); in mainland China (41.9%); in Korea (31.5%); in Euro-America (29.8%); and in Japan (18.7%). Such globally popular TV miniseries as *Band of Brothers*, and series such as *Everybody Loves Raymond, The X-Files, 24 Hours,* and the more recent *Desperate Housewives*, all of which were made in the US, have hit their high water mark in the Chinese television marketplace.

As mentioned earlier, the success of Hollywood blockbusters can be attributed to the technocratic logic of audiovisual effects and special stunts, which is universally attractive to the global audience, including those in China. However, in terms of television viewing, which pertains to what David Morley (1992) calls "the family's daily ritual," the cultural logic of local identities prevails as the determining factor of the audience response to certain media products. On a more macroscopic level, the medium of television has been widely used to construct what Benedict Anderson (1983) calls "imagined communities" in most of the modern nation-states, including the People's Republic of China. Put simply, cultural barriers and personal preferences hinder the globalization of the television marketplace. Television viewing stills remains an individualized or communitarian activity rather than a global endeavor. In this light, local, regional, national or ethnic identities largely shape the television audience's response in contemporary China.

The resistance to global communication can be developed into a nationalist or patriotic movement with the help of the Internet. In terms of the interrelationship between media and society, the concept of "netizen" seems to bear more political implications than the more neutralized "audience." While the audience—be it readers, cinema-goers, or television viewers—can merely exercise their power silently by means of dollar bills or remote control, the netizens can openly utter their voices, form alliances, and exert peer pressure over the media producers or administrative authorities. It is the netizens—the mass media audience in cyberspace—that can constitute a virtual pressure group in resistance to the hegemony of global communication.

Compared to readers, cinema-goers, and television viewers, the Chinese netizens appear more politically conscious and activated with resort to the officially sanctioned nationalism and patriotism than the audience of the "old" media. A telling example of this activation is reflected in their allied protest against supposedly anti-China commercials, that pertain to the consumer products of such transnational corporations as Nike and Toyota. For example, in one Toyota promotion, a Chinese-styled, stone-carved lion is depicted raising its claws, which is interpreted as paying tribute to a new type of land cruiser named "Prado" (which is transliterated as "hegemony" in Chinese) (Li, 2003). In another advertisement for Nippon paint, the image of traditional Chinese pavilions with painted pillars and carved dragons is evoked to attract local consumers. As known to all, Chinese people claim themselves as the "descendants of the dragon." To show how smooth the pillars become after the use of Nippon paint, the advertisement shows that the carved dragon cannot attach itself to the pillar and thus, slides to the ground (Wang, 2003).

Contrary to the advertisers' intention, these two graphic commercials, published via newspapers and magazines and obviously designed to court Chinese consumers, instigated anger and resentment among them. Given that both advertisements were produced by Japanese companies, the historical legacies of Sino-Japanese war in the late 19th century and mid-20th century exerted significant influences on their interpretation. For most Chinese netizens who voiced their anger via the internet, the Chinese lion's salutation to a Japanese land cruiser was understood as symbolizing China's submission to Japan's military conquest (Li, 2003). In the latter case, the Chinese dragon's sliding down because of Japanese-made paint was similarly indicative of Japan's everlasting ambition to dominate China (Wang, 2003).

In terms of visibility and extent of influence, these print advertisements cannot be compared to Nike's commercial entitled "The Chamber of Fear," aired via television and downloaded via its official website in October, 2004.

This commercial, unlike the previous ones, was not targeted toward Chinese consumers, but was used as part of Nike's global campaign for a new brand of basketball footwear, "Air Generation II." What matters here is the use of such Chinese icons as Kung fu (martial arts), Feitian (Chinese Bodhisattva), and again, the dragon. Wearing the new shoes, the featured NBA superstar LeBron James is endowed with such magic powers as to defeat the aged Kung fu guru, to strike the seductive Bodhisattva into pieces, and ultimately, to conquer the vicious dragon (see Zhu & Huong, 2005).

Based on the nearly 30,000 comments collected from different online chatrooms or BBS (Bulletin Board Services), over 92% of Chinese netizens identified the Nike commercial as "insulting or humiliating China." Under such a crushing power of public animosity, on December 3, 2004, Chinese regulators issued an official censure against this Nike commercial, claiming that "it annihilates China's national dignity and hurts Chinese people's self-esteem" (SARFT, 2004). Fearing a possible embargo, which had already been campaigned for among Chinese netizens, Nike finally self-censored this commercial and made a formal apology to the Chinese consumers via its official website on December 5, 2004.

By way of increasing global/local media encounters, the Chinese audience has developed an increasing awareness of nationhood and local cultural identities and more importantly, a strong sense of autonomy in the face of global media. They are no longer the stereotyped "silent majority" in the global media marketplace. It is not yet clear whether they can transcend the narrow-minded nationalism or locality so as to build up a more self-conscious "audience power." In point of fact, their ever-growing responses to global media could prevent China from falling victim to the homogenous Hollywoodization or Disneyfication, and more significantly, ensure that Chinese voices are heard in the sphere of global communication. Ironically enough, such "audience power" also can be abused to consolidate the heavy-handed system of official censorship in China and therefore, poses a significant obstacle to the free flow of global communication.

Conclusion

The complexities and intricacies of the global/local encounters have drawn increasing scholastic attention in the emergent studies of global media and communication. The current survey of the Chinese audience's conflicting responses to global media cannot but testify to the truism that globalization is not merely a process of homogenization, but rather what Roland Robertson (1992) calls "glocalization." Global media and communication, via the crushing power of the TMCs, restructure and reshape the mindset of Chinese audience, at least in terms of the news media and film industry. The changing audience response has consequently created a social ambiance to catalyze the implementation of an immediate press/media reform, which is oriented towards cultural diversity and media pluralization.

Paradoxically, the case studies of TV serials and anti-China commercials remind us of the countervailing trend of the ongoing media/cultural globalization: the further consolidation and increasing utterances of nationhood and indigenous cultural identities. The conflicting responses of Chinese audience are therefore indicative of their strategic negotiation of the global and the local. By dint of adopting the audience-centered perspective, this chapter aimed to pinpoint the urgency and necessity of transferring the scholastic focus in the current studies of global communication and China, namely, from the central theme of "what can media/cultural globalization do to China?" to that of "what can China do to media/cultural globalization?"

Author's Note

I thank the Tsinghua Asian Studies Fund for the provision of subsidies, which enabled me to be relieved of my daily teaching/administrative assignments and to focus on the completion of this chapter. I also thank my graduate assistants, Wu Yue, Zhu Dan and Huang Ruixi, for helping me with the data collection and processing.

References

Anderson, B. (1983). *Imagined communities*. London: Verso.

Chen, C. & Sun W. (Eds.) (1997). *Meijie ren xiandaihua* (Media, human beings and modernization). Beijing: Zhongguo shehui kexue chubanshe (China Social Science Press).

Chen, C., Sun, W., Zhang, X., Min, D. & Bo, W. (1999, November). *Shoujie quanguo shangxing dianshtai guanzhong zhuangkuang diaocha* (The first nationwide audience survey of terrestrial television stations in China). Unpublished document. Division of Audience Research, Chinese Association of Radio & Television Studies. Beijing.

CCTV (China Central Television). (2005). *Zhongyang dianshitai shouzhong diaochao niandu baogao* (The annual survey of CCTV's audience). Unpublished document. Divison of General Management, CCTV. Beijing.

Cui, B. (Ed.). (2005). *Zhongguo meijie chanye lanpishu* (The bluebook for Chinese media industry). Beijing: Zhongguo shehui kexuechubanshe (China Social Science Press).

Gurevitch, M. (1991). The globalization of electronic journalism. In J. Curran &

M. Gurevirch (Eds.). *Mass media and society* (pp. 179-193). London: Edward Arnold.

Hu, Y. & Zheng, L. (2002). Shouzhong guannian de bianhua dui chuanmei fazhan de tiaozhan: dui kuawehua Beijing shouzhong de yixiang shizheng yanjiu (The audience's changing perception and its challenge to media development in contemporary China: an empirical study of audiences in a cross-cultural context). *Xinwenjie* (The sphere of the news media), *2003(3)*, 12-16.

Huang, H., Yu, H. & Han, P. (2005). Guanyu Beijing yingshi shouzhong xuqiu de diaocha (A survey of the needs of the Beijing film and television audience). *Beijing Shehui Kexue* (Beijing Journal of Social Sciences), *2005(2)*, 140-146.

Jiao, J. (2006, January 18). CNNIC fabu di 17 ci hulianwang baogao (CNNIC issues the No. 17 report). *Xin Jing Bao* (New Beijing Daily). B06.

Li, Y. (2003). Fengtian badao che guanggao fenxi (An analysis of the advertisement for Toyota's "Prado" land cruiser). *Guoji Guanggao* (International Advertisement). 2003(4). 16-17.

Morley, D. (1992). *Television, audiences and cultural studies*. London: Routledge.

Robertson, R. (1992). *Globalization: social theory and global culture*. London: Sage.

Rantanen, T. (2005). *The media and globalization*. London: Sage.

SARFT (State Administration of Radio, Film and Television). (2004, December 3). *Guanyu liji tingzhi bofang "kongju doushi" guanggao pian de tongzhi* (A notice of halting the broadcasting of the commercial entitled "The Chamber of Fear"). Unpublished document. Division of Advertisement Administration, SARFT, Beijing.

Shi, A. (2005). The taming of the shrew: Global Media in a Chinese Perspective. *Global Media and Communication, 1(1)*, 33-36.

Tomlinson, J. (1991). *Cultural imperialism*. London: Pinter.

Xiao, Y. (2005). Dapian zhi lu (The road to blockbusters). *Sanlian Shenghuo Zhoukan* (Lifeweek), *342, 29-35*.

Wang, S. (2003). Libang qi guanggao fenxi (An analysis of the advertisement for Nippon paint). *Guoji Guanggao* (International Advertisement), *2003(10)*, 48.

Zhao, Y. (1998). *The party line is the bottom line*. London: Routledge.

Zhu, D. & Huang, R. (2005). Kuaguo guanggao zhong de wenhua chongtu: naike "kongju doushi" guanggao jinbo anli yanjiu (Cultural conflict in the transnational advertising: a case study of halting the broadcasting of Nike's ad entitled "The Chamber of Fear"). Unpublished manuscript. School of Journalism and Communications, Tsinghua University, Beijing.

CHAPTER SEVEN

ADVERTISING TO CHILDREN IN CHINA: SIMILARITIES AND CONTRASTS BETWEEN EAST AND WEST

MARK BLADES & CAROLINE J. OATES, UNIVERSITY OF SHEFFIELD, UK

In this chapter, we will consider the effects of advertising on children in China, and the implications of the rapid expansion of marketing aimed at Chinese children. In the first part of the chapter, we will discuss the concerns generated by any advertising aimed at children and suggest that much the same concerns will apply in China. In the second part of the chapter, we will consider children's understanding of advertisements and argue that the development of such understanding is likely to be similar in all cultures. We will also speculate how exposure to new forms of advertising may affect all children as new media technologies are adopted throughout the world. We will argue that, despite differences in tradition and regulation, there are good reasons to believe that the effects of advertising to children will be much the same in China as elsewhere, and that the issues related to advertising to children in other countries are likely to be the same issues that will need to be addressed in China now or in the near future.

It is conventional to begin papers on marketing with figures about population, economics, and media. Rather than go against convention we provide some figures here, but we note that although figures about population expansion and future economic growth may be useful approximations, any data about the use of different media are far less precise. There has been an explosion of media use in China in the last quarter of a century, and we can only assume that within a few more years the penetration of all media (television, computer, internet, mobile phone texting, and so on) will be as extensive as the same media in Western countries. There will also be new media that we cannot yet predict.

In the last quarter of a century, China's economic growth has exceeded that of most other countries (Yueh, 2005). Since the 1980s, China's GDP has increased by an average of about 10% per year, at a time when the mean rate for all countries has been about 3%. At the present rate of growth, China will be the world's largest economy by the middle of this century (Yueh, 2005). The current generation of Chinese children are therefore growing up in the fastest expanding and, soon to be, most powerful economy in the world.

There are 1300 million people in China including nearly 300 million children under 14 years of age (Chan & McNeal, 2006a). In 1979, the Chinese government introduced a policy of one child per family as an essential way to curb China's population explosion. Although the majority of children are now in one-child families, the birth rate is still declining (World Advertising Research Centre, 2006). However, the current decline in the birth rate is to some extent offset by a decline in infant mortality, and by an increase in life expectancy, so that the population of the country is estimated to top 1500 million by about 2030. This figure will include more than 350 million children.

More than 90% of Chinese households have television, so that in many areas nearly all households have access to television and in surveys of leisure time, two-thirds of respondents say that their favorite pastime in the evening is watching television with their families (Redl & Simons, 2002). There are 400 broadcasting stations including 60 national and local channels that broadcast up to 10 hours of programs for children each day (Chan & McNeal, 2004a, 2006a). Most households also have access to other media, and we will discuss these alternative forms of media at the end of this chapter. Researchers in both China and elsewhere, however, have focused almost exclusively on the effects of television advertising, which will be the focus in the first parts of this chapter.

After the 1949 revolution in China commercial advertising was limited, and following the Cultural Revolution in the 1960s, there was little or no advertising. It was not until the 1980s that there was a rapid increase in spending on all types of advertising and a corresponding increase in the number of advertising agencies (Wang, 1997, Zhou, Zhang, & Vertinsky, 2002) (See Yao, this volume). Spending on television advertising has grown rapidly since the year 2000; the amount has increased, on average, by more than 50% per year (World Advertising Research Centre, 2006). This additional spending has resulted in an increase in the total number of advertisements and Chan and McNeal (2004b) have estimated that a child who watches three hours of television per day will see 16,000 advertisements that year.

Chinese children comprise a very large market given that their numbers are much greater than the whole population of most other countries, and their notable direct and indirect spending power. Like children in other countries, Chinese children may have a regular allowance as well as gifts of money on special occasions. But unlike children in other countries, because of the one-child policy, Chinese children are likely to be only children and to be the focus of their families' ambitions. As only children, they can therefore expect to receive the sole attention of their parents and up to four grandparents, and the influence of such children has led to them being labeled "Little Emperors" (Chan & McNeal, 2004a). These children will have money to spend directly and money to save, and more importantly will influence a large proportion of family spending including for example, choice of foods, entertainment, and travel. McNeal and Yeh (1997) estimated that Chinese children influence up to two-thirds of family spending, which is a much higher proportion than in other countries. McNeal and Zhang (2000) also estimated that urban Chinese children (under 12 years of age) may influence $61 billion of family spending each year. As noted above, the Chinese economy is expanding rapidly and therefore the figures for children's influence will increase in the future. Given the powerful influence of children, it is not surprising that marketers have developed campaigns to target them (e.g. Bose & Khanna, 1996, O'Hanlon, 2000a, b).

In a comparatively short period, since the 1990s, Chinese television advertising has become more sophisticated. Early advertising often focused mainly on product information, prices, and details of where products could be purchased (Keown, Jacobs, Schmidt & Ghymn, 1992). More recent advertising has included greater emphasis on life-style and social status (Chan, 1995; Lin, 2001). Despite this, and in contrast to advertising in countries like the US, Chinese advertising still reflects traditional values, respect for family and the elderly, and frequent appeals to history and to harmony with nature (Lin, 2001; Zhou, Zhou, & Xue, 2005). Nonetheless, foreign influence on advertising style can be seen in the marketing of products from other countries, especially high status products, and in the use of foreign actors to express attitudes and emotional appeals that might not be appropriate if expressed by Chinese actors (Zhou & Belk, 2004). Zhou and Belk (2004) note that Western products in particular, might be marketed as high status, fashionable items appealing to the consumers as symbols of success and achievement.

Past researchers showed that, in general, Chinese adults held negative attitudes toward advertisements. For example, Zhao and Shen (1995) found that, in surveys carried out in the 1980s, more than two-thirds of people thought there were too many advertisements, and half believed that advertising was misleading. More recent researchers have found slightly more positive attitudes towards advertising. For example, Zhou, et al. (2002) questioned adults in five cities and found that only half thought there were too many advertisements. Half the sample said that they liked advertisements, a fifth disliked them, and the rest were neutral. The majority of the people surveyed said that they used information from advertisements to decide on purchases, although they did not always trust that information. About a quarter of the sample thought that advertising was often misleading. Nearly half the sample thought that advertising increased materialistic attitudes and prompted the making of unnecessary purchases.

Children in any country will always see many television advertisements that are aimed at adults (Chan, 2000;, Gunter, Oates & Blades, 2005). However, in most countries, children will usually see only a small number of advertisements for adults in periods of specific children's programs. In China, the majority of advertisements associated with children's programs are advertisements for adults (Chan & McNeal, 2004a). Chan and McNeal (2004a) listed the products marketed during children's programs including: medicine, furniture, household products, business advertisements, cars, clothing, mobile phones, and credit cards. The advertisements that were aimed at children included, in order of frequency: milk, jelly, vitamins, biscuits, drinks, food, sweets, and theme parks.

Chan and McNeal (2004a) found several differences between the style and content of children's advertisements in China and in the US, and they suggested that many of the differences reflected cultural factors. For example, Chinese advertisements were more likely to include male rather than female characters, and to have male voiceovers, reflecting China's more male oriented society. There was also more emphasis in Chinese advertisements on the shared or popular aspects of a product, rather than, as in the United States a focus on the personal or individual advantages of owning or using a product (see Zhou, et al. this volume). The most significant difference was that the proportion of food and soft drink advertisements in China was far higher than the proportion of such advertisements in the United States. More than four-fifths of the Chinese advertisements were for food and drinks. Chan and McNeal suggested that the priority of food advertisements over other advertisements for products such as toys or advertisements for entertainment may reflect the importance of food in a country that has experienced many famines.

Children in all cultures learn information about products from many sources as well as from television advertising (Gunter et al., 2005). These sources include parents, peers, information in shops at the point of sale, and more recently, from web sites. Yau (1994) suggested that parents and family are likely to be an important influence as a large proportion of children in China live in extended families and potentially have advice from parents, grandparents, and other relatives. Given the traditional emphasis on children respecting their elders, such advice is likely to be taken seriously (Yau, 1994). Children may also be influenced by their peers, because they may spend much time with other children in school, clubs, or in the course of collective activities (McNeal & Ji, 1999). Children are also likely to make frequent visits to markets and shops with their families, friends, or on their own where they can learn about products directly (Chan, 2005a). Some Chinese children may go to a market on their own from the age of about five or six, and nearly all children may do local shopping on their own from about eight years of age (McNeal & Yeh, 1997) which is earlier than would be the case in the urban areas of countries like the United States. If independent shopping does result in greater consumer knowledge, then young children in China may be developing consumer skills much earlier than children in other cultures.

Mcneal and Ji (1999) asked 400 children how they learned about new products, and found that their responses depended on the type of product. For example, children learned most about school and educational items from their parents. These were items, sometimes expensive ones, over which parents would be expected to have control. They were also items that were rarely featured in television advertisements (see above). However, for new products like foods and drinks that were widely advertised in the media, children were more likely to say that they learned about such products from television or at the point of sale, rather than from family or friends. When McNeal and Ji asked children to say what was, overall, their most important source of information about new products, half the children mentioned television. This finding is not surprising, because children aged 8 to 12 years, the age when they are developing as consumers, say that their favorite pastime is watching TV (Zhang, 2005) and therefore they are inevitably exposed to a very large number of advertisements. Children report that they do watch most of the advertisements shown on television, and that they like most advertisements and enjoy watching them (Chan, McNeal & Chan, 2002).

Concerns about the effects of advertising to children

In the West, advertising to children has generated many concerns. In this section, we will consider some of these concerns and discuss their applicability in the Chinese context. We will suggest that many of the issues are likely to be the same in both the West and in China with some differences. Such differences may be accounted for by the shorter history of advertising in China, and the different cultural context of that advertising.

A major concern in the West is whether advertising to children encourages unhealthy lifestyles. This concern focuses on the plethora of food advertisements aimed at children, and the type of food or drink that they encourage children to purchase (Gunter et al., 2005). In the US, there has been a large increase in the number of children with obesity, and a similar trend is evident in other Western countries (Hoek, 2005; Krishnamoorthy, Hart & Jelalian, 2006). The fact that Western children are growing larger and less healthy cannot automatically be blamed on the effects of advertising, as there could be many contributing factors. Indeed, marketers have argued that other factors, such as children's lack of exercise, or changes in family meals with a greater dependence on convenience foods are much more important factors than advertisements for food products (Clarke, 2003, Young, 2003).

Nonetheless, several researchers have argued that there is a direct relationship between food advertising and food consumption (Wiecha, et al., 2006) and there is empirical evidence for this claim. For example, Halford, et al. (2004) showed food or non-food television advertisements to healthy-weight, overweight, and obese children in the United Kingdom. The children watched the advertisements and were then allowed to eat as much as they liked from a selection of low and high fat foods (but not ones that they had seen in the advertisements). All three groups ate more food after they had seen food advertisements than they did after watching non-food advertisements, and the children were more likely to eat the high fat foods after watching the food advertisements. In other words, just watching food advertisements resulted in all children eating more food in general, and more high fat foods.

Hastings et al. (2003) reviewed all the research on food advertising to children and also concluded that food advertising has a direct effect on children's choice of food and the amount that they eat. As Hastings et al. indicated, the influence of food advertising could either be positive or negative. If children only see advertisements for high fat, sugar, and salt products then they will be influenced to eat these, probably to the detriment of their health. If children see only advertisements for healthy foods then they could be influenced to eat a well balanced diet, but as Hastings et al. pointed out, most governments do little to advertise healthy eating. By far, the largest proportion of all advertising aimed at children is for food products such as confectionery, breakfast cereals, snack foods, and soft drinks (Dalmeny, Hanna, & Lobstein, 2003; Hastings et al., 2003; Kunkel et al., 2004). The concern about food advertising is such that for the first time ever in the West, some countries, like the United Kingdom, have discussed a specific ban on advertisements for unhealthy foods that are aimed at young children (Ofcom, 2006). Such a ban would mean treating advertisements for unhealthy food in the same way as cigarette or alcohol advertisements, which in most Western countries cannot be shown to children (Gunter et al., 2005).

In a content analysis of advertisements aimed at Chinese children, Chan and McNeal (2004a) found that more than 80% were food products. Some of these (such as milk products) were not necessarily unhealthy products, but many others were for items with high sugar or high salt content. Chan and McNeal also found that a small number of advertised products were brands from the US and that with two exceptions (for entertainment and personal products) all the US brands were for high calorie food and drinks. Given the high proportion of food advertising aimed at children, and the likelihood that international food marketing companies will increase their share of marketing in China, we suggest that such advertising is likely to become a factor in contributing to Chinese children's unhealthy diets. Food advertising to children is still less developed in China than in the West, and therefore, China may be in a position to learn from the experiences of Western countries and limit such advertising before it adversely impacts on children's health.

Health related issues are not limited just to food advertising. For example, children in China may see advertisements for medicines and vitamins (Chan & McNeal, 2004a), in contrast to many Western countries where such advertising to children would be restricted or banned (Gunter et al., 2005). Children and adolescents may make comparisons between their own appearance and the appearance of actors and actresses in programs and advertisements, and such comparisons may lead to insecurities about self and body image that are targeted by further advertising for beauty, cosmetics, and slimming products (Chan, 2006; Fung, 2006). Children may also be exposed to advertisements aimed at adults for products like tobacco and alcohol, and children and teenagers who are too young to use or buy these products may develop positive attitudes to those products and develop brand preferences (Goldberg, 2003a, b; Peters et al., 1995). If tobacco and alcohol advertising encourage children to smoke or drink, especially at an early age, there are obvious health implications in allowing such advertising.

Children also see advertisements for entertainment products (music, films, video games, books), for clothes and fashion items, for sports equipment, and for toys (Chan & McNeal, 2004a; McNeal & Ji, 1999). In themselves, advertisements for these products do not carry the same risk implications as unhealthy food advertisements, but the purpose of all advertising is to generate wants and desires in children. These desires can only be satisfied by children spending money, or by pestering others to spend money on them. The latter may lead to family conflict, depending on whether parents are willing to buy the desired products. Many countries, including China, have regulations prohibiting advertisements that encourage children to pester parents (Chan & McNeal, 2004; Gunter et al., 2005). However, the specific aim of advertising to children is to get them to influence family spending (Chamberlain, Wang, & Robinson, 2006; Pilgrim & Lawrence, 2001; Shoham & Dalakas, 2005), and as noted earlier, in Chinese family households that center on only children as "Little Emperors," the children have a great deal of influence and may well be indulged by parents and grandparents. In the West, by contrast, children who pester are often in competition with brothers or sisters to gain the attention of their parents and they may have less influence. Whether as a result of these family differences, advertising generates more conflict in China or in the West is a debatable point that would merit further research.

Promoting a desire for products, especially the desire for specific brands that might have high status associations has been described as encouraging materialism in children (Buijzen & Valkenburg, 2003; Chan, 2003, 2004, 2005b). Materialism is a term that includes a number of attitudes such as placing concern for material goods before people, assessing people on the basis of what they own, setting goals that focus on material wealth, and in general adopting selfish, possessive attitudes, rather than sharing, altruistic ones. Such attitudes, though not perhaps explicitly encouraged, are not out of place in Western cultures that have a long tradition of capitalism, competition, and individualism. Advertising also has been an accepted part of most Western cultures for more than a century (Gunter et al., 2005). In contrast, China has a tradition that places strong emphasis on a person as part of a culture, within a network of family, social, and national obligations (Lin, 2001) and these traditions are at odds with the materialistic nature of advertising. There also have been recent periods (1960s-1970s) when virtually all advertising was banned in China (Wang, 1997) so there has been no continuous history of advertising, and therefore no assumption that advertising is always an inevitable part of the culture. However, it seems likely that, with the very rapid economic development of China, advertising will become as extensive and as inevitable as in the West.

Concern that advertising will make children more materialistic is one of the fears expressed by parents when they are asked their opinion about advertising to children (Chan & McNeal, 2004a). Parents in China generally hold a negative view of advertising aimed at children. For example, parents thought that advertisements encouraged bad eating habits, caused family conflict, and that children were too easily seduced by free gifts and special offers. Parents thought that there was too much advertising aimed at children, that it was misleading, and that it should be banned during children's television (Chan & McNeal, 2004a). Such attitudes were very similar to the attitudes expressed by parents in other countries. Young, de Bruin, and Eagle (2003) asked parents in the United Kingdom, New Zealand, and Sweden about their thoughts on advertising to children. Just like parents in China, the parents in other countries thought that advertising led to unhealthy eating, encouraged children to want things that they did not need, was a major cause of children pestering, and that advertisers used tricks and gimmicks to sell their products.

The parents in other countries also wanted more regulation of advertising aimed at children. For example, most of the respondents in the United Kingdom group and three quarters in the Swedish group wanted stronger regulation (Young et al., 2003). Thus, if parents are concerned about what they perceive to be the negative effects of advertising, then it is not surprising that a large majority of parents in all countries want greater regulation. However, it is somewhat surprising that such a large proportion was found in Sweden, because Sweden already has stricter regulation than most countries, and already bans some television advertising aimed at children (Advertising Education Forum, 2006). It may be the case that in all countries, and irrespective of the existing level of regulation, that parents will always want tighter control on advertising to children. If so, we anticipate that even if China tightens its regulations about advertising to children, parents in China will still maintain their opposition to such advertising.

Children's understanding of advertisements

In the West there has been a growing concern about young children's ability to understand the advertising messages that they see. There are two main aspects to understanding an advertisement (Oates, Blades, Gunter, & Don, 2003). First, children have to recognize that a particular message is an advertisement, and second, they need to realize that the aim of an advertisement is to persuade them to buy a product or a service. Understanding the latter aspect of advertising is usually referred to as understanding the "persuasive intent" of the advertiser. Children can distinguish television advertisements from television programs from about the age of four or five years (Gunter et al., 2005) at which time, children usually think that advertisements are just to provide a break between programs or are there to tell them what is available in the shops. It is only several years later that children become aware of the persuasive intent behind an advertisement, and realize that advertisements are biased and selective messages paid for by the manufacturer of the product being advertised (Oates, Blades, & Gunter, 2002).

We have argued previously that children's understanding of advertisements is closely linked to their cognitive development (Gunter et al., 2005), and children's cognitive development is universal, because all typically developing children achieve the same stages of development at roughly the same ages (John, 2002; Moses & Baldwin, 2005; Smith, Cowie, & Blades, 2003). If understanding advertisements is related to cognitive development (Chan & McNeal, 2006b), we would not expect much, if any, difference between children in China and children in the West in the development of their understanding of advertisements.

In a survey of Chinese 6- to 14-year-olds' understanding, Chan and McNeal (2004a) asked children several questions about television advertising. The children answered the questions by choosing one of five or six response options. In answer to the question "What are TV commercials?" only one-sixth of the 6-7-year-olds and less than one-third of the 8-9-year-olds chose the response stating that advertisements were designed to promote products. More than half the children in both age groups thought that advertisements were for entertainment or to provide a break. In answer to the question "What do TV commercials want you to do?" about one-third of each age group chose the response that advertisements were to get you to buy products. Such responses showed that the majority of children at these ages did not appreciate the persuasive intent of advertising. The findings from Chan and McNeal are similar to results found in the West. For example, Oates et al. (2002) asked children in the United Kingdom about the purpose of advertising and found that none of the 6-year-olds and only one-quarter of the 8-year-olds said that advertisements were meant to persuade.

On behalf of the American Psychological Association, Kunkel et al. (2004) reviewed much of the literature concerning advertising to children. Kunkel et al. concluded that children do not understand persuasive intent until about 8 years of age, and argued that advertising aimed at younger children is unethical because they do not have the cognitive abilities to understand how the advertiser intends to influence them. The American Psychological Association therefore called for a ban on advertising aimed at young children in the US. Kunkel et al.'s conclusion applies equally to all children, and a similar argument could be made about banning advertising to young children in China or any other country.

There is one way that children in China and in the West may have different experiences of advertising (Chan & McNeal, 2002). In most Western countries, television and print advertising is quite tightly regulated (see Gunter et al., 2005), and although advertisers may break or bend the regulations on occasions, these occasions are rare. By its nature, all advertising is biased, but in the West, television and print advertising often will not be deliberately misleading. In contrast, in China in 2000 there were nearly 70,000 illegal advertisements, many because they were misleading (Chan & McNeal, 2004a). Thus, children in China are more likely to be exposed to misleading advertisements than are children in the West. The application of the national regulations in China varies in different parts of the country. Chan and McNeal found that children in areas where the regulations were better enforced had a *poorer* understanding of advertisements because, as they suggested, children in areas with weaker regulation may have been given more explicit warnings about advertising by their parents. If this is the case, then as China extends or enforces advertising regulation, children's awareness of advertising may decline. Thus, as regulation increases, particular care will be needed to insure that children are educated about advertisements in other ways, for example by parents, or by media education programs (see Blumberg, et al., this volume).

Virtually all the research examining children's understanding of advertisements has focused on television advertising, and there is little or no research into children's understanding of advertising in other media. Children have long been exposed to advertising in other media, including print advertisements in comics and magazines, advertisements on the radio, ambient (i.e. street) advertising, point of sale advertising in shops, product placement in films, sponsorship for events, and viral (word-of-mouth) advertising. These forms of advertising are aimed at both children and adults, but with the exception of a few studies, they have received only limited attention in China (Chan, 2005a; McKechnie & Zhou, 2003; Prendergast & Chan, 1999; Prendergast & Man, 2005) or elsewhere. However, all these established forms of advertising are relatively minor compared to the recent development of the internet (Xin, 2002) and the advertising associated with it (Gong & Maddox, 2003).

Internet advertising is often aimed at children, but as yet we know very little about children's understanding of such advertising. As we noted above, children can recognize television advertisements from about 4 or 5 years of age, but most television advertisements are limited to specific "spots" between programs or within programs, and are usually a different style and length from those programs associated with it (Chan & McNeal, 2004a). These differences probably help young children distinguish television advertisements from programs. In contrast, internet advertisements are not so easily distinguished. A Web page advertising a product might look very similar to a page that is not an advertisement, and many Web pages that are not in themselves marketing a product may still carry advertising messages (e.g. in the banner of the page).

To find out if children could recognize advertisements on Web pages, we showed 6- to 11-year-olds in the United Kingdom several actual Web pages that had been designed for children (Blades, Oates, & Don, 2005). Some of the pages included advertisements and some did not. The children were asked to look at each Web page and point to anything that they thought was an advertisement. The 6-9-year-olds identified less than one quarter of the advertisements, and the 10-11-year-olds identified about half. All the children in the study were old enough to recognize advertisements in other media like television, and the older children should have had a good understanding of the persuasive intent of advertising (Oates et al., 2002). Nonetheless, all children showed difficulty recognizing the Web page advertisements. If children do not always realize that they are looking at advertisements they may be particularly vulnerable to internet advertising.

We anticipate that internet advertising will dominate all advertising to children in the near future, in both western countries such as the US and in eastern countries such as China. Unlike advertising in nearly all other media, which can be regulated to some extent, advertising on the Web is hard to regulate at all. As Xin (2002) pointed out when discussing the political implications of the Web,

> The Internet is unlike any of the traditional media, and this is what makes it so disruptive and troublesome. When one considers … its disregard of national boundaries, it is an extremely difficult, if not impossible, medium to control (p. 198).

Conclusions

In this chapter we have compared China and the West with reference to the advertising that is aimed at children. The concerns about such advertising and its effects on children are similar in both China and the West. These concerns are reflected in parents' attitudes towards advertising which, in general, are also similar in China and in the West. We also discussed children's understanding of advertising and indicated that such understanding is likely to develop in the same way in all children. In summary, there are many similarities between advertising to children in China and advertising to children in other countries.

When there are differences between China and the West, these can often be traced back to different cultural values and the unusual history of advertising in China. For example, Chinese parents had more concerns about making children materialistic, probably because advertising was often at odds with the traditional emphasis on a mutually supportive and communal society. Many parents in China also can remember periods when advertising was outlawed altogether, and therefore, they may not take advertising for granted in the same way as Western parents. However, China is changing so rapidly in the process of becoming the world's most important economic power, that past cultural values and past history may have less, if any, influence in the future.

On the one hand, China has a slightly less developed advertising environment than countries in the West. For example, advertising regulation and control is less sophisticated in many parts of China which may be to the disadvantage of children who are exploited by inappropriate or misleading advertisements. On the other hand, the fact that advertising to children is not quite so well developed, and not so dominated by multi-national marketing companies, may mean that effective intervention and better regulation now could help China to avoid some of the problems that have been associated with advertising in countries with more established marketing environments. In other words, China may have the advantage of benefiting from the less positive experiences of the West, and introduce preventative and educational measures early enough to reduce the negative aspects of advertising.

However, for one aspect of advertising, China has no advantage over other countries. All countries constantly have to come to terms with the effects of new media technologies, and all new technologies spawn new advertising initiatives. China has political reasons for trying to control and influence the spread of new technology, especially the internet, but it seems unlikely that any country or political party can control such technologies for very long, and as these technologies become more dominant so will the advertising that they carry. If children are to be protected from the negative effects of that advertising, then initiatives and policies that go beyond national boundaries will be needed. Thus, China and the West will need to be part of shared global agreements to monitor marketing to children.

Acknowledgements

We are grateful to Moondore Ali and Jacquie Don who collected data for some of the studies referred to in this paper. We are also grateful to Maria Chu who helped to collect material for the literature review and interpreted some of the references to the research carried out in China.

References

Advertising Education Forum (2006). http://www.aeforum.org/

Blades, M., Oates, C. J., & Don, J. (2005, April). Children's awareness of print, ambient and internet advertising Poster present to the Society for Research in Child Development Conference, Atlanta, GA.

Bose, A., & Khanna, K. (1996). The little Emperor. A case study of a new brand launch. Paper presented to ESOMAR Congress, Istanbul, September. Available from http://www.warc.com

Buijzen, M., & Valkenburg, P. M. (2003). The effects of television advertising on materialism, parent-child conflict, and unhappiness: A review of research. *Applied Developmental Psychology, 24*, 437-456.

Chamberlain, L.J., Wang, Y., & Robinson, T. R. (2006). Does children's screen time predict requests for advertised products? *Archives of Pediatric Adolescent Medicine, 160*, 363-368.

Chan, K. (1995). Information content of television advertising in China. *International Journal of Advertising, 14*, 365-373.

—. (2000). Hong Kong children's understanding of television advertising. *Journal of Marketing Communications, 6*, 37-52.

—. (2003). Materialism among Chinese children in Hong Kong. *International Journal of Advertising and Marketing to Children, 4*, 47-61.

—. (2004). Material world: attitudes towards toys in China. *Young Consumers, 6*, 54-65.

——. (2005a). Store visits and information sources among urban Chinese children. *Journal of Consumer Marketing, 22,* 178-188.

——. (2005b). Hong Kong children's perception of material possessions. *House of Tomorrow, 13,* 1-5.

——. (2006). Advertising and adolescents. In K. Chan (Ed.), *Advertising and Hong Kong Society.* Hong Kong: Chinese University Press.

Chan, K., & McNeal, J. U. (2002). Children's perceptions of television advertising in urban China. *International Journal of Advertising and Marketing to Children, 3,* 69-79.

Chan, K., & McNeal, J. U. (2004a). *Advertising to children in China.* Hong Kong: Chinese University Press.

Chan, K., & McNeal, J. U. (2004b). Chinese children's attitudes towards television advertising: Truthfulness and liking. *International Journal of Advertising, 23,* 337-359.

Chan, K., & McNeal, J. U. (2006a). Children and media in China: An urban-rural comparison study. *Journal of Consumer Marketing, 23,* 79-88.

Chan, K., & McNeal, J. U. (2006b). Chinese children's understanding of commercial communications: A comparison of cognitive development and social learning models. *Journal of Economic Psychology, 27,* 36-56.

Chan, K., McNeal, J. U., & Chan, F. (2002). Children's response to television advertising in China. *International Journal of Advertising and Marketing to Children, 4,* 43-53.

Clarke, B. (2003). The complex issue of food, advertising and child health. (Interview with Jeremy Preston, Director of the U.K. Food Advertising Unit). *International Journal of Advertising and Marketing to Children, 5,* 11-16.

Dalmeny, K., Hanna, E., & Lobstein, T. (2003). *Broadcasting bad health. Why food marketing to children needs to be controlled.* A report by the International Association of Consumer Food Organizations for the World Health Organization consultation on a global strategy for diet and health. http://www.who.int/en/

Fung, A. (2006). Gender and advertising: The promotional culture of whitening and slimming. In Chan, K. (Ed.), *Advertising and Hong Kong society.* Hong Kong: Chinese University Press.

Goldberg, M.E. (2003a). American media and the smoking-related behaviours of Asian adolescents. *Journal of Advertising Research, 43,* 2-11.

——. (2003b). Correlation, causation, and smoking initiation among youths. *Journal of Advertising Research, 43,* 431-440.

Gong, W., & Maddox, L. (2003). Measuring web effectiveness in China. *Journal of Advertising Research, 43,* 34-49.

Gunter, B., Oates, C. J., & Blades, M. (2005). *Advertising to children on TV. Content, impact, and regulation.* Mahwah, New Jersey: Erlbaum.

Halford, J. C. G., Gillespie, J., Brown, V., Pontin, E. E., & Dovey, T.M. (2004). Effect of food advertising for foods and food consumption in children. *Appetite, 42*, 221-225.

Hastings, G., Stead, M., McDermott, L., Forsyth, A., MacKintosh, A.M., Raynor, M., Godfrey, C., Caraher, M., & Angus, K. (2003). *Review of research on the effects of food promotion to children.* Report prepared for the Food Standards Agency. http://www.food.gov.uk/

Hoek, J. (2005). Marketing communications and obesity: A view from the dark side. *New Zealand Medical Journal, 118 (1220).*

John, D. R. (2002). Consumer socialization of children—A retrospective look at twenty-five years of research. In F. Hansen, J. Rasmussen, A. Martensen, & B. Tufte (Eds.), *Children—Consumption, advertising and media.* Copenhagen: Copenhagen Business School Press.

Keown, C. F., Jacobs, L.W., Schmidt, R.W., & Ghymn, K-I. (1992). Information content of advertising in the United States, Japan, South Korea, and the People's Republic of China. *International Journal of Advertising, 11*, 257-267.

Krishnamoorthy, J.S., Hart, C., & Jelalian, E. (2006). The epidemic of childhood obesity: Review of research and implications for public policy. *Society for Research in Child Development Social Policy Report, 19, Number 2.*

Kunkel, D., Wilcox, B.L., Cantor, J., Palmer, E., Linn, S., & Dowrick, P. (2004). *Report of the American Psychological Association task force on advertising and children.* http://www.apa.org/

Lin, C. A. (2001). Cultural values reflected in Chinese and American television advertising. *Journal of Advertising, 30*, 83-94.

McKechnie, S. A., & Zhou, J. (2003). Product placement in the movies. A comparison of Chinese and American consumers' attitudes. *International Journal of Advertising, 22*, 349-374.

McNeal, J., & Ji, M.F. (1999). Chinese children as consumers: An analysis of their new product information sources. *Journal of Consumer Marketing, 16*, 345-364.

McNeal, J. U., & Yeh, C.H. (1997). Development of consumer behavior patterns among Chinese children. *Journal of Consumer Marketing, 14*, 45-59.

McNeal, J., & Zhang, H. (2000). Chinese children's consumer behaviour: A review. *International Journal of Advertising and Marketing to Children, 2*, 31-37.

Moses, L. J., & Baldwin, D.A. (2005). What can the study of cognitive development reveal about children's ability to appreciate and cope with advertising. *Journal of Public Policy and Marketing, 24*, 186-201.

Oates, C., Blades, M., & Gunter, B. (2002). Children and television advertising. When do they understand persuasive intent? *Journal of Consumer Behaviour*, *1*, 238-245.

Oates, C., Blades, M., Gunter, B., & Don, J. (2003). Children's understanding of television advertising: A qualitative approach. *Journal of Marketing Communications, 9*, 59-71.

Ofcom (2006). Advertising food and drinks to children on television. A consultation on possible new restrictions. http://ofcom.org.uk/

O'Hanlon, T. (2000a). Building a "kid contract" with Chinese children: Truths and trends. *International Journal of Advertising and Marketing to Children, 2*, 123-127.

——. (2000b). Building a "kid contract" with Chinese kids: Part II. *International Journal of Advertising and Marketing to Children, 2*, 205-209.

Peters, J., Betson, C. J., Hedley, A. J., Tai-Hing, L., Say-Gark, O., Chit-Ming, W., & Fielding, R. (1995). Recognition of cigarette brand names and logos by young children in Hong Kong. *Tobacco Control, 4*, 150-155.

Pilgrim, L., & Lawrence, D. (2001). Pester power is a destructive concept. *International Journal of Advertising and Marketing to Children, 3*, 11-21.

Prendergast, G., & Chan, C. H. (1999). The effectiveness of exterior bus advertising. *Journal of Consumer Marketing, 11*, 33-50.

Prendergast, G., & Man, Y.S. (2005). Perceptions of handbills as a promotional medium: An exploratory study. *Journal of Advertising Research, 45*, 124-131.

Redl, A., & Simons, R. (2002). Chinese media—One channel, two systems. In S. H. Donald, M. Keane & Y. Hong (Eds.), *Media in China. Consumption, content and crisis*. London: Routledge Curzon.

Shoham, A., & Dalakas, V. (2005). He said, she said ... they said: Parents' and children's assessment of children's influence on family consumption decisions. *Journal of Consumer Marketing, 22*, 152-160.

Smith, P. K. Cowie, H., & Blades, M. (2003). *Understanding children's development. Fourth edition*. Oxford: Blackwell.

Wang, J. (1997). Four hundred million to more than one billion consumers: A brief history of the foreign advertising industry in China. *International Journal of Advertising, 16*(4).

Wiecha, S., Peterson, J. L., Ludwig, K.E., Kim, D.S., Sobol, J., & Gortmaker, A. (2006). When children eat what they watch–Impact of television viewing on dietary intake in youth. *Archives of Pediatric and Adolescent Medicines, 160*, 436-442.

World Advertising Research Centre (2006). Demographic data for China. http://www.warc.com

Xin, H. (2002). The Surfer-in-Chief and the would-be kings of content. In S. H. Donald, M.Keane, & Y. Hong (Eds.), *Media in China. Consumption, content and crisis*. London: Routledge Curzon.

Yau, O. (1994). *Consumer behaviour in China: Consumer satisfaction and cultural values*. New York: Routledge.

Young, B. (2003). Does food advertising make children obese? *International Journal of Advertising and Marketing to Children, 4*, 19-26.

Young, B., de Bruin, A., & Eagle, L. (2003). Attitudes of parents toward advertising to children in the U.K., Sweden, and New Zealand. *Journal of Marketing Management, 19*, 475-490.

Yueh, L. (2005). The challenge for marketing in China. *Market Leader, 28*, 42-46.

Zhang, G. J. (2005). Youth trends in China. *Young Consumers, 6*, 28-33.

Zhao, X., & Shen, F. (1995). Audience reaction to commercial advertising in China in the 1980s. *International Journal of Advertising, 14*, 374-390.

Zhou, D., Zhang, W., & Vertinsky, H. (2002). Advertising trends in urban China. *Journal of Advertising Research, 42*, 73-81.

Zhou, N., & Belk, R.W. (2004). Chinese consumer readings of global and local advertising appeals. *Journal of Advertising, 33*, 63-76.

Zhou, S., Zhou, P., & Xue, F. (2005). Visual differences in US and Chinese television commercials. *Journal of Advertising, 34*, 111-119.

CHAPTER EIGHT

EFFECTS OF CULTURE-CONGRUENT VISUALS ON AFFECT, PERCEPTION AND PURCHASE INTENTION

SHUHUA ZHOU, YINJIAO YE, & JIE XU, UNIVERSITY OF ALABAMA

International advertisers and researchers have long been intrigued by the peculiarities as well as commonalities in advertising strategies between Western and Eastern societies. A recent issue of the *Journal of Advertising* focused on the strategies, cultural values, narrative styles, as well as visual differences in the contexts of different societies. Among these comparative studies was our pilot study on visual differences between US and Chinese commercials. (Zhou, Zhou, & Xue, 2005). We conducted the study because few had attended to the *visual* strategies embedded in commercials created in occidental and oriental markets. Our content analysis uncovered five categories of visual discrepancies in US and Chinese commercials; namely, US commercials used more visual stories, stronger emotional appeal, more product comparisons, and acknowledged brand earlier, whereas Chinese commercials displayed stronger veneration of tradition and history, and used more individual images. We argued that these findings of visual manipulation were perhaps reflective of their respective cultural values.

A logical next step was to investigate the effects of some of these visual differences on the perception of commercials, as well as viewers' affective and behavioral reaction to commercials and the advertised products. Such research not only contributes to our theoretical knowledge regarding how viewers process culture-congruent visual elements, but also enlightens international marketers to conduct culturally-based advertising campaigns, which have been proven to work better than "generalized" advertising campaigns (Mueller 1994; Taylor, Wilson & Miracle, 1997).

The importance of visuals in television commercials lies in their effectiveness to convey meanings and messages, because many consider visuals to be more concise than words, and that they can be more easily and quickly processed than verbal language (Berger 1998; Lester 2000). Barry (1997) contends that images contained in visuals touch the primal sense of human beings and that all images are by nature, gestalts that have the potential to imply more than the sum of their parts. As such, the skillful use of visuals in advertising may convey the advertised message, and achieve more by appealing to viewers' aesthetic sensibilities, emotion, and cultural affinity. This appeal, may, in turn, affect viewers' emotional reaction and perception of the commercial, and consequently, intention to purchase the advertised product.

In our pilot study, we assumed that people in different societies perceived and utilized visual images in accordance with the norms and values of their own culture. Theoretically, visual images are both agents and artifacts of human behaviors within a society (Newton, 2001). They are agents in the sense that they are part of the cultural dialectic of formation and change. They are artifacts in that they tell us something about a culture, its people, and their values.

Accordingly, we designed a number of visual variables that were theoretically motivated within the contexts of different cultural circumstances; that is, low-context versus high-context and individualistic versus collectivistic cultures. In that deductive exercise, theories of context as well as individualism and collectivism were utilized to rationalize variables of interest. The following sections explain these two theories and how we utilize them to motivate our constructs.

High- versus low-context cultures

High- versus low-context

Contextuality is a construct often used to describe global cultural differences. There are high-context (HC) and low-context (LC) cultures, between which exist significant differences in how people relate to informational content, in particular, information that is implicit or explicit. In LC cultures, most information is vested within explicit codes, such that entities and constructs are spelled out as concisely and thoroughly as possible (Hall & Hall, 1987). In contrast, a HC culture is one in which the communicators assume a great amount of shared knowledge and views, such that less explanation is necessary. In HC cultures, intimate human relationships, social hierarchy, and social norms all influence human communication, rather than the message alone. Most Asian countries belong to a HC cultural group that is characterized by the use of symbolism and nonverbal and indirect verbal expressions, whereas the US and most western European countries are considered LC countries accustomed to explicit information and direct speech (Hall & Hall, 1987; Zandpour, Chang, & Catalane, 1992).

The framework of high- versus low-context has important implications for both communication styles and persuasive appeals. Gudykunst et al. (1996) postulated that LC communication would be characterized as direct, precise, open, dramatic, and based on feelings or true intentions, whereas HC cultures would more likely prefer communication that is indirect, ambiguous, reserved, and understated. Some researchers using the high/low context demarcation have confirmed that context can be a predictor of advertising content (Cho, Kwon, Gentry, Jun, & Kropp, 1999; Lin, 1993). Miracle and his colleagues (Miracle, Taylor, & Chang, 1992), for example, found that advertising in a HC culture frequently used affective elements to establish context, whereas advertising in a LC culture often used direct or even confrontational statements to differentiate products. Other researchers have also pointed to the instinctive and reflective nature of HC culture, and found that its advertising regularly employed indirect messages and stressed depth rather than breath, whereas advertising in LC cultures was more likely to use unequivocal messages and stress breadth rather than depth as it aimed for explicit communication (Lin, 1993; Roth, 1992; Tai & Pae, 2002).

Individualism versus collectivism

Another way to differentiate culture is the concept of individualism and collectivism (Hofstede, 1980). In an individualistic culture, a person mainly has concerns for self and immediate family, emphasizes personal autonomy and self-fulfillment, and identifies on the basis of one's personal accomplishments. Thus, the worldview of individualism emphasizes the personal and peripheralizes the social. Individuals' uniqueness and self-determination are valued, and people who show initiative or work well independently are admired. Collectivism, on the other hand, assumes that groups bind and mutually obligate individuals, and is marked by closely linked individuals who see themselves as belonging to one or more collectives, and are inclined to give priority to the goals of the groups before their own. Collectivist societies expect individuals to identify with and work well in groups; the group offers protection in exchange for loyalty and compliance (Triandis, 1995). Research has shown, for example, that a difference on the individualism-collectivism dimension represents a primary distinction between Chinese and US cultures (Chan, 1986; Ho, 1979). Historically, as a collectivistic culture, China has emphasized the importance of family, social interests, and collective actions, while deemphasizing personal goals and accomplishments (Li, 1978; Oh, 1976). The US, however, is known for its rugged individualism, and the belief that each person is an entity separate from others and the group (Spence, 1985).

This individualism and collectivism framework has important implications for the content of advertisements. Content analyses of magazine advertisements, for example, suggested that Korean advertisements tended to use more collectivistic appeals, whereas US advertisements tended to use more individualistic appeals (Han & Shavitt 1994). Similar results were found between Japanese advertisements and US advertisements (Javalgi, Cutler, & Malhotra 1995). As Lin (1993) suggested, communication in a collectivist society concentrates more on achieving group consensus and harmony. In an individualistic culture, however, competition is often encouraged in pursuit of the goal to achieve personal excellence.

In our work, three sets of variables were designed in accordance with the two theories discussed above (see Zhou, Zhou & Xue, 2005). Of relevance to the current chapter are three: visual story line, product acknowledgement, and individual/group images. The first one, visual story line, was designed to measure the completeness of information. A complete story line denotes that the visuals of a commercial display a story with a beginning, middle, and an end. Obviously, the shortest way to a direct story in a 30-second commercial is to juxtapose a series of shots such that a visual story is self-evident. A visual story line is strictly defined as a complete shot sequence, which shows a problem solved even without the aid of audio information. For example, a beer commercial may show a complete visual story in which a man is shown in a grocery store checkout without enough money to pay for his two selected items, beer and toilet paper. At the conclusion of the commercial he decides to buy the beer. The whole commercial is complete even without the aid of any audio. We argued that commercials in a LC culture would utilize more such direct and forceful propositions. Findings showed that more US commercials than Chinese commercials had visuals that could stand alone; 47% versus 32%, respectively (Zhou, Zhou, & Xue, 2005).

The second variable of interest to this chapter is brand acknowledgement. Because LC cultures typically offer more explicit information so as to relate thoughts and actions more concretely (Hall & Hall, 1987), it would stand to reason that to avoid confusion, such information should be presented as early as possible by quickly acknowledging the brand names so the audience knows what products are being advertised. To assess this hypothesis, we divided a commercial into three parts and coded whether the brand name appeared in the first, second, or last third of the commercials. Results showed that 47% of US commercials acknowledged the brand name in the first third while only 34% of Chinese commercials did so (Zhou, Zhou, & Xue, 2005).

A third variable of interest to this chapter is the use of group versus individual shots. We rationalize that an individualistic culture is more affinitive to individual shots than group shots. Therefore, a shot showing at least three people was coded as a group image. Findings indicated that 66% of US commercials contained group images, while 16% contained individual images; the percentages from Chinese commercials in this category were 47% and 30% respectively. However, these results were contrary to the original hypotheses, a point we will revisit at the end of this chapter (Zhou, Zhou, & Xue, 2005).

The results of our study are interesting but remain descriptive. In other words, viewers' responses to these images are unknown. Against the background of advertising globalization, it is especially interesting to examine how viewers respond to visuals that are congruent or non-congruent with their culture. This goal motivated our study below.

Such studies are warranted as research on high/low context points out that effective communication in one context may not work in the other context. For example, Hall and Hall (1987) noted that people from HC cultures might become impatient and irritated when people from LC cultures insist on giving them more information than they expect. Conversely, people from LC cultures may feel lost when they are not given enough information. In the same vein, research has demonstrated that individualism correlates with clear, goal-oriented communication, whereas collectivism correlates positively with concern about a target's feelings, tendency to avoid negative evaluation of the target, and desires to minimize imposition on the target (Kim, Sharkey, & Singelis, 1994). The cultural background along the dimension of individualism versus collectivism also influences people's evaluation of persuasive messages. For example, Lee and Boster (1992) found that US participants rated fast-talking male speakers as more competent than those speaking at a slower rate, but the reverse was true for Korean participants. Presumably, for Americans, rapid speech implies that the speaker makes true and uncensored statements, whereas slow speech suggests to Koreans a careful consideration of others and the context.

Purposes and hypotheses of the current study

To our knowledge, no study has been specifically conducted on culture-congruent visual elements and their effects. Culture-congruent visual elements may provide affinity otherwise absent in commercials with non-congruent elements. As such, they may influence viewers' affective responses, perception of the commercials, and purchase intention of the advertised products.

A majority of the research testing the effect of culture congruence focuses on organizational communication. The key concern here lies on the consonant interplay between individual and organizational value systems. Boxx, Odom, and Dunn (1991) found that greater perceived congruence was associated with greater job satisfaction, commitment, and cohesion in a given organization. Thus, organizational commitment and job satisfaction would be maximized when congruence occurred between the two value systems (Harris & Mossholder, 1996).

Researchers also examined the attitudinal and behavioral responses induced by congruence. For instance, in a study on the effectiveness of product placements in TV shows, Russell (2002) found that the degree of connection between a brand and the plot was positively correlated with the degree of persuasion. Dolich (1969) proposed that individuals tended to relate the brand symbol to self concepts, which reflected a congruency between self images and product brands. In light of these positive effects of congruency, the current study tests the following hypotheses:

H1: Commercials with culture-congruent visuals (complete visual story line, early product acknowledgment, and individual images) generate more positive affect than those commercials without culture-congruent visuals among US audiences.

H2: Commercials with culture-congruent visuals (complete visual story line, early product acknowledgment, and individual images) generate more positive perception than those commercials without culture-congruent visuals among US audiences.

H3: Commercials with culture-congruent visuals (complete visual story line, early product acknowledgment, and individual images) generate higher purchase intention than those commercials without culture-congruent visuals among US audiences.

Method

Participants

A total of 228 undergraduate students in a large university in the Southeastern part of the US were recruited to participate. More females (69%) than males (31%) took part in the experiment. Participants' ages ranged from 16 to 25, with a mean of 20.

Study design

Eight commercials representing all permutations of the three manipulations in this study were selected from thousands of commercials recorded off network television. The three factors in this study included complete/incomplete visual story lines, early/late brand acknowledgment, and individual/group images.

Thus, the 2 x 2 x 2 factorial design yielded eight combinations, each represented by a commercial satisfying three respective conditions in each combination. As such, the experiment was a 2 x 2 x 2 x 8 repeated measure design in which all participants watched all eight commercials and saw all combinations. The commercials were burned to DVD-R discs directly from a DVD recorder to preserve quality. Four discs were recorded to correspond to four experimental orders to randomize order effects.

Manipulation of variables

Within each of the commercials used, a visual story line was conceptually defined as a sequence of shots that told a complete story. To ensure successful manipulation, we purposely turned off the audio track to examine the shots. If the visual story showed a beginning, middle, and an end, or if the visuals showed a problem or conflict resolved through the visual sequence, the commercial as a unit was considered to reflect a complete visual story.

To assess product acknowledgement, we evenly divided a commercial into three parts and checked if the brand name appeared in the first, second, or last third. For half the commercials in the study, brand acknowledgement was made in the first or last third.

A commercial that showed at least three people in all the shots was considered one with group images. Conversely, a commercial that showed only one person in all the shots was considered one with individual images.

Affect measure

Participants' affective responses were measured by having them rate the commercial using the Self-Assessment Mannequin (SAM) developed by P. J. Lang (Bradley et al., 1992). The SAM is a pictorial valence and arousal scale which translates into two 9-point scales, from very negative to very positive for valence, and from very calm or sleepy to very aroused or excited for arousal.

Perception measure

Three items using a 7-point semantic differential scale were created to measure participants' perceptions of each commercial. The three items were appealing/unappealing, enjoyable/not enjoyable, and entertaining/not entertaining, with a low score representing low enjoyment of the commercial. Reliabilities (α) for the scales across the eight commercials ranged from .70 to .93, with an average of .86. For each commercial, responses were summed and divided by three to create a mean response for each participant.

Purchase intention measure

Four 7-point Likert-type items were created to measure participants' purchase intentions. The four items were "I would try this product," "I would buy this product," "I would actively search for this product," and "I would buy this product for myself or as gift." Reliabilities for the scales across commercials were high, ranging from .88 to .94, with an average of .92. For each commercial, responses were summed and divided by four to create a mean response for each participant.

Procedure

Participants were randomly assigned to one of the four orders, and were told that they would view some commercials and be required to complete a questionnaire before and after viewing. Each participant was given an informed consent form to sign.

Participants were then shown eight commercials. After viewing each one, the experimenter paused the disc and asked participants to provide answers regarding affect, perception, and purchase intention. This procedure was repeated until all eight commercials were viewed and questionnaires completed. When all procedures were completed, participants were thanked and debriefed.

Results

Hypothesis one predicted that commercials with culture-congruent visuals would show greater positive affect than commercials without culture-congruent visuals. Our findings showed that visual story line had a significant effect on viewers' affect, F (1, 225) = 18.85, p < .001, ε^2= .08, as they reported significantly more positive feelings for commercials with visual story lines (M = 7.01, SD = 1.61) than for those without such story lines (M = 6.68, SD = 1.63). A significant main effect of visual story line on viewers' reported arousal was found, F (1, 225) = 81.45, p < .001, ε^2= .27, as viewers were more excited after watching commercials with visual story lines (M = 5.29, SD = 2.08) than those without (M = 4.52, SD = 2.13).

A main effect of brand acknowledgement on viewers' reported valence and arousal was found. In terms of valence, viewers reported significantly higher positive feelings for commercials with early acknowledgement (M = 7.10, SD = 1.56) than for those with late brand acknowledgement (M = 6.59, SD = 1.68) with F (1, 225) = 51.06, p < .001, ε^2= .19. In terms of arousal, viewers were more excited after watching the commercials with early brand acknowledgement (M = 5.16, SD = 2.08) than those with late brand acknowledgement (M = 4.66, SD = 2.13) with F (1, 225) = 36.85, p < .001, ε^2= .14.

As for individual/group images, the main effect was statistically significant, but in the opposite direction of our hypothesis. In terms of valence, viewers reported higher positive feelings after watching commercials with group images (M = 6.98, SD = 1.63) than those with individual images (M = 6.71, SD = 1.61) with F (1, 225) = 17.64, p < .001, ε^2 = .07. Similar results were found for arousal, as viewers were more excited after watching commercials with group images (M = 5.44, SD = 2.05) than those with individual images (M = 4.37, SD = 2.15) with F (1, 225) = 162.22, p < .001, ε^2= .4. Therefore, H1 was partially supported.

Hypothesis two postulated that the perception of commercials with culture-congruent visuals would be more positive than the perception of culture-incongruent commercials. Our results also partially supported this hypothesis. Specifically, the main effect of complete visual story line was statistically significant, F (1, 226) = 69.67, p = .001, ε^2= .24. Viewers rated the commercials with complete visual story lines more favorably (M = 4.60, SD = 1.38) than they did those commercials without visual story lines (M = 3.98, SD = 1.61). As for brand acknowledgement, the main effect was also statistically significant, F (1, 226) = 4.36, p = .038, ε^2= .02. Viewers reported more favorable perceptions of commercials with early brand acknowledgement (M = 4.35, SD = 1.32) than they did for those with late brand acknowledgements (M = 4.22, SD = 1.69). Finally, the commercials featuring individual images were perceived less favorably (M = 4.14, SD = 1.63) than those with group images (M = 4.43, SD = 1.61), with F (1, 226) = 23.53, p = .001, ε^2= .09.

Hypothesis three predicted that culture-congruent visuals would generate higher purchase intentions than culture-incongruent visuals. A significant main effect of visual story line on purchase intention was found, F (1, 221) = 126.69, p < .001, ε^2 = .36. Participants were more likely to purchase the products promoted with a visual story line (M = 4.62, SD = 1.62) than those promoted without visual story lines (M – 3.86, SD = 1.70). Secondly, brand acknowledgement also had a significant effect on purchase intention, F (1, 221) = 19.53, p < .001, ε^2= .08. Respondents reported higher purchase intentions for products promoted with early brand acknowledgement (M = 4.41, SD = 1.70) than for those with late brand acknowledgement (M = 4.07, SD = 1.62). Thirdly, the main effect of image was statistically significant on purchase intention, F (1, 221) = 40.63, p < .001, ε^2= .16. However, results were opposite to our hypotheses as viewers reported higher purchase intention after watching the commercials with group images (M = 4.43, SD = 1.61) than those with individual images (M = 4.07, SD = 1.71).

Conclusions and discussion

Overall, our study yielded partial support for the hypotheses that culture-congruency in advertisements would predict consumers' affective responses, perception, and purchase intention. Both visual story line and brand acknowledgement consistently predicted positive effects in affect, perception, and purchase intention. In response to culture-congruent visuals, viewers reported higher valence and arousal, better perception of the commercials as well as higher purchase intention for the advertised products. However, commercials with group images generated more positive affect, perception, and higher purchase intention than those with individual images as had been expected.

A conclusion that culture influences people's perception of commercials can be drawn from the results, with a caveat. The first two manipulations (visual story line and brand acknowledgement) are in line with previous research that shows effective communication in a low-context culture to be explicit, direct, and complete (Gudykunst et al., 1996). Commercials that told a complete visual story and identified the product early in the commercial were considered culture-congruent and influenced participants' behavior.

However, results of this study also showed that commercials with group images were more positively related to affect, perception, and purchase intention than those with individual images. One explanation is that individualism is best manifested in a group setting, as we speculated in the pilot content analysis in which we found that US commercials utilized more group images than Chinese commercials (Zhou, Zhou, & Xue, 2005). Research has shown that although relationship and group membership are impermanent and non-intensive for individualists (Kim, 1994; Shweder & Bourne, 1982), they still need relationship and group membership to attain self-relevant goals (Kagitcibasi, 1997). As such, advertisers may position an individual within a desired group to highlight a unique image (Roth, 1992; 1995). Accordingly, in comparison to commercials with individual images, commercials with group images may, in fact, be more congruent with individualistic culture than collectivistic culture. If this assumption is correct, the reverse effects of individual images render a set of rather consistent findings regarding the effectiveness of culture-congruent visual elements.

As far as the US market is concerned, the managerial implications for international advertisers are that commercials with culture-congruent visuals have an advantage over those with culture-incongruent visuals. It remains to be seen whether such effects translate into other elements of commercials, such as its narratives, or into other cultures.

References

Barry, A.M.S. (1997). *Visual intelligence: Perception, image and manipulation in visual communication.* New York: State University of New York Press.

Berger, A.A. (1998). *Seeing is believing: An introduction to visual communication* (2nd ed.) CA: Mayfield.

Boxx, R., Odom, R., & Dunn, M. (1991). Organizational values and value congruency and their impact on satisfaction, commitment, and cohesion: An empirical examination within the public sector. *Public Personnel Management, 20,* 195-205.

Bradley, M.M., Greenwald, M.K., Petry, M.C., & Lang, P.J. (1992). Remembering pictures: Pleasure and arousal in memory. *Journal of Experimental Psychology, 18*(2), 379-390.

Chan, W. (1986). *Chu Hsi and Neo-Confucianism.* Honolulu, HI: University of Hawaii Press.

Cho, B., Kwon, U., Gentry, J. W., Jun, S., & Kropp, F. (1999). Cultural values reflected in theme and execution: A comparative study of US and Korean television commercials. *Journal of Advertising, 28*(4), 59-73.

Dolich, J. (1969). Congruence relationships between self images and product brands. *Journal of Marketing Research, 6,* 80-84.

Gudykunst, W., Matsumoto, Y., Ting-Toomey, S., Nishida, T., Kim, K., & Heyman, S. (1996). The influence of individualism-collectivism, self construals, and individualistic values on communication styles across cultures. *Human Communications Research, 22,* 510-543.

Hall, E.T., & Hall, M.R. (1987). *Hidden differences: Doing business with the Japanese.* New York: Anchor Press.

Han, S-P., & Shavitt, S. (1994). Persuasion and culture: Advertising appeals in individualistic and collectivistic societies. *Journal of Experimental Social Psychology, 30*(4), 326-350.

Harris, S., & Mossholder, K. (1996). The affective implications of perceived congruence with culture dimensions during organizational transformation. *Journal of Management, 22,* 527-547.

Ho, D. (1979). Psychological implications of collectivism: With special reference to the Chinese case and Maoist dialectics. In L. H. Eckensberger, W.J. Lonner, & Y.H. Poortinga (Eds.), *Cross-cultural contributions to psychology* (pp. 143–150). Amsterdam: Swets and Zeitlinger.

Hofstede, G.H. (1980). *Cultural consequences: International differences in work-related values.* London: Sage.

Jawalgi, R.J. Cutler, B.D., & Malhotra, N.K. (1995). Print advertising at the component level: A cross-cultural comparison of the United States and Japan. *Journal of Business Research, 34,* 117-124.

Kagitcibasi, C. (1997). Individualism and collectivism. In J.W. Berry, M.H. Segall, & C. Kagitcibasi (Eds.), *Handbook of cross-cultural psychology: Vol. 3, Social behavior and applications* (pp. 1-50). Needham Heights, MA: Allyn and Bacon.

Kim, M. S., Sharkey, W. F., & Singelis, T. M. (1994). The relationship between individuals' self-construals and perceived importance of interactive constraints. *International Journal of Intercultural Relations, 18*, 117-140.

Kim, U. (1994). *Individualism and collectivism: Theory, method, and applications*. Thousand Oaks, CA: Sage Publications.

Lee, H.O., & Boster, F.J. (1992). Collectivism-individualism in perceptions of speech rate: A cross-cultural comparison. *Journal of Cross-Cultural Psychology, 23*, 377-388.

Lester, P.M. (2000). *Visual communication: Images with messages*. CT: Wadsworth.

Li, D. J. (1978). *The ageless Chinese*. New York: Charles Scribners.

Lin, C. A. (1993). Cultural differences in message strategies: A comparison between American and Japanese TV commercials. *Journal of Advertising Research, 33*(40), 40-48.

Miracle, G.E., Taylor, C.R., & Chang, K.Y. (1992). Culture and advertising executions: A comparison of selected characteristics of Japanese and US television commercials. *Journal of International Consumer Marketing, 4*(4), 89-113.

Mueller, B. (1994). Degrees of globalization: An analysis of the standardization of message elements in multinational advertising. *Current Issues in Advertising, 12*(1), 119-133.

Newton, J.H. (2001). *The burden of visual truth the role of photojournalism in mediating reality*. Mahwah, NJ: Lawrence Erlbaum Associates.

Oh, T.K. (1976). Theory Y in the People's Republic of China. *California Management Review, 19*, 77-84.

Roth, M.S. (1992). Depth versus breadth strategies for global brand management. *Journal of Advertising, 21*(2), 25-36.

—. (1995). Effects of global market conditions on brand image customization and brand performance. *Journal of Advertising, 21*(2), 25-36.

Russell, C. (2002). Investigating the effectiveness of product placements in television shows: The role of modality and plot connect congruence on brand memory and attitude. *Journal of Consumer Research, 29*, 306-318.

Shweder, R.A., & Bourne, E.J. (1982). Does the concept of person vary cross-culturally? In A.J. Marsella & G.M. White (Eds.), *Cultural conceptions of mental health and therapy* (pp. 97–137). Boston, MA.: Reidel.

Spence, J.T. (1985). Achievement American style: The rewards and costs of individualism. *American Psychologist, 40*, 1285-1295.

Tai, S.H.C., & Pae, J.H. (2002). Effects of TV advertising on Chinese consumers: Local versus foreign-sourced commercials. *Journal of Marketing Management, 18*(1/2), 49-72.

Taylor, C.R., Wilson, D.R., & Miracle, G.E., (1997). The impact of information level on the effectiveness of US and Korean television communication. *Journal of Advertising, 26*(1), 1-19.

Triandis, H.C. (1995). *Individualism and collectivism.* Boulder, CO: Westview.

Zandpour, F., Chang, C., & Catalane, J. (1992). Stories, symbols, and straight talk: A comparative analysis of France, Taiwanese, and US TV commercials. *Journal of Advertising Research, 32*(1), 25-38.

Zhou, S., Xue, F., & Zhou, P. (2002). Self-esteem, life-satisfaction and materialism: Effects of advertising images on Chinese college students. *Advances in International Marketing, 12*, 243-261.

Zhou, S., Zhou, P., & Xue, F. (2005). Visual differences in US and Chinese commercials. *Journal of Advertising, 34*(1), 111-119.

CHAPTER NINE

CULTURE, CONTAINMENT, AND GLOBAL CONTEXT: *CHINA DAILY* COVERAGE OF RELIGION IN CHINA

KURT M. DENK, S.J., JESUIT SCHOOL OF THEOLOGY, GRADUATE THEOLOGICAL UNION

In early 2006, global media devoted significant attention to the decision by Google and other web firms to self-censor the Chinese version of their search engines for topics deemed too sensitive by China's government (Barboza, *New York Times*, 2006, January 25; Huanxin, *China Daily*, 2006, February 15; Japan Economic Newswire, 2006, February 14; Kahn, *New York Times*, 2006, February 12; Lee, *San Francisco Chronicle*, 2006, February 2; 2006, February 22; Zeller, *New York Times*, 2006, February 15 & 16). Among such censored references were China's control of Tibet and treatment of its traditional spiritual leader, the Dalai Lama, and China's banned Falun Gong spiritual movement. The media's attention to these specifically religious topics reflects one example of religion's salience both within China and as a point of interest in a broader global context.

The discussion that follows analyzes media treatment of factors reflected in and impacting upon China's contemporary religious reality, with the goal of providing a framework for future study of media coverage of religion in China. This content analysis was based on 40 religious-themed articles in *China Daily* pertinent to China proper or to China's relations with other nations which appeared between October 7, 2004 and June 3, 2005. Two articles serve to introduce the discussion. The remaining articles to be discussed are sorted into three thematic categories: 15 articles primarily emphasized religion in China as a cultural phenomenon in general; 11 articles primarily evinced the long-standing Chinese tendency to privilege state dominance of religion (Bays, 2004), and the "control and containment" (Spiegel, 2004) of religious impulses seen as potentially destabilizing to Chinese society; and 12 articles either explicitly or implicitly addressed religion within a broader global context of contemporary social, religious, and political issues. Comparison and contrast analysis of additional non-Chinese media coverage of topics paralleling those in *China Daily*'s articles, and reference to some material outside the timeframe specified, is included to qualify or shed further light upon the main findings of the analysis. *China Daily*'s eye for both endogenous and exogenous contexts made it particularly appropriate for use in this analysis. Specifically, *China Daily*'s website identifies itself as the "voice of China" and its mission as "committed to helping the world know more about China and the country's integration with the international community" as specified in the overview of the newspaper on its website (see *About China Daily*). Overall, the findings of this content analysis suggest how media's own salience today, especially in light of globalization, exerts two important and related effects germane to religion in China. First, media impact is likely to support religion's "staying power" (Liu, 2004) among China's populace, in the sense that the media's influence and capacity to transmit ideas will serve as a carrier for religion's own influence within Chinese culture. Second, the growth of the Chinese media along with international media interest in China means that China's evolving religious identity will increasingly impact global religious and political consciousness.

Religion in China today: A snapshot of internal realities and external influences

Most pertinent to contemporary China's internal religious reality is the marked increase in religious belief and practice amidst ongoing social change (Kindopp, 2004; Regulations better safeguard, 2004). Some commentators have characterized this as a full-scale spiritual revival (BBC News, 2004, December 19). Just 30 years ago, following Mao's Cultural Revolution (1966-76), religion in China was moribund if not extinct, at least at a visible level (Kindopp, 2004). However, China's government had indicated there were over 200 million religious worshipers there in 2000, while outside authorities such as the US State Department offered higher estimates (Kindopp, 2004). Five religions are officially recognized by the Chinese government: Buddhism with 100 million followers; Catholic Christianity with 12 million followers; Islam with 18 million followers; various Protestant Christian denominations collectively with 30-60 million followers; and though Taoism, whose figures are difficult to verify, but which claims tens of millions of followers (Kindopp, 2004). Quasi-religious groups not recognized by the state—the banned Falun Gong spiritual movement most notable among them—claim millions of followers.

Further, as Shi submits in this volume (see Chapter 6), the explosive growth of communications mechanisms in China is well-documented. Thus, while state controls still exist, the expansion of China's media market makes information more publicly accessible, including that pertaining to religion.

China's contemporary religious reality also reflects exogenous, indeed global, dimensions. For example, the increasingly complex Sino-US relationship has served to elevate and intensify the two nations' differences over religious freedom (Center for Religious Freedom, 2005, March 24; China rejects US, 2005; Kindopp, 2004; Hamrin, 2004; Liu, 2004; Rice, 2005, November 20; US Commission on International Religious Freedom, 2005). Policy analysts also cite China's 2001 entry into the World Trade Organization and, since 9/11, increased focus on religion's role in international relations, as catalysts for focusing a broader, global spotlight on China's internal realities, including religion (K. Chan, 2004; Hamrin, 2004; Liu, 2004).

Coverage of religious themes in *China Daily*: Culture, containment, and global context

China's promulgation of new regulations on religious affairs in the autumn of 2004, which were set to take effect in March of 2005 (Religious affairs, 2004), serves to contextualize this chapter's analysis of *China Daily* coverage of religious themes. A corresponding opinion article, "Regulations better safeguard religious freedom in China" (2004), presented the new regulations as "the first comprehensive ones of their kind concerning religious affairs promulgated by the Chinese Government," specifically emphasizing that the guidelines derived from a consultative process that

> conscientiously listened to comments from involved parties and experts in the fields of law, religion and human rights, especially comments from representatives of religious circles and those citizens who are religious.

It described the regulations as "based on China's actual conditions and abundant experience from long-term practice" and "on the reality of the sites for religious activities in China," and acknowledged the existence of "vast numbers of religious citizens." The new policies were further contextualized with reference to China's "rapid socio-economic development" and implementation of governance according to the rule of law.

Notably, the article announcing the new regulations included statements in favor of the right to religious freedom which the Chinese Communist Party (CCP) enshrined in Chinese constitutional law in 1982, stating that "the rules are regarded as a significant step forward in the protection of Chinese citizens' religious freedoms" (Religious affairs rule, 2004). In its title alone— "Regulations better safeguard religious freedom in China"—the Opinion article (Regulations better safeguard, 2004) also positively cast the new regulations in terms of promoting religious freedom, and was noteworthy in its specifically confirming that

> the promulgation and implementation of these regulations will be beneficial to the protection of Chinese citizens' freedom and rights of religious belief according to law, and to the respect and safeguarding of human rights as well.

At the same time, however, that *China Daily*'s coverage of the new religious rules emphasized themes of human rights and religious freedom, the Opinion article's closing paragraph firmly cast this human rights terminology within the framework of the state's right and responsibility to enforce the law against anything that would compromise public order:

> The regulations include provisions on stopping illegal and criminal activities carried out in the name of religion. In order to safeguard State and public interests, maintain harmony among and between religions and preserve social concordance, and better protect citizens' rights to freedom of religious belief and normal religious activities, these regulations provide that anyone who engages in illegal and criminal activities shall be stopped and punished according to law if they make use of religion to endanger State or public security, infringe upon citizens' rights of the person and democratic rights, obstruct the administration of public order, or encroach upon public or private property.

These words portray a phenomenon that policy analysts outside China regularly highlight: China's longstanding state control and containment of religion (Spiegel, 2004).

In short, the aforementioned articles on China's new religious regulations encapsulated the three characteristics of *China Daily* coverage of religion considered in this chapter. First, the references to long-term experience, contemporary religious demographics, and new social realities in China suggest, at a minimum, that *China Daily* acknowledged the salience and complexity of religious culture in China today. Second, this sensitivity is nonetheless followed up by a strict restatement of the state's right to control religious expression—a view long-imprinted in Chinese cultural-political consciousness, even prior to the Communist Revolution (Bays, 2004). Notably, outside observers such as Spiegel (2005) and the United States Commission on International Religion Freedom (2005) have argued that the new guidelines actually serve to strengthen the state's hand in controlling religious practice. Third, the repetition of phrases like "human rights" and "religious freedom" and the references to conscientious listening to religious (and other) constituencies are significant. These phrases and terminology may well indicate an intentional sensitivity on the part of *China Daily* editors (not to mention the CCP itself, in selecting the new regulations' language) to a context of global pressure on China over religious freedom. Such pressure increasingly comes from independent human rights groups (Center for Religious Freedom, 2004, 2005; Panchen Lama Resource Center, 2006), though policy analysts also have highlighted the role of human rights and religious freedom as a central point of contention in China's present-day relations especially with western nations (Kindopp, 2004). During the interval encompassed in this analysis, five other *China Daily* articles explicitly addressed human rights and religious freedom issues (Chan, 2005; Beijing slams US, 2004; Model forum, 2005; Nation holds human rights, 2005; A balance between, 2005), while three additional *China Daily* articles of this sort appeared within close proximity to the formal timeframe of this analysis (Zhe, 2005; White paper, 2004; China rejects, 2005).

A comparative perspective was offered by BBC News (2004, December 19) that covered China's new religious regulations and also emphasized the characteristics of religious culture in general, religious control and containment, and global context. The BBC's account discussed the new rules in light of China's "spiritual revival—much of it outside the government's control" and as a consequence of the "social change unleashed by economic reforms in China." Citing its own correspondent in Shanghai, Francis Markus, the BBC noted that

> while the official reports say the new rules will protect the people's legitimate religious rights, the word 'legitimate' makes clear that there will be no basic relaxation of policy.

The BBC also explicitly mentioned international human rights groups' and foreign governments' pressure on China with regard to religious freedom, emphasizing that "many critics are likely to dismiss this move as window-dressing at best, or at worst as an attempt to actually tighten state control."

The preceding analysis of media coverage of China's new religious affairs regulations has served to introduce the three-fold thematic lens for analyzing *China Daily* religious coverage, focusing on the role of religion in broader Chinese culture, state control and containment of religion, and the global context that enmeshes contemporary Chinese religious realities and media coverage of them. The ensuing sections address each of these foci in turn.

Religious culture in general

Yang's (2004) sociological analysis of China's contemporary "desecularizing reality" has described how

> culture is an all-encompassing and esteemed term in the Chinese context ... [with] its own significance and its own life. Religion as a part of culture has its own reasons for existence and its own logic (p. 108).

Yang and others (e.g., Bays, 2004; Liu, 2004; C.K. Yang, 1961) specify that culture in general, and religious culture in particular, are important in Chinese society. Those emphases help make sense of the fact that, as will be shown, *China Daily*'s coverage tended to characterize religious topics as reflecting topics in Chinese culture in general. Indeed, more than one-third of the articles in this category appeared in *China Daily*'s "Arts and Culture" section (Cheng, 2005; Young Panchen, 2004; Oldest handwritten Koran, 2004; Tibetan legend, 2005; Timeless mountain, 2005; Tibetan history, 2005)

Sun's (2002) study of communications in China, which also attends to cultural aspects, sheds light on a second characteristic of *China Daily*'s articles. According to Sun, media and communications in China have followed the traditional route of Chinese scholarship in general, guided by the cultural principle of "practical *zhi*" which holds that knowledge ought to transmit information that lends itself to realistic problem-solving more than abstract theorizing. Traditionally, then, Chinese media is meant to serve a practical educative purpose.

The articles reflected in this first category echoed both Yang's and Sun's points. Typically, they investigated religious phenomena as salient features of Chinese culture, and were primarily educative in nature, presenting readers with background information about the religious topics being reported. For example, an article entitled "Timeless mountain" about grottoes of ancient Buddhist sculptures in China's Gansu region (*China Daily*, 2005, April 16) concluded that "the worth of the Maiji Mountain grottoes in terms of the history of Chinese art, religion, folk customs and philosophies is immeasurable." Sub-headings in the article respectively addressed "cultural exchanges," the impressive "legendary skills" of the "ancestors of the Chinese, Fuxi and Nuwa, the Adam and Eve of the East" who constructed the grottoes, and the historical "spread of Buddhism." A news article indicating that "China is building up its own list of intangible cultural heritage to protect ethnic minorities' languages, art, music, dance, and religion" (Intangible cultural heritage, 2004) also demonstrated *China Daily*'s location of religion within China's broader cultural milieu.

Cheng's (2005) article, "Thriving Christian communities," demonstrated a cultural ethnographic approach in its vivid description of the daily life of a Christian village in China's Nujiang River Canyon. In an educative tone, the reporter explained that "for historical reasons and the isolation of the mountains, Christianity is one of the common religions among the Lisu people in the Nujiang Canyon." Indeed, this twinned religious-cultural ethnographic and educative approach appeared to be the dominant theme in most articles. One, "Young Panchen immersed in studies," detailed the study habits and daily religious routine of the young Panchen Lama (2004, October 12). The Panchen Lama is the term for the second highest-ranking lama (or "teacher") in Tibetan

Buddhism, directly after the Dalai Lama. Who Tibetan Buddhists recognize as the legitimate Panchen Lama is a matter of controversy, as the one recognized by the Chinese government differs from the one recognized by the exiled Tibetan government (see Panchen Lama Resource Center website).

Xu's (2004, October 14) lengthy article, "Cultural centre answers the call," portrayed the cultural and religious significance of a young Chinese woman's conversion to Islam in preparation for marrying a Muslim man and, en route, addressed the history of Islam in China:

> By the 15th century, Islam had become rooted in the Chinese soil as an inseparable part of the Chinese culture. Muslims are now found everywhere in the country, in all walks of life, though most of them live in Northwest China. Islam is the religious belief for 10 of the 56 ethnic groups in China—the Hui, Uygur, Kazakh, Ozbek, Kirgis, Tata'er, Tajik, Dongxiang, Sala and Bao'an, which have a combined population of 20 million.

By typifying *China Daily*'s tendency to report on religion as a subset of Chinese culture at large, Xu has contextualized a certain aspect of Chinese *religious* history—the spread of Islam—in terms of China's broader *cultural* history, the implications of which this chapter's conclusion will explore.

China Daily's religious-cultural ethnographic approach also appeared in "Tibetan legend lives on" (2005, February 15). In describing the cultural and religious traditions of an ancient Tibetan settlement in China's Sichuan Province, the article interpreted the significance, "in a religious sense," of inscriptions about the great hero king, Gesar. An article reporting on the China's People's Political Consultative Conference's statement in favor of the state encouraging religious groups, similarly linked religion, ethnicity, and culture (CPCC delegates, 2005). Finally, also demonstrating *China Daily*'s characterization of religion as embedded in Chinese culture, Soiqoin's (2005, May 26) article, "Tibetan history preserved in old photos," detailed the lives of three of Tibet's first photographers, surveying how their "lenses captured" aspects of Tibet's religious and cultural history.

Other *China Daily* articles emphasized the cultural, architectural, or artistic merits of religious items or sites. For example, "Oldest handwritten Koran in China needs funds," stressed historical and cultural values of preserving China's oldest-known Islamic text (2004, October 20). Li's (2004, November 24) article, "Shanghai's Buddhist monastery expanded," cited government officials' view that the upkeep of popular religious sites was necessary, while Fangchao's (2004, December 10) article, "Harbin to rebuild Orthodox church," argued that that city "should well preserve historical relics" as reflected by this church. Zi's (2005, April 15) article, "Facelift for ancient Tibetan buildings," reported on the architectural details and financial outlays for renovations of palaces belonging to former Dalai Lamas in China's Tibetan Autonomous Region, and noted that the renovations were meant to preserve both the buildings' appearance and "historical and cultural value." Jing's (2005, April 26) article, "Niujie mosque in Beijing gets facelift," addressed specific details of the mosque's renovation, and included historical information about Islam's arrival in China and demographic information about the number of practicing Muslims in Beijing today. Each of these articles portrayed, at some level, *China Daily*'s tendency to conceive of religion as an important component embedded in China's broader cultural history.

Two articles further emphasized the dynamism of China's culture vis-à-vis non-Chinese contexts. A. Chan's (2004, October 19) *China Daily* article, "Buddhism in China illustrates cultural integration," opened with the declaration that

> the spread of Buddhism from India to Japan and Korea after the religion's development in China exemplifies the compatibility of Chinese and foreign cultures.

China Daily's (2005, April 18) article, "Sino-Indian agreement paves way for new temple," addressed Buddhism's importance to Chinese culture, and argued that Sino-Indian cultural connections are relevant to contemporary bilateral relations. Citing comments by China's director of religious affairs in Luoyang, Henan Province, the article contextualized the Sino-Indian agreement as follows:

> the two countries have a long history of Buddhist cultural exchanges. And construction of the temple is an important symbol of enhanced Buddhist cultural exchanges in a new historical age.

The "new historical age" was immediately specified by detailing a recent important meeting between Chinese Premier Wen Jiabao and Indian Prime Minister Manmohan Singh. Here, we observe *China Daily*'s awareness that religion's cultural salience transcends national boundaries.

Before concluding this section, comparative analysis of commentary and reporting on general religious themes in China by media sources other than *China Daily* highlights how *China Daily*'s coverage is notable for its preponderant focus on religion as a cultural phenomenon, to the exclusion of addressing possible reasons for religion's recent growth or the impact that religion itself exerts upon Chinese culture. As the discussion below will detail, a variety of other media sources tend to emphasize the impact of outside influences on religious phenomena internal to China, and pursue a more exploratory approach to religion in China than has been found in *China Daily*, in the sense that these other sources try to explain *why* China's cultural landscape is manifesting rapid growth in religious belief and practice. To cite a first example, *China Rights Forum* devoted their 2003 issue to China's spiritual revival. Whitehead and James (2003) also have traced how an apparently growing spiritual hunger in Shenzhen, China has yielded new forms of spiritual expression, which they have attributed to that industrialized, cosmopolitan region's rapid socioeconomic development and correspondent social dislocations. More recently, Zakaria's (2005, May 9) *Newsweek* cover story, "Does the future belong to China?" identified religion as one of the more prominent features of change internal to China, paralleling China's rise in the world. Similarly, Grant's (2005, May 5) article for CNN.com, "Glimpses of hope in the new China," analyzed religious faith in China against the backdrop of evolving faith and cultural traditions and the impact of the Cultural Revolution and communist ideology on present-day faith practice. Grant also linked the recent growth of religion in China to rapid economic growth and social change.

Of particular note is the extent to which these non-Chinese sources have interpreted religion's cultural salience in contemporary China somewhat differently from a state-supervised media source such as *China Daily*. Whereas the *China Daily* articles emphasized phenomenological details, characterizing religion in terms of its being an expression of Chinese culture, outside sources, such as those cited above, *explained* the role of religion in the ongoing evolution of Chinese culture within a globalized context. This difference will be revisited later in the chapter.

Control and containment of religious impulses

The second category of *China Daily* articles on religion is best understood in light of the state dimensions of Chinese religious history. From ancient times, religion has been subordinate to state power (Bays, 2004; Chan, 1992). In China's modern imperial era, state concern for containing religion and its popular expression was a response to western states' imposition of their own power on China, which often included granting special privileges to religious missionaries (Bays, 2004). During the governing period of Mao Zedong's in 1949, state enforcement of atheism reflected Communist Party ideology, and served to contain religion's social force and emancipate China from western influences (Spiegel, 2004). During the Cultural Revolution (1966-76), Mao made efforts to eradicate religion through brute force, such that by the late 1970s all religious venues had been forcibly closed if not destroyed (Kindopp, 2004).

In 1978, Deng Xiaoping initiated major reforms, and religion was re-embraced by the state, to some extent, to facilitate social cohesion (Spiegel, 2004). In 1982, while retaining its official atheism, the Chinese Communist Party openly acknowledged religion's cultural potency in an official statement, referred to as Document 19, that cited various "characteristics" of religion in socialist China including longevity and popularity, complex links with ethnicity, and impact on international relations (Potter, 2003; Spiegel, 1992, 2004). China's revised constitution officially provided for freedom of religious belief, insofar as it did not impinge on state security and the good of society (People's Republic of China, 1982; Spiegel, 2004). Accompanying these changes were a series of mechanisms for maintaining state control over religious practice, all of which remain in place today: the Religious Affairs Bureau (renamed in 1998 the State Administration for Religious Affairs) which manages the everyday regulation and supervision of religious groups; state-supervised "patriotic associations" which formally govern the five recognized religions of Buddhism, Taoism, Catholic and Protestant Christianity, and Islam; the Ministry of Public Security which polices religious practice in tandem with local agencies; and various other state apparatuses that maintain official registration of religious venues, oversee clergy, and control religious media publication and distribution (Spiegel, 2004, 2005). Thus, while religion has been allowed to resurface in China over the past three decades, state "control and containment" of religion (Spiegel, 2004) remains a pervasive characteristic of its operation in China's broader socio-cultural milieu.

Articles in *China Daily* during the timeframe of the analysis presented here highlighted this dynamic, as over a quarter of the 40 articles either addressed or reflected some aspect of the control and containment of religious impulses. A good example of this theme was a feature article (President Hu meets Panchen Lama, 2005) covering President Hu Jintao's meeting with the Panchen Lama. The article described Buddhist ceremonies and tradition, thus underscoring *China Daily*'s fundamentally educative editorial approach to religious topics. But, the article also alluded to state power by quoting President Hu's encouragement to the religious leader to live "with full love to the country and his religion," by specifying that China's State Council "confirmed and approved" the Panchen Lama's status, and by referencing the government's "assistance and support" to the Tibetan Autonomous Region—long viewed by critics of China's government as religious repression rather than as a source of religious support (Panchen Lama Resource, 2006).

This perceptual difference between the Chinese state's support versus repression of religion stands out all the more when *China Daily*'s articles are compared with non-Chinese media coverage of the state's stance towards Buddhism. For example, a BBC article, "Tibetan monk 'broken' in China"

(2005, January 26), appeared 10 days before the above-cited *China Daily* article and summarized a Human Rights Watch report on Tashi Phuntsog, a Tibetan monk imprisoned for ties to a prominent lama who China branded a "terrorist" and sentenced to death (a sentence which was later commuted). According to the BBC, Tashi Phuntsog entered prison healthy, and was released three years later unable to walk or speak clearly. In short, the BBC presented the Tashi Phuntsog incident as an example of China's suppression of religion, while *China Daily* made no mention of it.

The case of China's Falun Gong (also referred to as Falun Gong or Falun Dafa), a spiritual movement with Buddhist and Taoist roots that emphasizes holistic improvement of the mind, body, and spirit (Falun Dafa, n.d.; Li, 2001), serves as a prime example of a *China Daily* editorial approach that mirrors state interests in the control and containment of religious impulses perceived as dangerous to maintaining state order. The Falun Dafa Information Center website claims 100 million worldwide followers or more at present, the majority of them in China (http://www.faluninfo.net/index.asp). Outside experts estimate tens of millions of Falun Gong practitioners prior to a state-sponsored crackdown that began in 1999, and still many millions in China even today, several years since the crackdown began (Kindopp, 2004; Tong, 2002). The state's main concern is over the group's capacity to assemble large numbers of people in public spaces, which has led to a crackdown and official outlawing and branding of the group as an "evil" and "heretical cult" based on "superstitions" intended to deceive followers. According to Falun Dafa, other governments, and international human rights organizations, the group also has been subjected to widespread arrests, persecution and torture. The state has used its ability to control media communications throughout China as a significant means of containing Falun Gong (Spiegel, 2004; 2005, July 21). Recalling that *China Daily* is a state-supervised media outlet, comparison with non-Chinese coverage of Falun Gong also demonstrates how the regime uses media to contain religious impulses.

On the whole, *China Daily* articles on Falun Gong during the interval encompassed in this analysis were negative, if not polemic, in tone: negatively referencing Falun Gong in a Hong Kong court case (Chan, 2005; A balance, May 7, 2005); accusing Falun Gong as posing a danger to Hong Kong's ordinary mechanisms of social protection (Strengths of basic law, 2005); accusing Falun Gong of communications satellite sabotage (Falun Gong hijacks, 2004; In brief, 2004; Falun Gong accused, 2005); and reporting the arrest of Falun Gong members (In brief, 2005). Two other articles (Tian'anmen suicide, 2005; Falun Gong followers, 2005) covered public-protest suicides of Falun Gong protesters in Tiananmen Square, and detailed how jailed Falun Gong leaders connected with the episode had "repented" of their actions and of their membership in "the evil cult." Beyond simply portraying Falun Gong negatively, a further sign of state control and containment of undesired religious activity occurred in *China Daily*'s reporting of the state's manipulation of media and communications technology. This was evidenced in an article (Google steps up, 2005) chronicling Google's attempts to expand its China market which explicitly cited the need, if foreign web technology firms like Google were to succeed in China, to voluntarily to filter out

> sensitive topics from the Falun Gong spiritual movement to the June 4, 1989, crackdown on pro-democracy protesters in Tiananmen Square.

As noted earlier, Google's acquiescence to China's control of religion reverberated worldwide months later.

Comparative analysis of non-Chinese media reporting on China's treatment of Falun Gong revealed a different interpretive approach than found in *China Daily*. Western media in particular have portrayed China's treatment of Falun Gong as persecution, and its use of media in this regard as one of classic manipulation. Ping's (2003) survey of "The Falun Gong phenomenon" sympathetically concluded that "it is rare to see such a meek and mild group of people as Falun Gong practitioners taking on one of the world's most vicious political powers" (p. 23). More recently, Yardley's April 25, 2005 *New York Times* article, "A hundred cellphones bloom, and Chinese take to the streets," cited Falun Gong as a primary target of the Chinese government's

> powerful filtering devices that can screen cellphone and e-mail messages … [and which] can separate messages with key words such as Falun Gong, the banned spiritual group, and then track the message to the person who sent it.

About two weeks later Yardley (2005, May 9) published another article which detailed China's jailing of Falun Gong practitioners without due process afforded by Chinese governing law.

In short, many global media sources portray Falun Gong as a major international human rights cause rather than as a cult-based threat to Chinese public order. Ian Johnson's 2001 Pulitzer Prize for a *Wall Street Journal* investigative series on China's persecution of Falun Gong (Pulitzer Prizes, 2005) exemplifies this case. Benjamin Sand's (2004) Voice of America News feature, "China arrests 11 Falun Gong members for posting torture photos on internet," also represents western critical attention to China's handling of Falun Gong. Patsy Rahn's (2005) *Asia Media* article, "Media as a means for the Falun Gong movement," also explicitly represented the view that media has the capacity to report on, and serve as a vehicle for, battling perceptions of contentious religious issues such as Falun Gong. Finally, Adam Liptak's (2005)

New York Times article, "Chinese TV director sued by Falun Gong claims free speech protection in the US," revealed the extent to which globalization allows otherwise-endogenous religious phenomena such as the Falun Gong to hold sway beyond the confines of one nation. Notably, in the months following the timeframe of the present content analysis, *China Daily*'s mention of Falun Gong was practically nonexistent, whereas non-Chinese global media sources like the *New York Times* continued to track China-Falun Gong issues (Kahn, 2005, December 3 & 13; Marshall, 2006).

Global context

As noted above, religion in general increasingly occupies both Chinese and global consciousness (Beckford, 2003; K. Chan, 2004; Hamrin, 2004; Whitehead & James, 2003). As Laurie Goodstein of the *New York Times* reported January 9, 2005:

> Almost anywhere you look around the world, with the glaring exception of Western Europe, religion is now a rising force. Former Communist countries are humming with mosque builders, Christian missionaries and freelance spiritual entrepreneurs of every possible persuasion. In China, underground "house churches" are proliferating so quickly that neither the authorities nor Christian leaders can keep reliable count.

Clearly, media's global reach can facilitate increased focus on religion. Hamrin (2004) notes that the autumn 2001 statement at a CCP conference on religion by Chinese president Jiang Zemin "that religion is here to stay as an important issue affecting all societies and international relations," had a significant effect:

> one positive result of the media coverage of the conference was the demise of a long-standing taboo against public discussion of religion in today's China (p. 175).

During the timeframe of the content analysis offered here, 12 *China Daily* articles directly spoke to a complex connection between the demographic fluidity and cultural salience of religious phenomena in China, and forces affecting or interpreting these phenomena from the outside, such as bilateral cultural affinities, political debates in the international arena, or the stance of governments critical of China's religious policies.

As mentioned above, the editorial approach of *China Daily* articles treating religious themes as representative of Chinese culture at large tended to emphasize history and ethnography. At face value, Cheow's (2005) article discussing the role of Buddhism in linking the two nations' cultural

development over time, would appear to fit that first categorization, for in it
Cheow asserted Chinese cultural pride:

China and India have "met" and held dialogue with each other for more than a
thousand years through Buddhism and the Silk Road. This historical "civilization
dialogue" was then extended (thanks to China) to Japan and the rest of East or
Confucianist Asia.

Most notable, however, was the sentence used to *introduce* the article:

the buzz today is over the rise of China and India in the big global power shift, as
witnessed during the recent Davos World Economic Forum.

Thus, it might be observed that *China Daily*'s coverage of religion did not
always simply limit the salience of religion to China's internal milieu. Cheow's
article cast an item of religious interest—the historical spread of Buddhism—as
germane not just to China's domestic identity, but to its rise on the world scene.

Another globally contextualized, religious-themed news item evinced a
critique of religion's place amidst the exigencies of global politics. *China
Daily*'s "Millions celebrate Christmas across globe" (2004, December 26)
acknowledged a religious event, but contextualized it as existing in no uncertain
tension with broad political realities:

worshippers brought hopes for greater peace in the coming year as they flocked
to Manger Square in Bethlehem to hear Christmas messages urging an end to
violence, particularly in the Middle East. But from Indonesia to Iraq, fear
overshadowed the festivities.

Here, one observes *China Daily*'s apparent awareness of religion's cultural
force within and outside of China, and as enmeshed in global power dynamics.

China Daily articles also have addressed religion within the global context
of human rights, reflecting an apparent awareness of and sensitivity to
international criticism of China's human rights record. For example, one article
(2004, October 7), "Beijing slams US report on human rights," referred to
religion twice, and directly quoted the Chinese foreign ministry's response to a
US Congressional report deeply critical of China:

the report issued in Washington, "ignores the facts and makes preposterous
accusations on human rights, religion, Tibet, Hong Kong and other issues,"
foreign ministry spokesman Kong Quan said in a statement.

In the ensuing months, *China Daily* published what might be seen as further
rejoinders to the US accusations. Particularly notable in "Model forum promotes
human rights" (2004, November 11) was a quote from Jin Yongjian, president

of the United Nations Association of China, that "full realization of human rights is a common aspiration of the peoples all over the world, including the people of China." Yongjian insisted that China's government and people "have always attached great importance to the protection of human rights," as evidenced by the spring 2004 insertion of a clause "respecting and protecting human rights" into China's Constitution. Yongjian also asserted that, while religion was a universal phenomenon, international understanding of human rights was never univocal:

> As countries have different historical, cultural, religious backgrounds, social systems and are at different levels of economic development, their concepts of and approaches to human rights are bound to be diverse. Such differences should not be used to justify the politicization of the issue of human rights, which often causes confrontation between states.

Several months later (2005, April 14), *China Daily*'s publication and commentary about the Chinese government's 2004 report on human rights, "Nation holds human rights in high esteem," also cited religion in particular, and focused largely on descriptions of religious activity. This article appeared within weeks of a high-profile visit to China by US Secretary of State Condoleezza Rice. Thus, it may have represented *China Daily*'s editorial recognition of the religious freedom issue's salience in a broader global context which casts a watchful eye on China's religious reality (cf. Center for Religious Freedom, 2005). Notably, an article (2004, March 30) about the previous year's report included similar language, but devoted about one-third of the space of the 2005 article.

Another topic illuminating the global context of *China Daily* media coverage of religion appeared in its spring 2005 coverage of China and the Catholic Church, the latter an institution with a significant presence in China and worldwide (Madsen, 2004; Wiest, 2004). Specifically, Pope John Paul II's death and Pope Benedict XVI's election catalyzed Sino-Vatican diplomatic maneuvers, a development followed in *China Daily* and worldwide media. (Since China's communist revolution, the Vatican has maintained diplomatic relations with Taiwan, but not with Beijing.) That *China Daily* understood John Paul II's global appeal was typified by the headline announcing his death, "Pope John Paul II dies, world mourning" (2005, April 3). Two days later, "Pope's funeral set for Friday" (2005, April 5), mentioned Catholics' rituals honoring the late pope, both in China and abroad, and reflected on the implications of the pope's reign by noting that in Rome the pope's body

> was displayed ... for prelates, ambassadors and other dignitaries ....up to 2 million mourners are expected in Rome to pay tribute to the Polish-born prelate

who reigned over his church for 26 years with unbending loyalty to its ancient precepts.

China Daily addressed the impact of John Paul II's death and Sino-Vatican relations in a manner that attended both to its impact on China's internal religious reality (i.e., acknowledging the import of the event to China's 12 million Catholics), as well as to its salience for China's global image. Thus, *China Daily*'s 2005 article on April 4, "Pope passes away from heart and kidney failure," confirming the cause of the pope's death, noted Beijing's appreciation for John Paul II's apology for harms China experienced at the hands of missionaries, but quickly emphasized that improvement in ties would not occur gratuitously. Rather, effecting diplomatic relations required that the Vatican meet China's "two principles" of terminating diplomatic relations with Taiwan, and promising non-interference "in China's internal affairs, including any intervention under the pretext of religious affairs." The second principle refers to a longstanding dispute over whether the Vatican or Beijing should have final say in the appointment of bishops for the Catholic Church in China (Madsen, 2004).

Similarly, the article "Pilgrims flock to see the pope's final farewell" (2005, April 9) noted the extensive global complement of people, famous and ordinary, at the funeral but also emphasized China's "strong dissatisfaction" with the Vatican for granting a visa for Taiwan's leader Chen Shui-bian to attend the funeral and "setting new obstacles" to Sino-Vatican ties.

During and following the conclave to elect a new pope, *China Daily*'s coverage continued to dwell on Sino-Vatican differences over Taiwan and non-interference issues, while never evading critique of the Vatican stance. For example, its coverage of Joseph Cardinal Ratzinger's election as Pope Benedict XVI, "China congratulates Ratzinger as new pope" (2005, April 20), re-printed the Chinese Patriotic Association's congratulatory message to him. The Chinese Patriotic Association oversees officially-sanctioned Catholic worship, though it should be noted that a significant "underground" Catholic church has operated in China throughout the Communist era. Madsen (2004) notes that the once-sharp distinctions between the "open" vs. "underground" (or "official" vs. "unofficial") Catholic communities are beginning to blur given, in large part, increased Sino-Vatican dialogue over issues pertinent to Chinese Catholics, such as government vs. Vatican approval of Chinese Catholic bishops. In this historical light, the tone and content of *China Daily*'s coverage of the Spring, 2005 developments in Sino-Vatican movements towards regularizing diplomatic relations is especially noteworthy.

The article also indicated that the Chinese government "hopes [that] the Vatican under the new pope and China will work to improve strained relations," and reiterated China's critique of the Vatican's "so-called diplomatic relations with Taiwan" and "intervention" in China's internal religious affairs. *China Daily*'s coverage of Sino-Vatican relations in the wake of Pope Benedict XVI's election in particular portrayed the complex connections and sometimes opposition between internal concerns of, and outside influences on, China's contemporary religious reality. Thus, the benefit of formalizing diplomatic relations with a potential global partner such as the Vatican was simultaneously relevant to, and influenced by, China's longstanding religious-cultural sensibility that required state control and containment of religion. Perhaps indicative of this complexity, one day after officially congratulating Pope Benedict, *China Daily* (Ratzinger is elected as new pope, 2005) reprinted a BBC account of his election that included rather critical editorial remarks on the direction of the Catholic Church:

> The Catholic cardinals did not after all choose an African or Latin American pope who would have spoken directly to the concerns of the developing world. They chose Joseph Ratzinger, a theologian who's spent many years at the Vatican in Rome, at a time when it faces strong attacks over church scandals, suffocating bureaucracy and claims that it's grown out of touch with the lives of people, both in the secular west and the needy south.

Worldwide coverage of Pope John Paul II's death after a momentous 26-year reign presumably had the capacity to stimulate feelings of affinity among Chinese Catholics for fellow Catholics beyond China's borders—the growth of which clearly would interest the Vatican, but potentially exacerbate church versus state loyalty conflicts in China among its Catholics.

Of particular relevance to this text's broader look at cross-cultural differences in media impact, is the difference in editorial approach when comparing *China Daily* and non-Chinese sources on Sino-Vatican diplomatic maneuvers in the spring of 2005. For example, *China-Daily*'s coverage emphasized the CCP party line: diplomatic relations are desired, but only on China's grounds. Non-Chinese media more comprehensively speculated on the impact of global influences upon China's internal decision-making. Thus, McGeown's (2005) BBC article on China's approach to Pope John Paul II's death, "China's tense links with the Vatican," noted that the growth of religion in China—Catholicism included—clearly interested both the Vatican and China's leaders. McGeown also observed that while Pope John Paul II's anti-communist record had taxed Sino-Vatican relations, the election of a new pope gave China's leaders new impetus to press for diplomatic relations.

Sisci's (2005) *Asia Times Online* feature, "China, Catholic Church at a crossroads," covered similar issues to McGeown's BBC report, and offered in-depth coverage of the history and socio-cultural context of Chinese Catholicism, going so far as to conjecture that the role that Chinese Catholics have played in China's economy could, analogously, parallel their role in the Church: that is, Chinese Catholicism, by its sheer numbers, could significantly impact global Catholicism. Rosenthal's (2005) *New York Times* article also moved beyond the greater mass-appeal coverage of John Paul II's death, to address Sino-Vatican relations' salience within a broader, even globalized context. Specifically, he noted that "in re-establishing ties with the Vatican, China would strengthen its prestige as a world power."

The awareness of a global context to Sino-Vatican relations continued to appear in both *China Daily* and other media beyond Pope Benedict XVI's election. *China Daily* has maintained a cautiously optimistic stance, reporting that China has remained "sincere" about formalizing ties with the Vatican (China "sincere," 2005, May 18) and attentive to opportunities to improve China's relationship with the Vatican (Qin, 2005; Vatican decision criticized, 2005). Both Chinese and non-Chinese media also have continued to follow the issue. However, *China Daily* has not covered issues pertaining to repression against Chinese Catholics documented by human rights advocacy groups such as the Cardinal Kung Foundation (http://www.cardinalkungfoundation.org), or by policy analysts (Madsen, 2004) and journalists (Williams, 2005).

By way of postscript, the global salience of Sino-Vatican relations appeared again in Fisher and Bradsher's (2006) *New York Times* article, "Pope picks 15 cardinals, one a China critic," covering Pope Benedict XVI's first selection of new cardinals (top papal advisers). Beyond the singling out of a Chinese context in the article's title alone, of further note is the fact that 7 of the article's 19 paragraphs exclusively dealt with cardinal-designate Joseph Zen of Hong Kong and the implications of that choice for advancing Sino-Vatican relations. In contrast, only one paragraph was allocated to discussion of Archbishop William Leveda, who became the highest-ranking American ever to serve in the Vatican when he filled the high-level Vatican post vacated by Benedict XVI upon his election. Archbishop Sean O'Malley of Boston, Leveda's fellow American cardinal-designate, was mentioned in passing only. Fisher and Bradsher's decision to highlight above all others the one Chinese cleric elevated to the cardinalate suggests an editorial conclusion that Sino-Vatican relations remain of considerable interest, if not significance, in a broader global context. Notably, global media sources such as BBC (2006, February 23) reported within days of the new cardinal appointments that Chinese foreign ministry spokesman Liu Jianchao had quickly sought to warn cardinal-designate Zen "to avoid politics." *China Daily* did not cover this issue.

Implications: Religion in China, media, and global theological flows

As the preceding analysis of the three facets of religious-themed reporting in *China Daily* and other media sources illustrates, China's experience of the growth of religious belief and practice among its people and the salience of its internal religious reality to global media attention and political dynamics suggests a series of present and impending challenges. Specifically, one also may argue that media's own salience in China and the world at large can have two important, related effects. One effect entails supporting and stimulating religion's "staying power" (Liu, 2004) in China. The other effect entails affecting and influencing new trends in global religious and political consciousness as China's own evolving religious reality occupies more space in global consciousness. In light of these observations, this final section serves to outline the types of emergent questions that could serve as a valuable interpretive lenses for future studies of media and religion in China.

The lens that *China Daily* and other media have used for examining religious themes salient to China today first suggests that religion in China will sustain itself. As this chapter's analysis demonstrates, and as analysts of China's religious history have portrayed (Kindopp, 2004; Liu, 2004; Yang, 1961), the religious impulse is embedded in Chinese culture. Sociologists of religion emphasize that such impulses are fundamental to human coping with cultural stress factors (Berger, 1990), a dynamic particularly germane to the rapid socio-cultural change overtaking China. K. Chan (2004) argues that

> in such times of radical social transformation, people tend to search for some
> form of permanency ... [and] religion has returned as an attractive source of
> meaning for many facing often-traumatic social change (p. 61).

Given that China's social transformation shows few signs of slowing, growth in religious belief and practice are also unlikely to wane.

Religion's likely staying power in Chinese culture spells difficulty for any long-term state attempts to "contain" religious belief and practice. For example, as this chapter's section on *China Daily* coverage of religious culture in general portrayed, the Chinese state permits certain religious expressions and even admits, to some degree, to religion's cultural salience. However, as the discussion of Falun Gong portrayed, the state cracks down on or manipulates such expressions when they ostensibly contradict its policies or power. In so doing, however, "China's leaders may not fully comprehend the power of religious belief" (Spiegel, 2004, p. 54). By way of contrast, in addition to offering stability in turbulent times, China's religious movements offer ethical systems to critique state power, or to propose different interpretations of the values inherent in China's contemporary socio-cultural and political milieu. According to Yang (2004),

> the effervescence of cultural discourses in religion in effect pushes leftist ideologues to the margins, for the stifled reiteration of atheism and antireligious position, still backed by certain Party and government officials, appeals to few people in the market of ideas (p. 108).

That in February 2006 a number of retired high-level Chinese authorities (even some from Mao's era) warned China's present administration about the dangers of reactionary policies like stepped-up media censorship suggests that many Chinese with experience of the state's longstanding control and containment policies, are well aware of the benefits of moderation (BBC, 2006, February 14; Kahn, 2006).

China cannot escape the reality of the growth and diversification of religious belief and worship. Nor should its leaders presume that the spread of religious discourse and practice only spells the potential for chaos. Citing a variety of contemporary studies of religion and culture (e.g., Berger & Huntington, 2003; Fukuyama, 1995; Harrison & Huntington, 2000; Witte & van der Vyer, 1996), Hamrin (2004) argued that a greater openness to religion by the Chinese state would both strengthen its domestic social fabric, and cohere with international growth in religion itself and the concomitant global movement to emphasize human rights and define freedom of religious belief as essential to social harmony.

To the extent that China continues to loosen internal social and information controls and opens itself up to outside influences, media communications will continue to serve as an important carrier for the market of ideas, including religious phenomena. More news from the outside also is bound to impact the religious consciousness of Chinese citizens and communities. Hamrin (2004) offers a striking portrait of the potential direction of such evolving religious and cultural consciousness:

> Chinese churches and temples are filled with highly educated clergy and lay professionals with family members scattered globally who regularly interact with counterparts in China. Chinese religious networks help open up the market for values and ideas, along with goods and services. A new modern Chinese cultural identity is being constructed among the diaspora (p. 181).

At the very least, developments such as those that Hamrin portrays will be important subject matter for media, and for studies of media impact.

Increased availability to Chinese of broader forms of documentary and human interest style reporting also is likely to provide a context in which more human interest stories about religion can emerge. Such developments are, in turn, more likely to influence actual religious *behavior* than are stories that simply report statistics and events. Notably, during the timeframe of this content analysis very few documentary-style articles appeared in *China Daily*. Its June 3, 2005 article "Thriving Christian communities" was one exception. Thus, future research in the Chinese media may trace and document phenomena such as that studied by Shanghai sociologist Lizhu Fan (as cited in Whitehead & James, 2003), who indicated that,

> confronted by new questions of meaning and purpose, Shenzhen respondents …
> gave very personal expression to their spiritual search in the age-old idiom of
> China's common spiritual heritage (p. 12).

Will media sources such as *China Daily* simply report the fact that religious growth is occurring, or explain and measure how religious practice both reflects and then acts back upon broader socio-cultural realities? It will be important for subsequent studies of religion in China, especially those more longitudinal in nature, to gauge *how* media, of both the state-supervised Chinese and independent global varieties, cover the diversity of religious and spiritual practice in China.

Finally, a variety of constituencies should pay attention, over the coming years, to how continued media coverage of religious issues in China and across the world might cause global shifts. For example, Worthley (2006) recently proposed that the likelihood of Beijing and the Vatican establishing diplomatic relations would change Catholicism in China, *and* the universal church. Worthley advanced a theological argument by speculating that "divine providence may be using developments in China to guide the worldwide church into the future" (p. 10). Critically, from a religious belief standpoint, many people of faith may come to conceive shifts in Chinese Christianity affecting global Christianity as exactly that: evidence of God working in the world. Both sociologists and media analysts, whether they accept a theological reading, would do well to consider how the growth of religion "with Chinese characteristics"—to play off Deng Xiaoping's now-famous advocacy of socialism—will have a global impact.

Indeed, current international flows of media communication about religious issues have the capacity to facilitate what theologian Robert Schreiter (1997) terms "global theological flows." Schreiter's concept, and specifically his identification of human rights as one of the four "flows" (or dynamics) serving to transcend time-old boundaries of distance, theological worldview, and specific faith confession, helps to frame this chapter's conclusion. As globalization impacts religion, and impacts China, it is reasonable to conclude that global theological flows will continue to impact upon China's religious milieu. Of greatest significance for shifting China's religious and political culture may be those influences that advocate open and diverse religious practice as a fundamental human right. Since media likely will be the means by which much of this interaction will occur, future media studies of religion in China—and elsewhere—will benefit from attending to the emphasis, as presented in this chapter, on how global forces (e.g., advocacy groups, other governments) that highlight human rights, are capable of impacting both religious behavior in China, and the state's policy decisions to accommodate it.

More broadly, the "play" of religion within the globalization context suggests that future analyses of media treatment of religion—both inside and outside China—need to address more than the *fact* of various religious worldviews' burgeoning accessibility to the populace at large. Rather, they must take into account broader, now-globalized shifts in religious consciousness as a whole. Just as globalization impacts religion, so too does religion exert global influence (Hamrin, 2004; Goodstein, 2005; Worthley, 2006). Crucially, globally interconnected mass media can play both a reporting *and* a causative role. Media reports religious phenomena. By broadcasting powerful religious sentiments, however, the media also may facilitate *specifically religious* behavioral effects, as demonstrated by the religious furor in the winter of 2006 over western nations' publication of cartoons satirizing Islam.

China, and other powers, could perceive growth in religion ipso facto as an extremist threat. Or, as the kinds of human-interest themed stories of religious culture cited in this analysis suggest, China and other global powers might recognize, and use media to communicate, the capacity of localized religious belief and practice to ease the social and psychic tensions which globalization can produce. If indeed

> religious freedom is the best antidote to religious extremism, for such freedom contributes to the construction of social justice and national security—two sides of the same coin (Hamrin, 2004, p. 180),

then the globally interwoven matrices of religion and media present today's world with a unique opportunity to witness religion as a potent positive force within a global culture. If time-old religious differences have sown today's violence (religious and otherwise), media's capacity to communicate positive, peace-building global religious flows such as those that emphasize human rights is something of potential value to the international community at large.

References

A balance between protesters' rights and public interest needed. (2005, May 7). *China Daily Hong Kong Edition*. Retrieved May 23, 2005, from http://www.chinadaily.com.cn/english/doc/2005-05/07/content_439864.htm

Barboza, D. (2006, January 25). Version of Google in China won't offer e-mail or blogs. *New York Times,* C3.

Bays, D. H. (2004). A tradition of state dominance. In J. Kindopp & C. L. Hamrin (Eds.), *God and Caesar in China: Policy implications of church-state tension* (pp. 25-39). Washington, DC: Brookings Institution Press.

BBC News. (2004, December 19). *China rules on religion "relaxed".* Retrieved May 20, 2005, from http://news.bbc.co.uk/go/pr/fr/-/1/hi/world/asia-pacific/4109051.stm

—. (2005, January 26). *Tibetan monk "broken" by China.* Retrieved May 22, 2005, from http://news.bbc.co.uk/go/pr/fr/-/2/hi/asia-pacific/4207989.stm

—. (2006, February 14). *Party elders attack China censors.* Retrieved February 25, 2006, from http://news.bbc.co.uk/2/hi/asia-pacific/4712134.stm

—. (2006, February 23). *China warns Hong Kong cardinal.* Retrieved February 25, 2006, from http://news.bbc.co.uk/1/hi/world/asia-pacific/4742834.stm

Beckford, J. A. (2003). *Social theory and religion.* Cambridge, UK: Cambridge University Press.

Beijing slams US report on human rights. (2004, October 7). *China Daily.* Retrieved May 20, 2005 from: http://www.chinadaily.com.cn/english/doc/2004-10/07/content_380153.htm

Berger, P. L. (1990). *The sacred canopy: Elements of a sociological theory of religion.* New York: Anchor Books.

Berger, P. L., & Huntington, S. P. (Eds.). (2003). *Many globalizations: Cultural diversity in the contemporary world.* New York: Oxford University Press.

Center for Religious Freedom. (2004, August 25). Press release. APEC should press china on religious freedom: repression of Christians, Buddhists, and Falun Gong members reportedly increasing. Retrieved on May 20, 2005 from http://www.freedomhouse.org/religion/news/bn2004/bn-2004-08-25.htm

—. (2005, March 24). Press release. *Secretary of State Rice sends mixed message on religious freedom in China.* Retrieved on May 20, 2005 from http://www.freedomhouse.org/religion/news/bn2005/bn-2005-03-24.htm

Chan, A. (2004, October 19). Buddhism in China illustrates cultural integration. *China Daily Hong Kong Edition.* Retrieved May 20, 2005, from http://www.chinadaily.com.cn/english/doc/2004-10/19/content_383578.htm

Chan, K. (1992). A Chinese perspective on the interpretation of the Chinese government's religious policy. In A. Hunter & D. Rimmington (Eds.), *All under heaven: Chinese tradition and Christian life in the People's Republic of China* (pp. 38-44). Kampen, NL: J.H. Kok.

—. (2004). Accession to the World Trade Organization and state adaptation. In J. Kindopp & C. L. Hamrin (Eds.), *God and Caesar in China: Policy implications of church-state tension* (pp. 58-74). Washington, DC: Brookings Institution Press.

Chan, T. (2005, May 6). Gov't respects rights and freedoms. *China Daily Hong Kong Edition*. Retrieved May 24, 2005, from: http://www.chinadaily.com.cn/english/doc/2005-05/06/content_439716.htm

Cheng, W. (2005, June 3). A glimpse of Shangri-La: Thriving Christian communities. *China Daily*. Retrieved on June 4, 2005 from: http://www.chinadaily.com.cn/english/doc/2005-06/03/content_448170.htm

Cheow, E. T. C. (2005, February 24). Cultural factors bind China and India. *China Daily*. Retrieved January 6, 2006, from: http://www.chinadaily.com.cn/english/doc/2005-02/24/content_418894.htm

China congratulates Ratzinger as new pope. (2005, April 20). *China Daily*. Retrieved May 23, 2005 from: http://www.chinadaily.com.cn/english/doc/2005-04/20/content_435912.htm

China rejects US rights report as meddling (2005, October 13). *China Daily*. Retrieved January 6, 2006 from: http://www.chinadaily.com.cn/english/doc/2005-10/13/content_484621.htm

China "sincere" about ties with Vatican. (2005, May 18). *China Daily*. Retrieved May 23, 2005 from: http://www.chinadaily.com.cn/english/doc/2005-05/18/content_443377.htm

CPPCC delegates urged to help religious groups. (2005, March 2). *China Daily*. Retrieved May 22, 2005 from: http://www.chinadaily.com.cn/english/doc/2005-03/02/content_421050.htm

Fangchao, Li. (2004, December 10). Harbin to rebuild Orthodox church. *China Daily*. Retrieved May 21, 2005, from: http://www.chinadaily.com.cn/english/doc/2004-12/10/content_398921.htm

Falun Dafa. (n.d.). *Falun Dafa: Truthfulness, benevolence, forbearance.* Retrieved May 21, 2005, from http://www.falundafa.org/eng/index.htm

Falun Gong accused of satellite interception. (2005, March 16). *China Daily*. Retrieved May 22, 2005 from: http://www.chinadaily.com.cn/english/doc/2005-03/16/content_425420.htm

Falun Gong followers: Hatred for Li Hongzhi. (2005, January 20). *China Daily*. Retrieved May 22, 2005 from: http://www.chinadaily.com.cn/english/doc/2005-01/20/content_410723.htm

Falun Gong hijacks HK satellite (2004, November 22). *China Daily*. Retrieved May 21, 2005 from http://www.chinadaily.com.cn/english/doc/2004-11/22/content_393776.htm

Fisher, I. & Bradsher, K. (2006, February 23). Pope picks 15 cardinals, one a China critic. *New York Times*, A24.

Fukuyama, F. (1995). *Trust: The social virtues and the creation of prosperity.* New York: Free Press.

Goodstein, L. (2005, January 9). More religion, but not the old-time kind. *New York Times*, A1.

Google steps up fight for the China market. (2005, May 11). *China Daily*. Retrieved May 23, 2005, from:
http://www.chinadaily.com.cn/english/doc/2005-05/11/content_441416.htm

Grant, S. (2005, May 5). Glimpses of hope in the new China. *CNN*. Retrieved May 23, 2005 from:
http://edition.cnn.com/2005/WORLD/asiapcf/05/05/eyeonchina.stangrant/index.html

Harmony and religious freedom thrive in multi-faith town. (2005, November 2). *China Daily*. Retrieved January 6, 2006, from:
http://www.chinadaily.com.cn/english/doc/2005-11/02/content_489711.htm

Hamrin, C. L. (2004). Advancing religious freedom in a global China: Conclusions. In J. Kindopp & C. L. Hamrin (Eds.), *God and Caesar in China: Policy implications of church-state tension* (pp. 165-85). Washington, DC: Brookings Institution Press.

Harrison, L. E., & Huntington, S. P. (Eds). (2000). *Culture matters: How values shape human progress*. New York: Basic Books.

Huanxin, Z. (2006, February 15). Regulation of internet in line with world norms. *China Daily*. Retrieved February 25, 2006, from:
http://www.chinadaily.com.cn/english/doc/2006-02/15/content_520394.htm

In brief. (2004, November 23). *China Daily*. Retrieved May 21, 2005, from:
http://www.chinadaily.com.cn/english/doc/2004-11/23/content_393809.htm

—. (2005, May 10) *China Daily*. Retrieved May 23, 2005, from:
http://www.chinadaily.com.cn/english/doc/2005-05/10/content_440536.htm

Intangible cultural heritage to be listed. (2004, November 17). *China Daily*. Retrieved May 21, 2005, from:
http://www.chinadaily.com.cn/english/doc/2004-11/17/content_392180.htm

Japan Economic Newswire. (2006, February 14). *China says foreign internet giants must help China block content. Technology Marketing Corporation*. Retrieved February 25, 2006, from:
http://www.tmcnet.com/usubmit/2006/02/14/1370203.htm

Jing, L. (2005, April 26). Niujie mosque in Beijing gets facelift. *China Daily*. Retrieved May 27, 2005, from:
http://www.chinadaily.com.cn/english/doc/2005-04/26/content_437378.htm

Kahn, J. (2005, December 3). Torture is "widespread" in China, U.N. investigator says. *New York Times*, A3.

—. (2005, December 13). Legal gadfly bites hard, and Beijing slaps him. Rule by law: The limit-tester. *New York Time*, A1.

—. (2006, February 12). So long, Dalai Lama: Google adapts to China. *New York Times*, A4-5.

—. (2006, February 15). Beijing censors taken to task in party circles. *New York Times*, A1.

Kindopp, J. (2004). Policy dilemmas in China's church-state relations: An introduction. In J. Kindopp & C. L. Hamrin (Eds.), *God and Caesar in China: Policy implications of church-state tension* (pp. 1-22). Washington, DC: Brookings Institution Press.

Lee, E. (2006, February 2). How Google censors its Chinese portal. *San Francisco Chronicle*, A1.

Li, C. (2004, November 24). Shanghai's Buddhist monastery expanded. *China Daily*. Retrieved on May 21, 2005 from:
http://www.chinadaily.com.cn/english/doc/2004-11/24/content_394155.htm

Li H. (2001). *Falun Gong* (4th ed.). Retrieved May 22, 2005 from
http://www.falundafa.org/book/eng/flg.htm

Liptak, A. (2005, January 2). Chinese TV director sued by Falun Gong claims free speech protection in the US. *New York Times*, A6.

Liu, P. (2004). Unreconciled differences: the staying power of religion. In J. Kindopp & C. L. Hamrin (Eds.), *God and Caesar in China: Policy implications of church-state tension* (pp. 149-164). Washington, DC: Brookings Institution Press.

McGeown, K. (2005, April 8). China's tense links with the Vatican. *BBC News Online*. Retrieved May 23, 2005 from:
http://news.bbc.co.uk/go/pr/fr/-/2/hi/asia-pacific/4423845.stm

Madsen, R. (2004). Catholic conflict and cooperation in the People's Republic of China. In J. Kindopp & C. L. Hamrin (Eds.), *God and Caesar in China: Policy implications of church-state tension* (pp. 93-106). Washington, DC: Brookings Institution Press.

Marshall, C. (2006, January 26). Businessman back in US after detention in China. *New York Times*, A16.

Millions celebrate Christmas across globe. (2004, December 26). *China Daily*. Retrieved May 21, 2005 from:
http://www.chinadaily.com.cn/english/doc/2004-12/26/content_403361.htm

Model forum promotes human rights. (2004, November 11). *China Daily*. Retrieved May 21, 2005, from:
http://www.chinadaily.com.cn/english/doc/2004-11/11/content_390380.htm

Nation holds human rights in high esteem. (2005, April 14). *China Daily*. Retrieved May 23, 2005, from:
http://www.chinadaily.com.cn/english/doc/2005-04/14/content_433948.htm

Oldest handwritten Koran in China needs funds. (2004, October 20). *China Daily*. Retrieved May 21, 2005 from:
http://www.chinadaily.com.cn/english/doc/2004-10/20/content_383891.htm

Panchen Lama Resource Center (2006.). Free the Panchen Lama—resource center (website). Retrieved on February 11, 2006 from: http://www.tibet.ca/panchenlama/resource.html

People's Republic of China (1982). Constitution of the People's Republic of China. Retrieved May 25, 2005 from: http://www.english.people.com.cn/constitution/constitution.html

Pilgrims flock to see the pope's final farewell. (2005, April 9). *China Daily*. Retrieved May 23, 2005, from: http://www.chinadaily.com.cn/english/doc/2005-04/09/content_432603.htm

Ping, H. (2003). The Falun Gong phenomenon. *China Rights Forum, 4,* 11-27.

Pope John Paul II dies, world mourning. (2005, April 3). *China Daily*. Retrieved May 23, 2005, from http://www.chinadaily.com.cn/english/doc/2005-04/03/content_430515.htm

Pope passes away from heart and kidney failure. (2005, April 4). *China Daily*. Retrieved May 23, 2005, from: http://www.chinadaily.com.cn/english/doc/2005-04/04/content_430632.htm

Pope's funeral set for Friday. (2005, April 5). *China Daily*. Retrieved May 23, 2005, from: http://www.chinadaily.com.cn/english/doc/2005-04/05/content_431044.htm

Potter, P. B. (2003). Belief in control: regulation of religion in China. *China Quarterly, 174,* 317-337.

President Hu meets Panchen Lama. (2005, February 4). *China Daily*. Retrieved May 22, 2005, from: http://www.chinadaily.com.cn/english/doc/2005-02/04/content_414865.htm

Pulitzer Prizes (2005). Archived press release: 2001 Pulitzer Prizes, International Reporting. Retrieved May 25, 2005 from: http://pulitzer.org/year/2001/international-reporting/

Qin, J. (2005, October 28). Vatican urged to translate words into action. *China Daily*. Retrieved on January 6, 2006 from: http://www.chinadaily.com.cn/english/doc/2005-10/28/content_488411.htm

Rahn, P. (2005, January 28). Media as a means for the Falun Gong movement. *Asia Media*. Retrieved May 22, 2005 from: http://www.asiamedia.ucla.edu/print.asp?parentid=20142

Ratzinger is elected as new pope. (2005, April 21). *China Daily*. Retrieved May 23, 2005 from: http://www.chinadaily.com.cn/english/doc/2005-04/20/content_435792.htm

Regulations better safeguard religious freedom in China. (2004, December 20). *China Daily*. Retrieved May 21, 2005, from: http://www.chinadaily.com.cn/english/doc/2004-12/20/content_401537.htm

Religious affairs rules promulgated. (2004, December 20). *China Daily*. Retrieved May 21, 2005, from:

http://www.chinadaily.com.cn/english/doc/2004-12/20/content_401512.htm
Rice, C. (2005, November 20). Press briefing by secretary of state Condoleezza
Rice on the president's visit to China. Retrieved on January 5, 2006 from:
http://www.whitehouse.gov/news/releases/2005/11/20051120-8.html
Rosenthal, E. (2005, May 22). Hints of thaw between China and Vatican. *New
York Times*. Retrieved May 23, 2005 from:
http://www.nytimes.com/2005/05/22/international/asia/22vatican.html
Sand, B. (2004, December 30). China arrests 11 Falun Gong members for
posting torture photos on internet. *Voice of America News*. Retrieved on
May 21, 2005 from:
http://www.voanews.com/english/2004-12-30-voa17.htm
Schreiter, R. J. (1997). *The new Catholicity: theology between the global and
the local*. Maryknoll, NY: Orbis Books.
Sino-Indian agreement paves way for new temple. (2005, April 18). *China
Daily*. Retrieved May 23, 2005, from:
http://www.chinadaily.com.cn/english/doc/2005-04/18/content_434979.htm
Sisci, F. (2005, April 12). China, Catholic Church at a crossroads. *Asia Times
Online*. Retrieved on May 23, 2005 from:
http://www.atimes/com/atimes/China/GD12Ad05.html
Spiegel, M. (1992). Document 19 (English translation of the Chinese
Communist Party's "Basic viewpoints and policies on religious issues during
our country's socialist period" [31 March 1982]). Appendix 2 in Freedom of
religion in China (pp. 33-45). Washington, London, Brussels: Human Rights
Watch/Asia.
—. (2002, January). *Dangerous meditation: China's campaign against Falun
Gong. Human Rights Watch*. Retrieved May 25, 2005, from:
http://www.hrw.org/reports/2002/china/
—. (2004). Control and containment in the reform era. In J. Kindopp & C. L.
Hamrin, (Eds.). (2004). *God and Caesar in China: Policy implications of
church-state tension (pp. 40-57)*. Washington, DC: Brookings Institution
Press.
—. (2005, March 14). *China's new regulation on religious affairs: a paradigm
shift? Testimony before the Congressional-Executive Commission on China*.
Retrieved on January 4, 2006 from:
http://www.cecc.gov/pages/roundtables/031405/Spiegel.php
—. (2005, July 21). *Freedom of thought, conscience, religion, and belief:
Testimony before the House Committee on International Relations. Human
Rights Watch*. Retrieved January 6, 2006, from:
http://hrw.org/english/docs/2005/07/25/china11426.htm
Strengths of Basic Law stem from being mixed constitution. (2005, April 11).
China Daily Hong Kong Edition. Retrieved May 23, 2005, from:

http://www.chinadaily.com.cn/english/doc/2005-04/11/content_432935.htm
Sun, Z. (2002). Communication studies in China: state of the art. In W. Jia, X.
    Lu, & D.R. Heisey, (Eds.). *Chinese communication theory and research:
    Reflections, new frontiers, and new directions* (pp. 3-19). Westport, CT:
    Ablex Publishing.
The Cardinal Kung Foundation. (2006, May 12). *The Cardinal Kung foundation.*
    Retrieved from http://www.cardinalkungfoundation.org/index2.html
Tian'anmen suicide masterminds repent. (2005, January 19). *China Daily.*
    Retrieved May 22, 2005 http://www.chinadaily.com.cn/english/doc/2005-
    01/19/content_410354.htm
Tibetan history preserved in old photos. (2005, May 26). *China Daily.* Retrieved
    on May 27, 2005 from http://www.chinadaily.com.cn/english/doc/2005-
    05/26/content_445786.htm.
Tibetan legend lives on. (2005, February 15). *China Daily.* Retrieved May 22,
    2005, from:
    http://www.chinadaily.com.cn/english/doc/2005-02/15/content_416533.htm
Timeless mountain. (2005, April 16). *China Daily.* Retrieved May 23, 2005,
    from:
    http://www.chinadaily.com.cn/english/doc/2005-04/16/content_434706.htm
Tong, J. (2002). An organizational analysis of the Falun Gong: structure,
    communications, financing. *China Quarterly, 171 (September)*, 636-60.
University of California at Berkeley, Graduate School of Journalism and School
    of Information Management and Systems. (n.d.). *China Digital Times.*
    Retrieved from http://www.chinadigitaltimes.net
United States Commission on International Religious Freedom (2005). *Annual
    report.* Retrieved February 11, 2006 from:
    http://www.uscirf.gov/countries/publications/currentreport/2005annualRpt.p
    df#page=1.
Vatican decision criticized. (2005, September 12). *China Daily.* Retrieved
    January 6, 2006, from:
    http://www.chinadaily.com.cn/english/doc/2005-09/12/content_476830.htm
White paper on human rights published. (2004, March 30). *China Daily.*
    Retrieved May 20, 2005, from:
    http://www.chinadaily.com.cn/english/doc/2004-03/30/content_319211.htm
Whitehead, E. E. & James, D. (2003). Nourishing the spirit: the search for
    meaning in Shenzhen. *America, 189 (5)*, 11-13.
Wiest, J-P. (2004). Setting roots: the Catholic Church in China to 1949. In J.
    Kindopp & C. L. Hamrin (Eds.), *God and Caesar in China: Policy
    implications of church-state tension* (pp. 77-92). Washington, DC:
    Brookings Institution Press.

Williams, H. (2005). China's Catholics: far from Rome. *BBC News Online.*
Retrieved   on   May   23,   2005   from   http://news.bbc.co.uk/2/hi/asia-
pacific/3343535.stm

Witte, J. Jr. & Johan D. van der Vyver, J.D. (eds.). (1996). *Religious human rights
in global perspective: religious perspectives.* Boston: Martinus Nijhoff.

Worthley, J. A. (2006). China's new role. *America, 194 (6),* 9-11.

Xu, B. (2004, October 14). Cultural centre answers the call. *China Daily.*
Retrieved on May 21, 2005 from:
http://www.chinadaily.com.cn/english/doc/2004-10/14/content_382167.htm.

Yang, C.K. (1961). *Religion in Chinese society.* Berkeley: University of
California Press.

Yang, F. (2004). Between secularist ideology and desecularizing reality: the
birth and growth of religious research in communist China. *Sociology of
Religion, 65* (2), 101-19.

Yardley, J. (2005, April 25). A hundred cellphones bloom, and Chinese take to
the streets. *New York Times,* A1.

—. (2005, May 9). Issue in China: many in jails without trial. *New York Times,*
A6.

Young Panchen immersed in studies. (2004, October 12). *China Daily.*
Retrieved May 21, 2005, from:
http://www.chinadaily.com.cn/english/doc/2004-10/12/content_381505.htm

Zakaria, F. (2005, May 9). Does the future belong to China? *Newsweek.*
Retrieved on May 26, 2005 from:
http://www.msnbc.msn.com/id/7693580/site/newsweek/
http://www.chinadaily.com.cn/english/doc/2005-11/11/content_493654.htm

Zeller, T. (2006, February 15). Internet firms facing questions about censoring
online searches in China. *New York Times,* C3.

—. (2006, February 16). Web firms questioned on dealings in China. *New York
Times,* C1.

Zi, M. (2005, April 15). Facelift for ancient Tibetan buildings. *China Daily.*
Retrieved on May 27, 2005 from:
http://www.chinadaily.com.cn/english/doc/2005-04/15/content_434309.htm

CHAPTER TEN

HUMAN COMPUTER INTERFACES FOR CHINESE USERS: FOCUS ON CELL PHONES

ZHANG XUE-MIN, YANG BIN, LI YONGNA[1], WANG BO, & ZHOU PENG, BEIJING NORMAL UNIVERSITY

Rapid growth in computer and communication technology has prompted the development of human-computer interfaces (HCI) and communication equipment for diverse mediums ranging from desktop computers to mobile communication tools. In China, mobile communication tools, such as cell phones, are widely used. For example, China had 140 million cell-phone users in 2001 (McMillan, 2001), over 300 million in 2004 (Dan, 2004), and likely remains the current largest cell-phone market in the world. The research studies reported here concern features of the cell phone interface that have implications for effective navigation among Chinese users. This work is necessitated as available research on mobile communication tool interfaces has yet to examine how best to present Chinese language content on a small screen.

The design of efficient screens presents an interesting challenge. Generally, the size of the cell phone screen is 3 cm x 3 cm, which is smaller than the size of a computer screen. Just from the angle of information presentation, the small screen results in small output graphs, fonts, and few words, that may impair the coherence and comprehension of the message and impose cognitive load on the user (Brewster & Murray, 2000). Cell phones also do not allow for whole page or whole line scrolling as allowed for in larger screen devices.

Kim and Albers (2003) investigated factors influencing the reading efficiency of a table displayed on a small screen and found that too many words in one line impaired users' ability to search for information. Sandfeld and Jensen's (2005) findings indicated that decreasing letter and target size impaired task performance; that is, participants did worse with small targets than they did with large ones in the same task. However, research by Chen and Chien (2005) indicated that font and font size had no effect on reading efficiency. They found that how the information was displayed and the speed in which it was displayed affected comprehension of a given message.

Not all research indicates impaired reading efficiency using small screens. For example, Dillon, Richardson, and McKnight (1990) found that although fewer lines of words could be displayed on a small screen as opposed to a larger one, no significant differences in reading and understanding of information were found. Laarni (2002) contrasted three kinds of small screen palmtop mobile devices, PDA, email devices and mobile phones, and found that on a 3 cm × 3 cm sized screen, reading efficiency was not impaired when 15 letters were displayed on one line, and that the efficiency was improved when the information was scrolled gradually as compared to a whole page at once. Melchior (2001) showed that the use of a *wiping* design (wiping alludes to the action of a windscreen wiper), whereby content to be scrolled off a screen was dimmed, helped users maintain the context of content presented on a small screen. Shieh, Hsu, and Liu (2005) also found that a pre-guiding presentation style combined with space between words helped promote reading efficiency and speed of content on a small screen.

Another factor linked to the ease of reading text on a small screen is the color of the font and of the background (Wang, Chen, & Chen, 2002). Research in our lab (Zhang et al., 2004) has found that comparable small font size on text and icons and green fonts presented on bright blue background enhances efficiency in reading among Chinese users.

Clearly, the design of a cell phone's interface must allow for multi-tasking and easy operation (Dong, Wang, & Dai, 1999; Duchamp, 1991). This issue looms larger as the functions of cell phones have expanded to include surfing the internet and sending and receiving emails. Thus, interfaces should be designed to maximize the users' ability to control it, to minimize the user's cognitive load, and to maintain the consistency of the interface (Chen, 2001). Three interface design types also need to be considered: framework, interaction, and visual which, as relevant to the research reported below, include color, font, and page format.

We briefly present below research from our lab investigating font size and different pairings of font and background color on Chinese users' ability to effectively read messages and navigate a cell phone interface.

The effects of background and font color on Chinese text presentation

This study considered color matching, which is of concern to cognitive science researchers interested in HCI, and to media interface designers, as good color matching can improve user efficiency and flexibility, and reduce optical fatigue (Fang, 1998; Fang, Wu, & Ma, 1998).

When designing visual computer interfaces, most designers select their matching colors according to their subjective sense or experience, without specific theoretical justification or experimental verification. The theory of optics can provide some theoretical support for color matching. In particular, interface designers can work on the principle of maximizing the difference in brightness between the background color and two or more dominant fonts (Zheng, 2000). Xu et al., (1997) further studied the quantitative selection of colors in interfaces, and the studies by Hua, Gong, and Zhao (2001) showed that color matching for cathode ray tube (CRT) displays could be generalized to liquid crystal displays (LCDs). Thus, to design an efficient interface using color matching, human color vision and personal preferences need also to be taken into account.

Computers are used extensively for reading text, and good color matching might be expected to enhance reading comprehension. Rapid serial vision presentation (RSVP) is a method of displaying letters, words or pictures one after another in a limited space. Xu and Zhu (1997a; 1997b) used this method with a fixed-rate moving display to study the key factors influencing Chinese text reading. Shen, Chen, and Tao (2001) studied the effects of scrolling, leading (in which the text scrolls from right to left on a single line), and RSVP on reading comprehension. These studies were, however, more concerned with the issues of presenting Chinese text, rather than color matching, which the present study addresses.

This study was designed to measure the effect of background-font color matching on the participants' reading time, subjective sense of fatigue, and their personal preference for color matches. A moving window paradigm was used. Participants were required to send short text messages. The time needed to send these messages was recorded. Fifteen matching schemes, as shown in Fig.10-1, were used.

Reading time was shortest with a black font on a white background, and longest with a red font on a black background. The background-font color pairings white-black, white-deep blue, blue-yellow, blue-white and white-deep green had shorter reading times than black-white, white-red, black-deep green and black-purple. Based on our findings and participants' reports of optical fatigue, we concluded that red should be avoided as a font color and that pairing two colors with small differences in brightness also should be avoided.

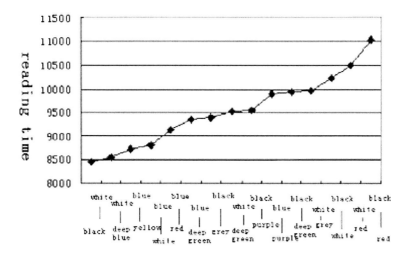

Fig. 10-1: Average reading time (ms) for different color matching pairs

Message reading efficiency using color screen mobile phones

As LCD technology has developed, color screen mobile phones are increasingly preferred by users, and are gradually replacing black and white phones. Like their black and white counterparts, color screen phones use whole-page or whole-line scrolling. One question concerns whether the scrolling style (whole-page, scrolling by line, or scrolling up and down) and screen background (whether there was a background picture) affects reading speed and comprehension.

For this study, we used a software Nokia mobile phone simulator with fixed brightness and contrast ratio, and a standard mobile phone keyboard, display, and operating system. The simulator's display was 100 pixels wide and 90 pixels high. The illumination level was 130 lux, and there was 30-50 cm distance between the participants and the display.

Participants were required to read 48 messages from different subject areas, and then answer 3 multiple choice questions, each with 3 possible answers. Each message was about 50 Chinese characters long. There were 3 reading styles (page at a time, line at a time, and constant scrolling) and 2 background styles (picture or no picture). Accuracy was measured by the number of correct responses to the questions. For the sample presented, the mean accuracy rate was 89%, and each message was read in less than 60 seconds. The variable of interest was reading time.

Across background conditions (picture or no picture), there was a significant effect of reading style as the one page at a time reading style resulted in significantly lower reading time than one line at a time or constant scrolling, in accordance with Laarni's conclusions (2002).

Across reading styles, there was a significant difference between the picture and no picture background conditions. The presence of the picture reduced reading time in the one line at a time reading style, and increased it in the one page at a time style. There were no significant differences found involving the constant scrolling style.

It is clear that in the one line at a time reading style, reading speed is enhanced by the presence of a background picture. The main reason for this finding is likely that the picture supplies background and spatial cues, making it easier for users to focus their attention on reading the messages, particularly when the content of those messages are presented one line at a time. In the constant scrolling reading style, there was no significant difference between picture and no picture background. In this reading style, the user has to control the movement of the message by repeatedly pressing a key, and users may get lost, resulting in decreased reading efficiency.

In the one page at a time reading style, reading efficiency was better when there was no background picture. In this style, the users scroll fewer pages and switch lines less frequently, and so have fewer opportunities for getting lost. Since there is no message movement, the background picture may interfere with the how the message is perceived. Although the picture was the same, participants may have treated it as a new stimulus, taxing their working memory and thereby, demonstrating weaker reading efficiency.

In situations when there was no background picture, there was no significant difference between the reading speed in the one line at a time and constant scrolling reading styles: however, both were significantly less efficient than the one page at a time reading style. The main reason for the similarity of the first two styles is the similar operation, frequent line breaks, and lack of spatial cues, with constant refocusing of attention on the relevant part of the message (Melchior, 2001). In fact, some correlative work on eye movement (Piolat, 1997; Baccino & Pynte, 1994) has shown that spatial cues contribute to better reading efficiency. However, because participants were unable to forecast successive parts of the message in both reading styles, and may have gotten lost (Melchior, 2001), a reduction in reading efficiency was found as compared to the reading style of one page at a time. When there was a background, the one line at a time and constant scrolling styles yielded significantly better reading efficiency than the one page at a time reading style.

Collectively, the findings of the studies from our lab may generalize from mobile phone message reading to other circumstances where there is a small screen interface, such as mobile web interfaces, palmtop computers, and electronic dictionaries. With the advent of increasing forms of technology incorporating small screen interfaces both in China and abroad, consideration of how best to design these interfaces will remain an issue.

Authors' note

The work reported here was funded through a 2005 grant to the Beijing Key Lab Project. The authors wish to extend their thanks to Lan Xue-Zhao, Lu Tian, Guo Xiamei, Rao Lilin, Zhang Yazi, Ran Tian, Sui Yi, and He Li.

References

Baccino, T. & Pynte, J. (1994). Spatial coding and discourse models during text reading. *Language and Cognitive Processes, 9*, 143-155.

Brewster, S.A., & Murray, R. (2000). Presenting dynamic information on mobile computers. *Personal Technologies, 4*, 209-212.

Chen, J. (2001). The up-to-date progress on HCI design. *Human Ergonomics, 1*, 40-42.

Chen, C.H., & Chien, Y.H. (2005). Effect of dynamic display and speed of display movement on reading Chinese text presented on a small screen. *Perceptual and Motor Skills, 100*, 865-873.

Dan, W. (2004, June 7). Cell phone use surges in China. Retrieved from: http://news.com/cell+phones+use+surges+in+China/2100-103935227836.html

Dillon, A., Richardson, J. & McKnight, C. (1990). The effect of display size and text splitting on reading lengthy text from the screen. *Behaviour and Information Technology, 9*, 215-227.

Dong, S., Wang, J., & Dai, G. (1999). *Human-computer Interaction and Multiple Channel User Interface* (pp. 145-159). Beijing: Science Press.

Duchamp, D. (1991) Issues in wireless mobile computing. *Proceedings of ACM SIGCOMM*, 235-245.

Fang, Zh.-G., (1998). A summary of the human-computer interaction technology. *Human Ergonomics, 4*, 64-66.

Fang, Zh.-G., Wu, X.-B., Ma,W.-J., (1998). The progress on the study of human- computer interaction technology. *Computer Engineering and Design, 19*, 59-65.

Hua, G.-W., Gong, J.-M., Zhao, N. (2001). The comparison of the color presentation efficiency between CRT, LCD and PDP. *Human Ergonomics, 7*, 5-9.

Kim, L., & Albers, M.J. (2003). Presenting information on the small-screen interface: Effects of table for formatting. *IEEE Transactions on Professional Communication, 46,* 94-104.

Laarni, J. (2002). Searching for optimal methods of presenting dynamic text on different types of screens. *NordiCHI, 10,* 19-23.

McMillan, A.F. (2001, December, 21). China cell-phone use hits 140 million. Retrieved from http://cnn.com/business.

Melchior, M. (2001). Perceptually guided scrolling for reading constant text on small screen devices. In M.D. Dunlop & S.A. Brewster (Eds.), *Proceedings of the Mobile HCI 2001: Third International Workshop on Human Computer Interaction with Mobile Devices.*

Piolat, A. (1997). Effect of screen presentation on text reading and revising. *Human-Computer Studies, 47,* 565-589.

Sandfeld, J. & Jensen, B.R. (2005). Effect of computer mouse gain and visual demand on mouse clicking performance and muscle activation in a young and elderly group of experienced computer users. *Applied Ergonomics, 36,* 547-555.

Shen, M.-W., Chen, X., & Tao, R. (2001). The research of the Chinese text reading efficiency in smooth scroll and RSVP pattern. *Psychological Science, 24,* 393-435.

Shieh, K.K., Hsu, S.H., & Liu, Y.C. (2005). Dynamic Chinese text on a single-line display: Effects of presentation mode. *Perceptual and Motor skills, 100,* 1021-1035.

Wang, A., Chen, C., & Chen, M. (2002). The effect of pre-guiding dynamic information presentation design on users' visual efficiency and optical fatigue. *Journal of the Chinese Institute of Industrial Engineers, 19,* 69-78.

Xu, B.-H., & Zhu, H. (1997a). The main factors influencing Chinese reading efficiency in RSVP presentation pattern. *Psychological Science, 20,* 11-15.

Xu, B.-H., & Zhu, H. (1997b). The research of the Chinese text reading efficiency in the fixed rate moving pattern. *Human Ergonomics, 3,* 21-23.

Xu, L.-P., Xie, W.-X., Li, Zh.-Y., (1997). The quantitative choice of color and the research of the color palette-gaining method in HCI. *Xi Dian University Journal, 24,* 45-51.

Zhang, X., He, L., Lan, X., Zhou, P., Lu, T. & Shu, H. (2004). A study of display efficiency of mobile user interface design. *Chinese Journal of Applied Psychology, 10,* 33-38.

Zheng, L.-H., (2000). The color choice in the multimedia CAI courseware and the function of multimedia CAI in physics teaching. *Guangxi Physics*, *21*, 51-54.

[1] Current address: Department of Psychology, University at Albany, NY, USA

PART III: MEDIA EDUCATION

CHAPTER ELEVEN

SCIENCE LITERACY, MEDIA LITERACY, AND THE INTERNET: CHANGE FORCES IN US AND CHINA

JOHN A. CRAVEN, III, DOWLING COLLEGE AND TRACY HOGAN, ADELPHI UNIVERSITY

The advancement of science education has a long, robust history in both the US and China. The driving force behind efforts in this domain is a widely-shared concern among scientists, economists, educators, and politicians that the general population is ill-equipped to 1) fully function in an increasingly complex scientifically and technologically-oriented society, 2) positively contribute to problem-solving for scientific and technological-based issues, and 3) adequately serve as advocates for the scientific and technological investments needed to ensure prosperity in the emerging global economy. Consequently, the US and the People's Republic of China have set "science literacy for all" on the national agenda. Unfortunately, despite massive educational investments over many past decades, the criticisms of science education have continued to outpace the strides towards achieving the goal of universal science literacy.

However, with the advent of the World Wide Web (WWW), spearheaded in the early 1980's by the English physicist Timothy Berners-Lee as part of the European Organization for Nuclear Research (CERN), the critical situation in science education may now be changing for the better. Indeed, the WWW and the internet now provide enabling conditions for science literacy (i.e., access to information and a forum for the critical exchange of empirically-based ideas) for millions more people around the globe each passing year. In fact, the media content available through the internet is exerting forces of change on scientific and educational communities in ways that few generations have witnessed. The global community of science educators is seeing accelerating changes in the design of curriculum and instruction as a result of the coupling of advancements in technologies, electronic-based content, and a remarkable propensity of youth to learn in and adapt to virtual environments. Perhaps more importantly, the internet is also shaping the way people of all ages and in all walks of life go about the process of acquiring, sharing, and, indeed, shaping new information. However, as with most technological advancements, there are challenges presented by unintended consequences of this new learning environment. These challenges to new educational enterprises in science emerge largely under three rubrics: literacy, access, and control.

The first rubric, literacy, entails the need to develop competencies as described by Aufderheide (1993) that enable one to function with "critical autonomy" within a sea of knowledge and media messages. These competencies, or core skills in media literacy, include the ability to "decode, evaluate, analyze, and produce both print and electronic media" (p. 9). Given the increasing porosity of the boundary between learner and knowledge communities, it is abundantly clear that achievements toward scientific literacy will be inextricably bound to achievements in media literacy.

The second rubric, access, entails the need to ensure equity in access to the internet and the technological infrastructure needed to function at efficient levels within the electronic learning environment. The links between global economic health and access to information are well documented (See American Association for the Advancement of Science, 1990; Armstrong, 1996; Department for Education and Skills, 2006; National Science Board, 2006). As societies become increasingly information-dependent, it is argued that two societal groups will emerge—those with access to information and those without. While the former may have more potential and greater possibilities in future job markets connected to knowledge-based industries (high-end service providers in dynamic, technology-driven enterprises), the latter will likely be relegated to low-end, low-paying, in-person service industries (Armstrong, 1996). The failure to address issues related to the gap between those who "have access" through technology and those who do not (commonly referred to as the "digital divide") will certainly result in a bifurcated citizenry. Such a situation is counterproductive for reaching the goal of scientific literacy for all.

Finally, the third rubric, control, entails newly emerging concerns regarding the diversity found through the internet. Recently, at the United Nations Educational, Scientific and Cultural Organization's (UNESCO) World Summit on the Information Society (WSIS, 2003), concerns were raised that efforts to close the digital divide may be unintentionally leading the media content found on the internet away from plurality and diversity toward a knowledge society that is more globally uniform (See Paolillo, Pimienta, & Prado; 2005). Recognizing the need to preserve cultural heritage, language, and local content, UNESCO and other global agencies are making efforts to ensure access and to preserve autonomy.

In this chapter, we use these three rubrics to discuss the intersections between science literacy, media literacy, and the internet, in the US and China. In doing so, we explore the ways in which the upcoming cyber-generation of young children may enter schools with radically different ideas about and orientations to knowledge acquisition. The chapter targets an audience interested in understanding 1) the commonality of goals of science education in the US and China, 2) learning about the current status and trends in internet access and use in both China and the US, and 3) localizing and versioning on-line applications and resources that promote science and media literacy. We begin with an overview of the goals of science education in the two countries. Next, we examine national survey data to explore trends in internet access and use in the two countries. We close the chapter with a discussion of the issues and challenges faced by providers and users of internet content.

Literacy

Science literacy

Curriculum and instruction in science education and the subsequent outcomes in terms of students' knowledge, skills, and attitudes is currently receiving great scrutiny on a global scale. Indeed, the idea of "Science for All" is now a common priority in both the US and China. This concept is grounded in a belief that the progress and betterment of society is highly dependent on a citizenry equipped with the knowledge and skills to use the tools of science and technology (American Association for the Advancement of Science, 1990). That goal requires the movement of science education away from what Schwab (1962) had coined "a rhetoric of conclusions" toward a functional literacy in the domain. The shift in this direction within science education is rooted in the following tenets:

1. New scientific and technological knowledge is being generated at exponential rates;
2. The environmental, health, and quality-of-life problems confronting societies are increasingly nestled within scientific and technological issues; and
3. To solve the increasingly complex, scientifically and technologically based issues, communities must rely on an engaged, scientifically, and technologically literate citizenry prepared to problem finding and solving.

Within the US, efforts to develop a scientifically literate population have focused on K-12 educational systems via a widely recognized set of national science education frameworks and standards. In 1991, for example, the

American Association for the Advancement of Science (AAAS) generated a list of recommendations that served as a guide toward scientific literacy for all. The endeavor, Project 2061, would later serve as the framework for two sets of national standards including Benchmarks for Science Literacy (American Association for the Advancement of Science, 1993) and the National Science Education Standards (National Research Council, 1996). The aim of Project 2061 was to ensure that all Americans were scientifically literate by the year 2061 (a date also marking the projected return of Halley's Comet). In that document, a science-literate person is

> one who is aware that science, mathematics, and technology are interdependent human enterprises with strengths and limitations; understands key concepts and principles of science; is familiar with the natural world and recognizes both its diversity and unity; and uses scientific knowledge and scientific ways of thinking for individual and social purposes. (pg. xvii)

While the National Science Education Standards (National Research Council, 1996) may serve as a recommended framework for the design of science education curriculum and instruction (with many states and districts using the national framework to guide the development of local frameworks), at this time there is neither a nationally mandated framework or a mandated set of standards to achieve the goal.

For China, the year 2049 has been set as the date when every member of the population will be scientifically literate. Unlike the US, the target population of governmental efforts to promote scientific literacy expands beyond K-12 audiences by reaching out to the broader community. For example, Channel 10 on China Central Television (CCTV-10) is dedicated to science and education. This broadcast is part of a larger effort of using mass media to reach and engage a broad segment of the population on the subject of science and technology (Pitrelli, 2005). Although there are content-similar broadcasts and documentaries in the US (e.g., Discovery Channel, Public Broadcast System, NOVA, Nature Channel), such programming has roots in either profit or non-profit enterprises rather than in a government-coordinated endeavor.

The organization behind this Chinese effort is the China Association for Science and Technology (CAST). CAST, composed of national societies, associations, research institutes and provincial associations for science and technology, is charged, in part, by the government to promote scientific literacy for the whole nation. CAST, founded nearly 50 years ago, is also charged with the task of popularizing knowledge of science and technology, promulgating scientific thinking and methods, and conducting activities of science and technology among the youth and teenagers (CAST, 2006).

In 1980, the State council authorized the formation of the China Research Institute for Science Popularization, or CRISP (Pitrelli, 2005). In recent years, CRISP has launched investigations relevant to the popularization of science in the nation such as

> science and technology communication and its contents, channels, target audience and mechanics, survey, monitor and explication of public science literacy, investigation and theoretical study on cultivation of juvenile creativity, science writing and science writers both within and outside China, theoretical study on informal science and technology education, investigation on science and technology weight in mass media, and evaluation theory and methodology on science popularization performances (ResearchSEA, 2005).

The relevant governmental agencies and departments in China are using the results of those surveys to inform policy-making decisions regarding science popularization.

Defining science literacy

Over the last few decades, there has been much debate about the definition of scientific literacy. Carl Sagan (1995) argued that scientific literacy, largely, requires a person to distinguish science from pseudoscience. In more common language, Sagan argued that the aim of science education should be to equip people with the habits of mind (e.g., ability as well as propensity to use critical, skeptical thinking skills) so that they would have a nonsense detector. Towards this end, science and technology education has been trending toward the inclusion of the nature of science (See Craven, Hand, & Prain, 2002; Graber, Nentwig, Becker, Sumfleth, Pitton, Wollweber, & Jorde, 2001) and media literacy (Potter, 2001; Osborne, 2002; Frechette, 2002).

The AAAS (1989) articulated the competencies for science literacy. In their document, *Capabilities of the Scientifically Literate High School Graduate*, those competencies included, in part, to:

1. Read and understand articles on science in the newspaper;
2. Read and interpret graphs displaying scientific information;
3. Engage in a scientifically informed discussion of a contemporary issue, e.g., should a child with AIDS be allowed to attend public school;
4. Assess the accuracy of scientific statements, e.g., the seasons change with the distance of the earth from the sun;
5. Be inclined to challenge authority on evidence that supports scientific statements;
6. Apply scientific information in personal decision making, e.g., ozone depletion and the use of aerosols; and
7. Locate valid scientific information when needed.

The vision set forth by this association concerning that of scientific literacy is highly congruent with that articulated in a document presented at the 2005 US-China Education Leaders Forum on Math and Science Education (http://internationaled.org/math&science.htm). In the document, *Chinese Science Curriculum Standards (Grades 3–6)*, science literacy is described as including

> the necessary science knowledge and skills, scientific thinking, understanding of science, scientific attitude and value system, and awareness and ability to solve problems using scientific knowledge (p. 3).

The standard of scientific literacy in Chinese education is nestled within the position that science literacy takes time and thus, science education must begin early in school life.

Technology and media literacy

With the advent of computers in classrooms, scientific and technological literacy have been inextricably woven together. The International Society for Technology in Education (ISTE), founded in 1979, is widely recognized as the flagship organization for the advancement of technology in education. Over the years, the complexity of the organization has reflected the growth in technology itself. Indeed, the special interests groups include: administrators, computing teachers, hypermedia and multimedia, innovative learning technologies, media specialists, and teacher educators. In the recent past, ISTE introduced a major initiative, The National Educational Technology Standards (NETS) Project. According to the NETS, capable information technology users are information seekers, analyzers, and evaluators; problem solvers and decision makers; creative and effective users of productivity tools; communicators, collaborators, publishers, and producers; and informed, responsible, and contributing citizens.

Today, with the saturation of the internet in classrooms across the US and the exponential growth in access in China, there is increasing recognition that a third strand, media literacy, is found in the fabric of science literacy (Craven, Hand, & Prain, 2002; Osborne, 2002; Frechette, 2002). Examining the NETS, it is clear that the boundaries between scientific, technological, and media literacy are becoming extremely porous. The NETS underscore the transition from mastery of content and skills in the knowledge domains toward the development of informed, engaged contributors with local and global communities. From a holistic perspective, there is great overlap between scientific literacy, technological literacy, and media literacy (hence, the three are typically grouped and identified as "the literacies"). Media literacy, as defined by representatives involved in the National Leadership Conference on Media Literacy, is the ability to access, analyze, and produce information for specific outcomes (Aufderheide, 1993). Furthermore, whether it is developing positive attitudes to support life-long learning, using technology to increase productivity and creativity, or using a variety of media tools to communicate information and ideas effectively to multiple audiences, in large part, technology literacy, as advocated by the ISTE organization depends upon media literacy.

Assessing the literacies

National Tests. Testing scientific, technological, and media literacy of K-12 students in the US is most often completed on the district level. However, performance outcomes are linked to federal funding through the 2001 No Child Left Behind Law. This federal law mandates that all students, regardless of race and/or ethnicity, will achieve basic competencies in reading and mathematics by the year 2010. During 2007, science will be added to this testing slate. While these tests indicate student understandings within each grade level, the tests are neither uniformly used as college entrance examinations or coordinated and administered at the national level. However, for Chinese students to move into the national university system, entrance exams in subjects such as mathematics and science are used to determine individual eligibility.

International Tests. In the US, the concerns about achievement in science education have deep roots in national defense and security and economic viability. As in the past, these concerns continue to fuel the international comparisons industry. The history of empirical international comparisons of education outcomes is now nearing a span of five decades. This record began with a splinter group of attendees at the United Nations Educational, Scientific, and Cultural Organization (UNESCO) Institute for Education in Hamburg in 1958 that founded the International Association for the Evaluation of Educational Achievement (IAE, n.d.). Recall, that at the time (1957), the former Soviet Union had successfully launched Sputnik I into orbit around the Earth.

The most notable international comparisons for science achievement include the First International Science Study (FISS; 1968–1972), the Second International Science Study (1983-84), and the Third International Mathematics and Science Study, or TIMSS, completed in 1995. The 1995 study examined achievement in the areas of biology, chemistry, and physics across three levels including 10-year-old students, 14-year-old students, and those students completing their final grade of secondary education. Since 1995, the period between international comparisons conducted by IAE has been greatly reduced to only a few years between test periods.

Following the increased frequency of these comparisons and the cachet in "product" recognition of the TIMSS, the acronym has since been changed to

Trends in International Mathematics and Science Studies. Originally designed to better understand and improve educational practices, these studies have, over the years, been used to suggest potential economic and academic advantages among the participating countries. The Asian countries most notably compared to the US now through the TIMSS series include: Japan, Republic of Korea, and Singapore (each participating in the TIMSS 1995, 1999, and 2003). In 2007, another Asian country, Mongolia, will participate in the TIMSS 2007 study (International Association for the Evaluation of Educational Achievement, 2006).

Although the evidence of international disparities continued to mount (a consequence of the escalation in testing and comparisons), there was growing dissatisfaction with both the methodology and accomplishments used by IAE. Specifically, a number of countries expressed concerns that the assessments measured knowledge out of context and not taught through the curriculum. For these reasons, some argued that the assessments were not valid (See Harlen, 2001). In response to these criticisms, the Organisation for Economic Co-operation and Development (OECD) has recently developed a cyclic (three-year) comparison of educational outcomes that includes problem-solving and science literacy. This international assessment is known as the Programme in International Student Assessment (PISA). In 1999, the OECD identified key points that distinguished PISA from the TIMSS student. According to Harlen (2001), the distinctions serving as advantage points over the TIMSS included that it:

> 1) comprised a program of surveys in which the ability to provide comparable data from one survey to another was built in; 2) concerned the outcomes from all aspects of basic education given to students during the years of compulsory education through age 15; and 3) assessed students based on common, international view of what the education system should provide to prepare its future citizens for adult life and for life-long learning and the skills and knowledge comprising this view, in the context of extended units designed to reflect real-life contexts rather than performance in isolated test items (pp. 50-51).

Similarly PISA was designed to focus on indicators of educational outcomes in support of policy analyses and to eventually move toward the assessment of cross-curriculum competencies and self-regulated learning.

These features underscore the effort by the OECD to develop a method of evaluating the degree to which various educational programs are preparing scientifically literate citizens. Thus, PISA was a deliberate attempt to move towards the evaluation of literacies and away from the assessment of a mastery of decontextualized knowledge bases. Indeed, the components of the PISA include mathematical, reading and scientific literacy, and problem-solving.

PISA. The Asian countries most notably compared to the US through the PISA program include Japan and the Republic of Korea. To date, two PISA studies have been completed. Data collection in the US for PISA 2006 took place from September to November, 2006 (NCES, n.d.). With the focus on the literacies, it was inevitable for researchers to expand the collection of information to computer use and fluency. In this way, the PISA has pushed the assessment envelope beyond the TIMSS. In doing so, the PISA provides valuable baseline data to understand media literacy. That is, the questionnaire administered to more than 280,000 in more than 41 countries (a number that increases to 57 in 2006) provides a window into a very poorly lit area; media literacy and science education.

According to Aufderheide (1993),

> Emphases in media literacy training range widely, including informed citizenship, aesthetic appreciation and expression, social advocacy, self-esteem, and consumer competence (p. 1).

In that the PISA includes survey instruments that gather information on those very topics, the PISA data also provide at least some of the basic information needed by those concerned with media literacy. Researchers and others interested in the PISA program should know that the organization is interested in disseminating the results of the PISA studies to support further analysis of the data (Organisation for Economic Co-operation and Development, n.d.). Towards that end, the OECD places downloadable survey instruments and results on the PISA internet site.

The PISA surveys asks 15 year olds to respond to questions on access (where access takes place), use (frequency and types of activities), and self-perceptions as they relate to internet use (skill/task-specific fluency, values, and interests). These surveys also provide insight about whom these adolescents view as their primary instructor in use of the Internet (See Table 11-1). The information in Tables 11-2—11-4 (below) provides much needed insight into this area of research through a comparison of the 15 year old 10 graders in US (N > 3300), Japan (N > 5000), and Korea (N > 4000). Although China does not currently participate in the PISA project, the Ministry of Education's Department of Development and Planning serves as one of the PISA National Project Managers for the consortium of cooperating countries.

Table 11-1. Instructor for Internet Use (Percentages of Users).

	Japan	Korea	United States
I don't know how to use the Internet.	0.1	5.5	0.2
My school.	2.7	30.6	10.6
My friends.	30.6	12.0	14.2
My family.	7.3	28.0	15.7
I taught myself.	54.3	20.2	58.2
Others.	5.0	3.5	1.2

Table 11-2. Frequency of Computer Use by 15-year old 10th graders (Percentages of Users).

		Almost every day	A few times each week	Between once a week and once a month	Less than once a month	Never
Home	Japan*	56.9	29.5	10.4	0.8	2.4
	Korea**	18.3	18.4	21.6	20.2	21.5
	US***	62.4	20.9	7.1	2.8	6.8
School	Japan	3.8	25.5	28.8	14.0	27.9
	Korea	2.2	24.2	32.8	15.8	25.0
	United States	18.4	22.3	29.5	21.4	8.4
At other places	Japan	3.8	17.3	32.4	29.5	17.0
	Korea	0.5	1.7	5.3	25.1	67.4
	United States	5.1	15.9	26.0	32.4	20.6

* Japan N > 5000
** Korea N > 4000
*** United States N > 3300

Table 11-3. Frequency of Use by Application (Percentages of Users).

How often do you use:		Almost every day	A few times each week	Between once a week and once a month	Less than once a month	Never
The internet to look up information on people, things, or ideas?	Japan	16.1	42.7	26.5	10.5	4.2
	Korea	6.5	13.0	22.4	38.6	19.5
	US	37.3	36.1	18.9	6.0	1.6
The internet to collaborate with a group or team?	Japan	19.5	29.6	22.6	15.1	13.2
	Korea	2.6	4.0	7.1	16.7	69.5
	US	20.9	20.5	20.6	14.4	23.3
The internet to download software (including games)?	Japan	16.9	30.7	23.3	15.5	13.5
	Korea	3.2	6.1	10.8	18.9	61.0
	US	27.3	23.4	20.5	13.6	15.2
The internet to download music?	Japan	36.9	42.4	14.5	3.8	2.4
	Korea	4.0	7.7	11.0	15.6	61.7
	US	41.0	23.9	12.1	7.9	15.1
A computer for electronic communication (e.g. e-mail or "chat rooms")?	Japan	38.6	35	16.3	5.9	4.3
	Korea	12.7	9.7	11.2	16.9	49.4
	US	50.2	22.3	11.7	6.4	9.3

Table 11-4. Fluency on Tasks (Percentages of Users).

How well can you do each of these tasks on a computer?		I can do this very well by myself.	I can do this with help from someone.	I know what this means but I cannot do it.	I don't know what this means.
Get on the Internet.	Japan	99.0	0.7	0.1	0.1
	Korea	72.8	15.2	7.4	4.6
	US	95.7	2.7	1	.6
Copy or download files from the internet.	Japan	96.7	2.6	0.4	0.3
	Korea	44.1	29.5	17.7	8.7
	US	86.4	9.9	2.8	.9
Attach a file to an e-mail message.	Japan	95.7	3.3	0.5	0.5
	Korea	37.5	27.2	22.9	12.5
	US	75.2	17.5	5.8	1.6
Play computer games.	Japan	92.7	5.0	1.7	0.5
	Korea	70.1	18.4	6.5	5.1
	US	95.1	3.3	1.1	0.5
Download music from the internet.	Japan	97.3	2.2	0.3	0.2
	Korea	35.3	32.4	22.9	9.4
	US	82.3	12.0	4.7	1.0
Write and send e-mails.	Japan	96.8	2.2	0.5	0.5
	Korea	57.2	21.6	13.8	7.4
	US	92.2	5.1	2.1	.7
Construct a web page.	Japan	19.1	53.8	21.3	5.8
	Korea	13.2	37.1	37.7	12.0
	US	45.0	35.3	16.6	3.0

By and large, the data above show that both Japan and the US adolescents have either taught themselves how to use the internet or have had friends instruct them on various aspects of internet usage (84.9% and 72.4%, respectively). Furthermore, a large majority of both US adolescents (62.4%) and their Japanese counterparts (56.9%) connect to the internet almost on a daily basis. Most of that time is spent either listening/downloading music and/or interfacing with friends and acquaintances through cyber-social networks. Interestingly, a large majority of both American and Japanese adolescents feel largely competent in many of the basic skills commonly used with the internet. It is important to note that the data come from self-reports. Thus, more needs to be understood about the actual skills versus perceived skills these adolescents possess and how adolescents are using the media content found on the Internet. Moreover, while the data shows that there is peer-to-peer communication, little is known about the purpose and content of these types of communication.

In short, while the PISA data is permitting greater understanding of adolescent access and use of the internet, we are at the nascent stage of understanding whether the skills and knowledge required for media and science literacy are being learned and applied in these virtual environments. Nor do we understand whether such users are accessing and using the tools and content designed to promote the development of science literacy.

Internet and science literacy

Currently, the ways in which the internet is used and the web-based resources that are available on the internet for the promotion of science literacy are abundant and ever expanding. While there are costs associated with such resources, the number of free and open-access resources is staggering. These internet-based educational tools and approaches provide unique opportunities for learners to develop deep conceptual understandings of scientific concepts (ranging from the basic to the highly sophisticated or abstract) through technologies that are described as virtual lab experiments or virtual manipulatives. Commonly referred to as internet "gizmos" and "gadgets," these virtual workstations allow users to move objects around the screen, take measurements, record data, manipulate variables, and conduct investigations ranging from dissections in biology to closed system experiments in physics.

Learners can go beyond the constraints inherent in the design of these gizmos and gadgets by designing investigations that use on-line databases to upload, download, store, and manipulate data collected in real-world investigations. The projects often use the context of local environmental topics and typically integrate on-line geographic information systems (GIS) technologies. Furthermore, given the global scale of data collection, many of these student-fed databases are used by practicing scientists. For example, in the GLOBE Program (Global Learning and Observations to Benefit the Environment), environmental data is collected and uploaded by thousands of students from more than 79 countries around the world. In one way, scientists are using data from student investigations of seasonal changes of life systems such as bud bursts, and green-up and green downs of vegetation (phenology) in statistical models for global climate change. The internet sites available through the GLOBE Program have multiple language capabilities including English, Chinese, French, Arabic, Dutch, and Spanish.

Another popular online database project is Journey North. This web-based program uses student observations to monitor and analyze wildlife migration patterns and seasonal changes on a global level. Just as there are students providing data to scientists, there is a vastly increasing number of scientific research agencies and organizations providing access to both real-time data and catalogued data to students as well as the general public. Such data includes GIS files, data from atmospheric and oceanic monitoring systems (e.g. buoys and weather stations).

Students and teachers involved in science investigations, whether web-based or not, also have access to a growing population of on-line scientists who serve as "expert" resources. Commonly referred to as "ask the expert," these sites often provide students with knowledge and insights into the enterprise of science. Teachers and students are also using the online search engines such as Google to develop webquests. Unlike a general search, webquests are more structured web-based inquiry modules that guide students to websites containing relevant information on a given subject. Currently, thousands of teachers are posting fully developed webquests online for use by others. Often, these webquests take advantage of another popular online aspect for science education—virtual field trips and web exhibits. As museums, historical societies, and other nonformal learning centers expand into the internet, access to collections and artifacts and other curios are being made accessible through electronic portals.

There are a number of other highly popular vehicles associated with the advancement of science literacy, including streaming videos on subjects within scientific disciplines. Media traditionally or originally developed for television broadcast as well as new materials developed strictly for dissemination through cyberspace are now accessible to millions of users. Clearly, as the number of internet users with high-speed connections increases, so does the number of users accessing these materials.

Another very popular use of the internet for science literacy is, of course, distance education. Today, distance education models are being used across the lifespan (See Setzer & Lewis, 2005). Thirty-one percent of those taking distance education courses in public schools (elementary and secondary) were in natural or physical sciences, computer science, and mathematics (enrollments are combined across these curriculum areas). Indeed, Setzer and colleagues (2005) report that 72% of districts within the US with students enrolled in distance education plan to increase distance education course offerings in the future. Within the US, adult education lies largely across two categories; work-related courses and personal interests courses (See Kim, Collins Hagedorn, Williamson, & Chapman, 2004; Craven, 2005; O'Donnell, 2006). As one might imagine, the growth in internet-based education (or "distance education") in China is phenomenal yet not new. For example, the Head of the World Bank's Education and Technology Team reported that in 1998, China was producing more than 100,000 graduates a year through distance education with nearly 46,000 in engineering and technology attaining degrees through on-line programs (Potashnik & Capper, 1998).

Institutions and organizations are providing open access to web-based educational modules and packages. For example, the Massachusetts Institute of Technology (MIT) currently operates a program, MIT OpenCourseWare (http://ocw.mit.edu/index.html). This initiative is dedicated to providing large-scale open access to graduate and undergraduate electronic course material. Meanwhile, New York University's Institute of Reconstructive Plastic Surgery, through a grant from *Smile Train* (a world wide charity targeting cleft palates) is using 3D animated technologies to create virtual surgery laboratories (Grayson, 2007).

A major initiative in Internet-based science and education was launched in 2004. That project, Little GLORIAD, is an advanced network linking China, Russia, and the US. The system was designed to meet lifetime learning needs of scientists and science educators (GLORIAD, 2004). The project has three main coordinating centers: in the US the network project is coordinated by the National Science Foundation (NSF), in China it is the Chinese Academy of Sciences (CAS), and in Russia it is a consortium of institutions led by the Russian Research Center Kurchatov Institute (with additional funding from the Russian Ministry of Education and Science). The network is described by the collaborative as

> a classroom serving as a large, curated information clearing house with services made available via a dynamically generated, browser independent web interface, a multi-lingual capacity, and extended search methods (GLORIAD, 2004).

Access

The degree to which the broad population has access to the internet and the ways in which the medium is being used represent a major concern in both

China and the US. In the US, several agencies have been involved in surveying populations to better understand computer access and usage patterns. Such agencies include the US Census Bureau, Economic and Statistics Administration (ESA), National Telecommunications and Information Administration (NTIA) and US Department of Education, and the National Center for Education Statistics (NCES). For example, supplementary instruments have been attached to subpopulations surveyed during the US Census Bureau's Current Population Survey since 1998. The findings from these surveys have been used for descriptive studies and to guide national policies on such topics as equity in access, internet safety, and education.

ESA and the NTIA within the US Department of Commerce have jointly issued several major reports on Internet use in America since 1998. In the latest report, *A Nation Online: Entering the Broadband Age* (Gallagher & Cooper, 2004), the agencies focused on broadband technologies, given its promise to enhance the nation's economic competitiveness as well as its capacity for providing health care information and education to all. Another significant source of light on internet use and access in the US comes from the US Department of Education, National Center for Education Statistics (NCES). In recent years, the NCES has disseminated several seminal reports on internet access and use in US public schools (See Wells & Lewis, 2006; Parsad & Jones, 2005).

Beginning in 1997, the government of China charged the China Internet Network Information Center (CNNIC) with the task of conducting national surveys of iInternet access and use in the country. The agency's most recent report, the *17th Statistical Survey Report on the Internet Development in China* (CNNIC, 2006) represents the most comprehensive portrait of Chinese internet access and use. Collectively, the comprehensive, government-supported reports shed much needed light on trends in access and use of the internet across both countries. These reports were used to compile a description (below) of internet access and use in the US and China.

China

Internet access and use in China continues to grow at exponential rates. Survey information has documented forms of access, gender differences in usage, age of users, and most typical sites where the internet is accessed. According to the most recent survey results (CNNIC, 2006), the number of internet users in the People's Republic of China totals 111 million (or slightly under 10% of the total population). Among the users, 64.3% use broadband access while others connect to internet through leased lines, or local area networks, (29.1%), which are higher speed. The slowest form of access, dial-up, is used by 51% of the citizens. There are gender differences found among the internet users in China with males representing 57.9% of all users and females representing 41.3% of all users. Age is also a factor in internet use in China with 82.6% of all users with an age of 35 and younger. Those with a college diploma and some form of college degree (bachelor's, master's, or doctoral) represent 24.4% and 29.2% (respectively) of all users. Those Chinese with access average 15.9 hours per week on the internet. Access occurs from a number of locations including the home (70.5%), workplace (37.6%), internet cafés (27.0%), school (19%), public places and other (0.9%).

Tables 11-5 and 11-6 lists the top ten services according to frequency of use among all internet users in China and the US (respectively). Six of those 10 activities are commonly used in the classroom and/or school settings. When comparing the frequencies of the top ten services used across China and the US, the similarities are quite notable. The minor discrepancy between the two groups is seen lower on the list as Americans may use the internet for shopping (purchasing products and/or services), searching for jobs, and online financing far more than their Chinese counterparts.

Table 11-5. Frequency of Services Used (China top ten)*.

Service	Frequency of Use (Percentage)
1. News**	67.9
2. Search Engine	65.7
3. Email**	64.7
4. Instant Message	41.9
5. BBS, Community Forum	41.6
6. Obtaining information (inquire about info of products, services, jobs, healthcare, government, etc.)**	39.8
7. Listening/Downloading music**	38.3
8. Watching/Downloading video**	37.1
9. Internet games**	33.2
10. School/class mates/ BBS	28.6

*Adapted from CNNIC (2006), p. 16.
**Also found on US list of top ten activities by frequency used.
Note: Percentages do not total to 100%

Table 11-6. Frequency of Services Used (2003 United States top ten)*.

Service	Frequency of use (Percentage)
News, Weather, Sports Information	66.0
Email	87.8
Product or Service Information	76.5
Search information on Health Services or Practices	41.6
Listening/Downloading music /Watching/Downloading video	21.7
Internet games	38.1
Search for information about government services or agencies	35.7
Purchase products or services	52.1
Search for a job	18.7
Online Financing	34.6

*Adapted from Gallagher & Cooper (2004), p. 8.

The survey data also sheds light on the perceptions and attitudes held by internet users in China. For example, the majority of users report a helpful or very helpful perception of the Internet for various activities including study, work, daily life, and entertainment (see Table 11-7). However, their overall attitude regarding speed, content, security and other aspects of connectivity apart from ease of use largely falls below satisfaction (see Table 11-8).

Table 11-7. Perception of usefulness of the internet (Percentage of Users)*.

	Very helpful to helpful	Average	Harmful to very harmful
Studying	85.8	12.2	2.0
Working	86.4	12.8	0.8
Daily Life	79.8	18.3	2.0
Entertainment	82.2	15.6	2.2

*Adapted from CNNIC (2006), p. 17.

Table 11-8. Attitudes towards the current internet (Percentage of Users)*.

	Excellent to satisfied	Average	Dissatisfied to disappointed
Speed	40.7	39.8	19.5
Cost and fee	23.4	43.7	32.9
Security	24.5	44.6	30.9
Authenticity of contents	30.6	47.4	22.0
Propriety of contents	27.5	47.7	24.8
Protection of individual privacy	28.2	45.4	26.5
Easy to use	60.7	34.0	5.3

*Adapted from CNNIC (2006), p. 17.

US

The most current information concerning trends and access use by American citizens comes from the US Department of Commerce. Gallagher and Cooper (2004) report that 61.8% of households in the US have at least one computer in the home; nearly the same percentage have household connections to the internet (61.5%). Among the connected, those with broadband access use the computer most often (66.1% connect to the internet each day). However, of those households with a computer, only 19.9% have broad-band connection. Thus, approximately 40% of households with access connect through slower, dial-up methods.

The data from a recent report, *A Nation on Line: Entering the Broadband Age*, (Gallagher & Cooper, 2004) sheds light on the age, educational degree, and income of those accessing and using the internet. For example, a steady increase in usage with age is documented in the report. Approximately 20% of three and four year olds are using the internet in some way while approximately 80% of adolescents aged 14-17 access the internet. Interestingly, among individuals older than 50 years, few are accessing the internet, especially those no longer in the work force (27.6% compared to 64.4% still in the labor force). Those with post-high school degrees and making over $150,000 per year are identified as the largest percentage of people in these categories of education and income to access the internet.

Digital divides

One continuing concern is the (growing) gap between those who have both access and resources to effectively use the internet and those who do not. Widely described as the "digital divide," this problem exists in the US and China, and across the globe. NTIA views the digital divide as sorting groups across attributes such as socio-economic status (income) and geographic location (urban versus rural), race, age, education, and household type (McConnaughey & Lader, 1998). In the US, concerns about the digital divide surfaced shortly after the creation and expansion of the internet. The commission charged by (then) Vice President Al Gore with analyzing the telephone and computer penetration across the US found that "The Least Connected" profiles were among rural poor, rural, and central city minorities, young heads of households (under 35 years of age), and female-headed households (McConnaughey & Lader, 1998).

More recently, the US Department of Commerce reported on the impact of access type (high speed versus low speed) as a factor impacting online behavior (Gallagher & Cooper, 2004). In the report, *A Nation Online*, the Department found that the frequency of use and the type (variety) of activity used on the internet was impacted by connection type. The data for the report was drawn from approximately 57,000 households completing a supplemental survey to the Census Bureaus' monthly Current Population Survey (CPS). The reasons for the disconnect from high-speed internet access included the belief that high speed services weren't available, or that they did not need and/or were not interested in the internet, the lack of high speed services or inadequacies of computer resources, and the expense of high-speed service. Notably, the survey included the population of age 3 and older; an indicator of how early internet access develops among users.

The Department of Commerce study also found that 51.2% of those surveyed indicated that they used the internet at least once a day as opposed to 66.1% among those with broadband access at home. Despite the rapid expansion in growth in the percent of households with access to the internet (from 18.6% in 1997 to 54.6% in 2003), a surprisingly large percentage of Americans (41.3%) still do not use the internet from any location (Gallagher & Cooper, 2004). Yet, in the US it appears that schools are serving a major function in closing the digital divide.

The National Science Board (2006) reports that while household factors such as income, parental education level, and race/ethnicity are related to home access to computers and the internet, the Board also recognizes that schools are serving a significant role in closing the gaps. Wells and Lewis (2006) found that nearly all US schools had access to the internet. In their comprehensive review of public schools and classrooms internet access from the years 1994–2005, they reported explosive expansions in internet access. The greatest growth rates occurred between the years 1996 and 2001. Since then, the growth rate has slowed in as much as the system, now nearing 100% connected, is considered saturated with internet connectivity. As the connectivity has increased, so has the use (by type and by frequency). Wells and Lewis (2006) also found that 97% of the schools with internet connectivity in 2005 were using broadband service.

Thus, there is growing acknowledgement that schools are helping to equalize access for disadvantaged students. In addition to providing computer time and internet access to nearly all students, schools are using the internet to communicate with students, parents, and the public at large. Schools are also using the internet for a variety of purposes including curriculum and instruction and the professional development of teachers (Wells & Lewis, 2005).

In China, the digital divide presents a problem as well despite massive national and foreign investments in the Information and Communications Technologies (ICT) in China. Harrington (2001) reports that Chinese internet users are typically well educated, young, predominantly male, and relatively wealthy. Harrington (2001) also reports that provincial use of the internet varies widely with some of the fastest growing provinces being among those with the lowest internet use. Other factors contributing to the disparity in internet access and use in China include inadequate human resource support, imperfect network legation, and information resource shortage in the Chinese language (Rong, 2001).

Diversity on the web

In December 2001, the United Nations General Assembly endorsed the organization of the World Summit on the Information Society (WSIS) to fathom the current status and development of information societies and to provide an opportunity for a broad coalition of global representatives to both discuss and shape the information society (UNESCO, 2005). Subsequent to a convention in December 2003, the United Nations Educational, Scientific, and Cultural Organization (UNESCO) and the WSIS adopted a framework, the Geneva Declaration of Principles, outlining the basic tenets upon which information societies should operate (UNESCO, 2005). That framework, entitled "Building the Information Society: A Global Challenge in the New Millennium," provides a vision and set of principles for the development of a global information society (WSIS, 2003).

One basic principle (B8) addresses cultural diversity and identity, linguistic diversity, and local content. The sections under this principle (52—54) provide a framework for internet media content designed to promote and preserve cultural identities, linguistic diversity, and preservation of heritage for future generations. According to WSIS (2003), these sections also speak to the need

> to promote the production of and accessibility to all content—educational, scientific, cultural or recreational—in diverse languages and formats. The development of local content suited to domestic or regional needs will encourage social and economic development and will stimulate participation of all stakeholders, including people living in rural, remote and marginal areas (p. 7).

The principles outlined by UNESCO and WSIS are certainly needed at a time when both the structure of the network as well as the media content of the internet is rapidly evolving.

Structure of the internet

The domain name system (DNS) of the internet is currently managed by a private-sector body called the Internet Corporation for Assigned Names and Numbers (ICANN). According to the organization (http://www.icann.org/), the vitality and viability of internet operations are dependent upon a carefully coordinated system of protocols and top-level domain identifiers (e.g., ".org," ".edu," ".gov,", and ".uk"—a national top-level domain). In 2006, the *People's Daily Online* (China adds top-level domain names), reported that China had created three top-level domains outside the coordination of ICANN, and expressed in Chinese characters (see *The Economist*, 2006, March 2), While this report subsequently proved false (ICANN disputes China domain report, 2006), it reflects global dissatisfaction with ICANN, which is seen to have too close ties to the US government (see *The Economist*, 2006, April 27).

Meanwhile, in the US, there is much debate about the development of a "two-tiered" internet system. In the proposed structure, commercial telecommunication organizations would bifurcate streams of information into high and low priority networks. Proponents of this system (typically telecommunications providers) argue that the tiered system will improve the efficacy of network operations. Alternatively, opponents fear the emergence of a system that squashes access, inhibits diverse expression, creates a hegemonic information system, and promotes economic monopolies (See *New York Times*, 2006; 2007).

The threat of cultural homogeneity to the point of monoculturalism also comes from the media content of the internet. The power of adolescents' need for socialization and the establishment of self-identify through interaction is evidenced by such new internet enterprises such as *MyFace*, *YouTube*, *MySpace*, and personal web spaces that serve as online diaries, journals, and/or weblogs. The explosive growth in teenage use of the internet for diversion is not unique to the US. For example, China now has more internet users than any country apart from the US and instant computer-to-computer messages in China have more than doubled since 2002 to around 87 million (*The Economist*, 2006, March 2). Blogs in China also exceeded more than 30 million (up from nearly non-existence a few years earlier). Moreover, *China Daily* recently reported that, according to a study published by the Central Committee of the Communist Youth League of China, more than 2 million of China's roughly 18 million teen users were internet addicts (Shanshan, 2007).

While understanding youth's use of traditional media and the internet has long been an interest among sociologists and educational psychologists, there are significant interests among advertisers, product developers, curriculum and instruction designers in the teenage market (La Ferle, Edwards, & Lee, 2000). La Ferle and colleagues argue that the teen market is rapidly expanding, and they attribute this expansion to adolescents' need for socialization and interaction. Nonetheless, these market interests and influences may be detrimental to the preservation of individuality and cultural heritage. Furthermore, it is apparent that the fluidity of the structure of the internet, the increasing technological abilities of adolescent users, the creativity demonstrated by youth to find ways to communicate with others, and increasing access, through cyber cafes, are combining to create a dynamic media system in both the US and China. However, the degree to which these interactions and uses lead to productive, educative, and beneficial enterprises remains an issue.

Unmistakably, localization and versioning of media content and applications in the aim of advancing scientific literacy while preserving cultural identify and heritage requires carefully planned, sustainable collaborations between stakeholders in both the US and China. There also is an ever-growing number of models providing insights into the ways these collaborations are coordinated and their outcomes. For example, one collaborative initiative is found in the US-China Cooperation Program in Science Policy, Research, and Education (George Mason School of Law, 2006). The program, now ten years old, links the National Science Foundation in the US and the National Natural Science Foundation of China.

In 2003, the program coordinated a seminar on science, society, and the internet. Participants included delegates from Japan, the US, and China. The objective of the conference was to explore the critical issues associated with the impacts of the internet on science and society (Blanpied, 2004). After a suite of presentations on a variety of topics including centrality of data, international codes of ethics, values and choices, internet governance, copyrights, cultural differences, and expertise, it became clear that much more empirical research was needed to understand the internet's impact on science, scientific research, and society (Blanpied, 2004).

Summary

In the US and China, the call for "science literacy for all" is well-documented. Grounded in the belief that advancement of the social and economic vitality of a nation is dependent upon an entire population who understands the processes and fruits of the scientific enterprise, the goal of science literacy serves as a focal point of educational and scientific policies in both countries. At the beginning of this chapter, we claimed that the internet, as a medium of mass communication, is moving science education closer to the endgame set for the years 2061 and 2049. However, our hopeful enthusiasm expressed at the beginning of this chapter should be curbed by the stark realities of human nature that exert oppositional forces on the educational endeavors described above. Indeed, we would argue that the internet should be considered an enabling environment rather than a panacea for science education.

In his book, *The Unnatural Nature of Science* (1992), Lewis Wolpert, Professor of Biology as Applied to Medicine, argues that the very way of thinking that makes science so successful is quite, as the title implies, "unnatural." As science educators we routinely see evidence of such reluctance (if not incapacity) towards critical examination and analysis from students. For example, the habit of students "cutting-and-pasting" information and data from the internet (taking electronic information directly from one medium and inserting it into another form) is ubiquitous. The propensity of students to take and use the first "hits" following a search and/or their failure to take a critical stance against claims found on the internet remain an impediment to science literacy. It follows that science educators should not confuse an ability to access information with the ability to critically analyze that information. Consequently, more needs to be understood about the developmental, attitudinal, and/or educational factors connected to such habits. Furthermore, more light needs to be shed on effective pedagogical strategies that target the development of skills and habits of mind associated with media literacy.

While more research is obviously needed in the areas identified above, we must not lose sight of other factors contributing to the problem of failure in critical stances. History is replete with the presence of mountebanks and charlatans eager to take advantage of the unsuspecting. Therefore, no one should be surprised to see the growth of electronic industries that, with technological sophistication, become very good at blurring the lines between science and pseudoscience. Thus, more needs to be understood about the relationships between the structural and deep features of electronic media and the ways in which learners attend to that electronic-based media. Certainly, this need will escalate alongside the advancing technological sophistication and savvy of those less scrupulous media providers.

Lastly, in recent years much light has been shed on the ways people learn. In science education, for example, the construct of "content-in-context" currently undergirds the design of many new approaches to curriculum and instruction. Content-in-context refers to the powerful influences that situation and context exert on learners as they connect to new ideas and information in the process of meaning making. Thus, designers of internet resources will need to consider ways in which local contexts, issues, and values can be embedded in the process of localizing and versioning web-based materials. In doing so, content providers can contribute to the preservation of locality, cultural identity, and heritage as well as the intellectual growth of the targeted users.

References

American Association for the Advancement of Science (AAAS). (1989). *Science for all Americans: A Project 2061 report on literacy goals in science, mathematics, and technology.* Washington, DC: AAACS.
—. (1990). *Science for all Americans: Project 2061.* New York: Oxford University Press.
—. (1993). *Benchmarks for science literacy: Project 2061.* New York: Oxford University Press.
Armstrong, R.B. (1996). The region's long-term economic and demographic outlook. In D. Hill (Ed.), *The Baked Apple?* (pp. 29-42). New York: The New York Academy of Sciences.
Aufderheide, P. (1993). *Media Literacy: A report of the national leadership conference on media literacy.* Queenstown, MD: Aspen Institute. (ERIC Document Reproduction Service No. ED365294)
Blanpied, W. (Ed.). (2004). Proceedings of the Trilateral Seminar on Science, Society, and the Internet (East-West Center, Honolulu, Hawaii, December 14-16, 2003). Published by George Mason University. Retrieved January 15, 2007, from:
http://www.law.gmu.edu/nctl/stpp/us_japan_pubs/internet_contents.pdf
China Internet Network Information Center (CNNIC) (2006). The 17th statistical survey on the Internet development in China. Retrieved December 8, 2006, from:
www.cnnic. net.cn/download/2006/17threport-en.pdf
China Association for Science and Technology (CAST). Retrieved November 23, 2006, from http://english.cast.org.cn/index.html
China Research Institute for Science Popularization (CRISP). Retrieved November 24, 2006, from:
http://www.scidev.net/ms/pcst2005/index.cfm?pageid=458

Craven, J. (2005). Personal and professional growth. In S. Farenga and D. Ness (Eds.), *Encyclopedia of Education and Human Development* (pp. 169-171). New York: M.E. Sharpe.

Craven, J., Hand, B., & Prain, V. (2002). Assessing explicit and tacit conceptions of the nature of science among pre-service elementary teachers. *International Journal of Science Education*, 24, 785-802.

Department for Education and Skills. (2006). *The supply and demand for science, technology, engineering and mathematics skills in the UK economy.* (Research Report No. 775). Nottingham, United Kingdom: DfES Publications.

The Economist. (2006, March 2). Internet Infrastructure. Retrieved December 5, 2006, from: http://www.economist.com/business/displaystory.cfm?story_id=5582257

—. (2006, April 27). Special Report: The party, the people and the power of cyber-talk—China and the Internet. Retrieved February 16, 2007, from: *http://www.economist.com/world/displaystory.cfm?story_id=6850080*

Frechette, J.D. (2002). *Developing media literacy in cyberspace: Pedagogy and critical learning for the Twenty-First century classroom.* Westport, CT: Praeger Publishers.

Gallagher, M.D., & Cooper, K.B. (2004, September). A nation online: Entering the broadband age. *United States Department of Commerce.* Retrieved November 5, 2006, from http://www.ntia.doc.gov/reports/anol/index.html

George Mason School of Law. (2006). US-China cooperation program in science policy, research, and education. Retrieved January 19, 2007, from http://www.law.gmu.edu/nctl/stpp/us_china.php

GLORIAD (2004). GLORIAD: Global Ring Network for Advanced Applications Development. Retrieved November 10, 2006, from http://www.gloriad.org/gloriad/index.html

Gräber, W., Nentwig, P., Becker, H. J., Sumfleth, E., Pitton, A., Wollweber, K. et al. (2001). Scientific literacy: From theory to practice. In H. Behrendt, H. Dahncke, R. Duit, W. Gräber, M. Komorek, A. Kross et al. (Eds.), *Research in science education: Past, present, and future (pp. 61-71).* Boston, MA: Kluwer Academic Publishers.

Grayson, B. (n.d.). The Smile Train Partners (United States); New York University: Institute of Reconstructive Plastic Surgery. Retrieved January 15, 2006, from http://medpro.smiletrain.org/medpro/partners/us/nyu.htm

Harlen, W. (2001). The assessment of scientific literacy in the OECD/PISA project. In H. Behrendt, H. Dahncke, R. Duit, W. Gräber, M. Komorek, A. Kross et al. (Eds.), *Research in science education: Past, present, and future (pp. 49-60).* Boston, MA: Kluwer Academic Publishers.

Harrington, J. (2001, November). *The Digital Divide: Lessons from the People's Republic of China*. Paper presented at the Midwest International Studies Association Meeting, St. Louis, MO.

Hepeng, J. (2002, July 10). *China promises universal science literacy*. Retrieved November 25, 2006, from: http://www.scidev.net/News/index.cfm?fuseaction=readNews&itemid=187 &language=1

IAE (n.d.). *Brief history of IEA*. Retrieved December 12, 2006, from: http://www.iea.nl/brief_history_of_iea.html

ICANN disputes China domain report (2006, March 1). *InfoWorld*. Retrieved May 28, 2007 from: http://www.infoworld.com/article/06/03/01/76004_030106HNicannchina_1. html

International Association for the Evaluation of Educational Achievement (2006). TIMSS 2007. Retrieved December 20, 2006, from: http://timss.bc.edu/TIMSS2007/about.html

Keeping a democratic web. (2006, May 2). *The New York Times*, A24

Kim, K., Collins Hagedorn, M., Williamson, J., & Chapman, C. (2004). Participation in adult education and lifelong learning: 2000–01 (NCES 2004–050). US Department of Education, National Center for Education Statistics. Washington, DC: U.S.Government Printing Office.

La Ferle, C., Edwards, S. M., & Lee, W.N. (2000). Teen's use of traditional media and the Internet. *Journal of Advertising Research, 40*(3), 55-66.

McConnaughey, J. W., & Lader, W. (1998*). Falling through the Net II: New data on the digital divide*. National Telecommunications and Information Administration. Retrieved December 24, 2006, from: http://www.ntia.doc.gov/ntiahome/net2/

National Research Council (1996). *National Science Education Standards.* Washington DC: National Academy Press.

National Science Board (2006). *Science and Engineering Indicators 2006*. Two Volumes. Arlington, VA: National Science Foundation.

NCES (n.d.). Program for International Student Assessment: Overview. Retrieved November 5, 2006, from http://nces.ed.gov/Surveys/PISA/

Organisation for Economic Co-operation and Development (n.d.). What PISA Produces. Retrieved December 14, 2006, from: http://www.pisa.oecd.org/pages/0,2966,en_32252351_32236130_1_1_1_1_ 1,00.html

Osborne, J. (2002). Science without literacy: A ship without a sail? *Cambridge Journal of Education, 32*(2), 203-218.

O'Donnell, K. (2006). Adult education participation in 2004-2005 (NCES 2006-077). U.S.Department of Education. Washington, DC: National Center for Education Statistics.

Paolillo, J. Pimienta, D., & Prado, D. (2005). Measuring linguistic diversity on the internet. UNESCO Publications for the World Summit on the Information Society. Retrieved January 15, 2007, from: http://unesdoc.unesco.org/images/0014/001421/142186e.pdf

Parsad, B., & Jones, J. (2005). Internet access in U.S.public schools and classrooms: 1994-2003 (NCES 2005-015). U.S. Department of Education. Washington, DC: National Center for Education Statistics.

People's Daily Online. (2006, February 28). China adds top-level domain. Retrieved May 28, 2007 from: http://english.people.com.cn/200602/28/eng20060228_246712.html.

Pitrelli, N. (2005). The new "Chinese dream" regards science communication. *Journal of Science Communication, 4*(2). Retrieved November 25, 2006, from http://jcom.sissa.it/archive/04/02/F040201/

Potashnik, M., & Capper, J. (1998). Distance education: Growth and diversity. *Finance & Development, March 1998,* 42-45.

Potter, W. J. (2001). *Media Literacy* (2nd Ed.). Thousand Oaks, California: Sage Publications.

Protecting Internet Democracy. (2007, January 3). *New York Times.* Retrieved January 8, 2007, from: http://select.nytimes.com/search/restricted/article?res=F20C11FD3C540C70 8 CDDA80894DF404482

ResearchSEA (2006). China Research Institute for Science Popularization. Retrieved on November 25, 2006, from: http://www.researchsea.com/html/institutions.php/ iid/43/research/china_research_institute_for_science_popularization_.html

Rong, L. (2001). *Seizing the opportunity to cross digital divide.* Retrieved November 30, 2006, from http://www.Asiasociety.org/speeches/rong.html

Sagan, C. (1995). *The demon-haunted world: Science as a candle in the dark.* New York: Random House.

Schwab, J. J. (1962). *The teaching of science as enquiry.* Cambridge, MA: Harvard University Press.

Setzer, J. C., & Lewis, L. (2005). Distance education courses for public elementary and secondary school students: 2002-03 (NCES 2005-010). U.S.Department of Education. Washington, DC: National Center for Education Statistics.

Shanshan, W. (2007, January 17). *Boys will be boys, but Net addicts younger than in the West.* Retrieved January, 18, 2007, from http://chinadaily.com.cn/china/2007-01/17/content_785210.htm

U.S. Department of Education, National Center for Education Statistics (n.d.) *Internet access in U.S.public schools and classrooms: 1994–2002,* NCES 2004-011, by Anne Kleiner and Laurie Lewis. Washington, DC. Retrieved December 10, 2006, from the U.S.Department of Education Website: http://nces.ed.gov/pubsearch/pubsinfo.asp?pubid=2004011

UNESCO (2005). UNESCO and WSIS: Toward knowledge societies. Retrieved December 1, 2006, from: http://portal.unesco.org/ci/en/ev.php-URL_ID=2128&URL_DO= DO_TOPIC&URL_SECTION=201.html

Wells, J., & Lewis, L. (2006). *Internet access in U.S.public schools and classrooms: 1994–2005.* Retrieved January 01, 2007, from the U.S.Department of Education Website: http://nces.ed.gov/Pubsearch/pubsinfo.asp?pubid=2007020

Wolpert, L. (1992). *The Unnatural nature of science.* London: Faber and Faber Limited.

WSIS (2003). Building the information society: A global challenge in the new millennium (Document WSIS-03/GENEVA/DOC/4-E 12 December 2003, Original: English). Retrieved November 20, 2006, from: http://www.itu.int/wsis/docs/geneva/official/dop.html

CHAPTER TWELVE

MEDIA LITERACY IN THE US AND CHINA

FRAN C. BLUMBERG, DANIEL P. AULD, LAUREN FRANKLE, SHERYL F. PACKMAN, AND ALLISON J. SCHWARTZ, FORDHAM UNIVERSITY

Media literacy is generally defined as the ability to "access, analyze, evaluate, and create messages" (Livingstone, 2004; p. 3; also see Alliance for Media Literacy, 2005) in diverse media contexts such as newspapers, TV, and the internet. Brown (1998) further characterizes media literacy as encompassing the ability to effectively analyze and use

> print journalism, cinematic productions, radio and television programming, and even computer-mediated information and exchange (including real-time interactive exploration through the global internet) (p. 44).

According to Messaris (1998), this overall ability should encompass an understanding of how media functions including

> their economic foundations, organizational structures, psychological effects, social consequences, and, above all, their "language," that is, the representational conventions and rhetorical strategies of ads, TV programs, movies, and other forms of mass media content (p. 70).

Implicit in these definitions, particularly that of Messaris, is that the media literate individual is aware of the cultural nuances and stereotypes that underlie media-based messages and content (see Heiligmann & Shields, 2005, for their related discussions of assumptions underlying magazine advertisements). Both Messaris (1998) and Hobbs (1998) also view media literacy as empowering individuals within a specific culture to negotiate the impact that a given media form has on their lives. This form of self-regulation is particularly salient as the transmission of media messages dissolves cultural and international boundaries;

a situation now confronting the US and China as the latter progresses toward
revenue based development of media products, and far greater economic
involvement with the former.

Accompanying this growing movement toward economic interdependency is
the negotiation of different values, and presumably, different goals for media
access and for media literacy education directed at young media users in
particular. For example, of greatest current agreement across both the US and
China is the perceived vulnerability of its children amidst the increasing
sophistication of media formats and increases in the sharing and dissemination
of information with offline friends and online strangers. This vulnerability,
which remains largely unsubstantiated from an empirical standpoint, is
presumed to reflect child and adolescent media users' lack of requisite
knowledge or cognitive ability to make informed decisions about the goals,
sources, and veracity of the information to which they now have access via mass
media (see Christ & Potter, 1998; Frechette, 2006; Livingstone & Bober, 2006).

A fairly recent demonstration of China's concern with media literacy was
reflected in a 2004 international media literacy conference that China hosted for
educators and media researchers to address the effects of mass media on
Chinese consumers (Media literacy crucial, 2004). Among the concerns raised
were how best to counter the implicit endorsements by television and the
internet of lives of excess, fallacious information about consumer products as
presented in advertisements, and violent or pornographic material content that
might be shown in popular video games. Internet exposure also garners much
attention in and outside China. For example, China has expressed strong
concerns about the perils of internet addictions that at times, warrant
hospitalization (Sebag-Montefiore, 2005).

However, the internet enjoys less usage than more dominant forms of
Chinese mass media; namely, print media as represented by the widely read and
distributed newspapers and, the advancing frontier of network television. This
chapter will provide snapshots illustrating differential prevalence of print media,
television, and the internet in both US and China, and discuss the implications
for media literacy goals and the education as both countries move toward
greater involvement and sharing of media with one another. (More extensive
information about the media industry in China is presented in Yao, this volume.)
Differential considerations of media literacy for both the US and China also will
be considered.

Print media: Emphasis on newspapers

China

At present, China publishes over 2000 newspapers and 9000 magazines (China First Media Service, 2004). Newspaper circulation in China reached 90 million readers in 2005, accounting for the largest share (22%) of the world's total (China First Media Service, 2004). Several types of widely-read newspapers are available to the Chinese public. Party newspapers are dedicated to consideration of political administration at the national, regional, district, and town level. This type of newspaper is exemplified by *People's Daily*, which as the main organ of the Central China Communist Party, has among the greatest circulation at 1,728,000 (see Massey & Luo, 2005). State newspapers cover issues relevant to all levels of administration such as the daily *China Economics Times*. English-language newspapers are intended for tourists and expatriates (BBC, 2006). *China Daily,* based in Beijing, exemplifies this particular form of newspaper and enjoys a fairly strong print circulation of about 800,000 (see Massey & Luo, 2005) and an increasing internet presence. Recent spin-offs of *China Daily* for children and adolescents include *21st Century,* which is designed as an educational supplement for teachers and students in Chinese classrooms. The goals of this supplement are to promote English comprehension, and facilitate exposure to colloquial expressions and trends in Western culture. For example, the June 7, 2005 edition of *21st Century Teens-Kids Edition,* headlined by an article, in English, about International Children's Day on June 1, was accompanied by a photograph of the Chinese president Hu Jintao talking to a group of young children. Another feature included a segment highlighting US colloquial expressions such as "Take heart" and "You can say that again."

Unlike most US newspapers, China has been relatively slow to publish online web companions to its papers. However, this situation is subject to change as Chinese newspapers move toward a more western model of advertising as the primary source of revenue. However, barriers to newspaper presence on the internet remain largely financial. In fact, *People's Daily* may be among the few newspapers with the financial resources available to develop a strong web presence (Massey & Luo, 2005).

US

Within the US and other Western countries such as the UK, the nexus of newspapers and internet is more common, although the latter is rapidly eclipsing the former as a source of news. The Newspaper Association of America (NAA), a nonprofit organization, compiles the statistics on daily and Sunday readership for the 1,452 daily and 6,659 weekly newspapers published in the US (NAA, 2007). Two of these daily newspapers are national (*USA Today* & *Wall Street Journal*). The majority of daily newspaper readers as of 2006, according to the NAA, were aged 35 and older, encompassing the baby boom generation. By comparison, the smallest group was that of individuals aged 18-24, which only comprised 13% of total newspaper readers. In fact, according to a 2005 report published by the NAA, only 54% of children aged 12-17 reported reading a newspaper for one or more hours over a given week, and for many, the section read was the comics. The relatively limited newspaper reading found among pre-adolescents and adolescents, most likely reflects greater enfranchisement of digital technology in which the activities engaged in are more social than information-seeking in nature (see Subrahmanyam, et al., 2001 for discussion of children's development in light of new forms of media). One also may advance the more obvious point that newspapers are designed primarily for adult readers.

Television

China

As noted by Yao (this volume), TV is the most popular form of media. The main venue for television in China is provided through China Central Television (CCTV), established in 1958 at the time of the Great Leap Forward. At the time of its establishment, CCTV was designed to disseminate governmental information, similar to the *People's Daily* (the national voice of the Party). More recently, CCTV has shown greater movement toward commercial and entertainment venues. However, television remains strongly linked to political and social goals.

The initial mandate for the Central Broadcasting Bureau had been propaganda, education, and cultural enrichment. However, that mandate was often compromised as television ownership during the 1960s was a luxury. In fact, at the time of its establishment in 1958, television viewing was a collective work activity, and most of the available television sets were the property of the party. By 1963, as Russian withdrawal of financial support was continuing, only television stations in major cities such as Beijing, Shanghai, and Tianjin remained in service. At the time of the Cultural Revolution in 1966, the development of television programming was at a standstill. This situation was somewhat rectified by 1967, at which time, programming was essentially dictated by party politics (Chang, 2002).

By the mid-1980s, CCTV clearly became entrenched as a political arm for transmitting news. At this time, cities and counties with sufficient revenue were now able to start their own television stations and CCTV's complete monopoly over television stations ended. Still, television largely remains a vehicle for education rather than revenue. In fact, only during the Deng Xiaoping era in the late 1970s was the ban on advertising lifted. In 1987, the first set of public service announcements was aired (Chang, 2002).

Television currently has far-reaching effects given its accessibility among the majority of China's population. Contributions to this increase in coverage may be attributed to the small but steadily expanding number of provincial television stations, and to the more rapidly increasing number of city and county level stations (Esarey, 2005). China potentially has the largest television audience in the world.

At present, 12 channels are offered through CCTV plus four additional channels dedicated to round-the-clock news, music, programming for children, and French and Spanish re-dubbings of the international news presented in Chinese on Channel 4, and a version of that news presented in English on Channel 9. Other stations outside CCTV include channels dedicated to news (Phoenix TV and Phoenix News & Finance broadcast out of Hong Kong), Chinese history (SunTV), music (Channel V), and general entertainment (StarTV which is owned by Rupert Murdoch's News Corporation) (Danwei, 2005).

The major CCTV channels are (adapted from Danwei, 2005):

- Channel 1: General News. This channel produces the main evening news broadcast.
- Channel 2: Business
- Channel 3: Arts
- Channel 4: International (Chinese language)
- Channel 5: Sports
- Channel 6: Movies
- Channel 7: Military and Agriculture with children's programming in the afternoon
- Channel 8: Dramatic series
- Channel 9: International (English version)
- Channel 10: Education
- Channel 11: Peking Opera
- Channel 12: Society and Law

US

As with newspapers, the lines between TV and the internet are increasingly blurred in the US as viewers can watch a television segment they may have missed on a late night talk show on youtube.com, a vastly popular free website for the sharing of video clips, recently purchased by Google. Television viewing still remains among the favorite leisure activities of Americans. The 2007 directory of both US radio and TV stations, prepared by *100000 Watt* (see www.100000watts.com) listed 1790 high power TV stations, 1682 digital TV stations, and 5080 low power TV and FM stations combined.

According to rating data provided by Nielsen for the week of February 12, 2007, the top-rated program on broadcast TV (*American Idol*, which is based on England's popular program *Pop Idol*) attracted 31.19 million viewers; the top-rated cable TV (the *National Basketball Association 2007 Allstar Game*) attracted 6.84 million viewers. According to the 2005 report prepared by the US Census Bureau (2006), over 94% of all Americans had watched TV during the week prior to being surveyed, with the largest percentage (97.3%) of viewers aged 65 and older, and the smallest percentage of viewers (92%) aged 18-24.

Internet

China

China also remains a growing market for internet users but lags behind the US in users given technology available and the prohibitive cost of computers and internet access for most users. According to June 30, 2006 statistics available through the China International Network Information Center (CNNIC), there were 123 million internet users in China, and 788,400 websites. As noted in their January, 2007, Statistical Survey Report on the Internet Development in China, the CNNIC operationally define an internet user as any Chinese citizen, at least 6 years of age, who uses the internet, on average, an hour per week. Thus, as in the US, recognition is made of the young internet user. Of these users, about 17% are under the age of 18. The largest age group represented among internet users (35%) ranges from 18-35 years of age. By educational status, the largest body of internet users is high school students (31%); the smallest body is that with doctoral degrees (4%). Despite prohibitive cost, the greatest point of access for internet users is the home (76%), followed by the work place (33%) and internet cafes (32%) (percentages do not total to 100% given potential for multiple responses).

Presumably, users under the age of 18 are of the greatest societal concern, as is evident in a 2004 *China Daily* article ("Media literacy crucial in 21st century"), which highlighted the launching of a nationwide campaign to block internet content deemed harmful to minors. The fall-out of this campaign also included the closing of internet cafes that provided services to minors (a point we refer to later in our discussion of media literacy).

US

The largest growing form of media in the United States is the internet. In 2005 (see Neilsen//NetRatings, 2006), there were 200 million internet users in the United States or 68%. A recent Kaiser Family Foundation survey among a representative sample of over 1000 US families indicated that 3% of children under the age of 6 had internet access in their bedroom and that 30% of 4-6 year olds had accessed a children's website on their own (Rideout, Vandewater, & Wartella, 2003).

According to the Nielsen//Net Ratings, as of November 2006 (Bausch & Han, 2006), 69.6% of the United States population or 210,080,067 people had used the internet. According to JupiterResearch (2006), the average consumer spent 14 hours a week online. Their findings also show that baby boomers (those individuals born between 1946 and 1964) comprise the largest population of "netizens", or 33% of all total users. More educated adults use the internet, including 91% of those with at least a college degree as compared to only 40% of those with less than a high school education. The Harris Interactive Poll, as reported in the *Wall Street Journal* (2006, May 24), reports that 70% of adults are now online at home and only 35% at are online at work; 22% of users access the internet at another location. These findings are reminiscent of those found among Chinese netizens.

Young children also are spending extensive amounts of time online per week according to a September, 2006 Nielsen//Net Ratings report. Specifically, children aged 2-11 spent nearly 9 and a half hours per week online, whereas children aged 12-17 spent nearly 27 hours online. According to a 2005 report prepared by the NAA, most adolescents used the internet to play games, followed by doing research for school.

Media literacy education in China and the US

As demonstrated at the opening of this chapter, definitions of media literacy are varied and reflect goals ranging from embracing media as a vehicle for democracy and global citizenship to avoiding media as a purveyor of misinformation and deception. An example of the latter extreme is reflected in the Center for Screen-Time Awareness' sponsorship of a US TV-turnoff week in April, 2007 (see www.tvturnoff.org) to promote, as indicated on their website, "empowering people to take control of technology and not letting technology take control of them so they can live healthier lives." China may be seen as promoting a similar, preventative stance toward the media as reflected in their efforts to actively monitor and regulate internet access and to protect its youth from video game and computer addictions. For example, the *South China*

Morning Post reported in 2004 of a 31 year old habitual internet game player who collapsed and died at his screen after playing a game for 20 consecutive hours ("Computer addict dies at screen," March 9). Collectively, these examples attest to a wariness (if not blatant disdain) of content available to children (and as the above news report indicates, adults) disseminated through television and the internet in China.

Clearly, media literacy, as a vehicle for the instruction of critical evaluation and monitoring of media content among vulnerable users, is increasingly a common concern among superpowers such as China, and the US, as well as the UK (arguably, the leader in advancing media literacy within the schools), Australia, Canada, Israel, and South Africa (see Lemish, 2007). The extent of this shared concern may even extend to young adults. For example, US undergraduates have been cited for their lack of diligence in checking the credibility of content acquired via the internet for their academic assignments (Metzger, Flanagan, & Zwarum, 2003).

How media literacy education will take shape in both China and the US as the two continue to explore their evolving relationship and sharing of media forms and content remains a question. As voiced by government ministers at a 2006 Cross Culture Communication Forum, China clearly has strong concerns about its current cultural deficit, and plans to make Chinese cultural products far more accessible internationally in the near future (Jing, 2006). This concern is all the more pressing in the wake of preparations for the Beijing 2008 Olympic Games which is intended by the Chinese to "let the real China be known to the world" (Zhang & Liu, 2007; p. 37).

Media literacy and media literacy education are relatively new in China, dating back only to 1997. However, both the US and China display similar concerns about how best to insure that the eyes and minds of those deemed impressionable are presented with information that promotes their psychological well-being, cognitive enrichment, and physical safety while adhering to culturally-sanctioned and globally-tolerant values.

Addressing these issues will remain elusive, in part, reflecting, on whom and what the onus is placed for media literacy instruction; parents, schools, the government. In the US, concerns about the increasing number of young children's computer, and more specifically, internet use, is reflected in the expanding roster of internet watchdog groups (e.g., Cyberangels.org) and guidelines for usage (e.g., National School Boards Foundation "Safe' Brochure) that have emerged as supplements to legislation such as *The Children's Online Privacy Protection Act*, which became effective in 2000, and specifies protocols to be followed by websites to insure the privacy of their child visitors. Collectively, these efforts are designed to protect child users from infringement of their privacy or safety and also to impart informal lessons on media literacy.

In China, similar preventative measures have emerged in the form of clinics to treat internet addictions and in 2004, the convening of the first International Conference on Media Education and Media Literacy in China (as noted at the beginning of our chapter). The Shanghai People's Congress set a precedent for other local authorities within China, by drafting regulations forbidding individuals younger than age 18 from visiting internet cafes and institutions providing internet services (Media literacy crucial, 2004).

However, the preventative measures put forth by the US and China are no substitute for educating students, young and old, about how best to evaluate the content encountered on the internet, (or presented through TV) so as to separate the wheat from the chaff. Clearly, the global accessibility now permissible through the internet has very positive ramifications for helping to build relations between countries such as the US and China. However, these positive outcomes will require the requisite media literacy skills.

As indicated at the start of our chapter, definitions of media literacy are varied. However, as presented by Lemish (2007), the media literacy skills seen as common to most media education programs largely focus on promoting an understanding that media messages are not created in a vacuum and reflect interests that are economic, social, political, historical, cultural, and aesthetic in nature. How these interests are perceived reflects an interaction between the interpreter, the message, and the cultural context.

How these goals will be incorporated in two countries with common goals to engage in more reciprocal sharing of cultural information, aside from cinema and cuisine (witness the actor Chow Yun-Fat and one of the world's largest US-based Kentucky Fried Chicken fast food restaurants in Beijing), but limited emphasis on media literacy instruction, should provide an interesting historical chapter in the study of media literacy in general. Of particular interest will be how US and China negotiate evaluation of the content that each receives from one another. Will the US continue to endorse the view of China as repressive and isolated? Will China continue to promote the view of the US as pre-occupied with lives of excess and material wealth?

Stay tuned!

Authors' note

We wish to thank John Randall for his insightful comments on points raised in this chapter.

References

Alliance for Media Literacy (2005). What is media literacy? Retrieved October 3, 2005 from www.amla.org/home/media-literacy

Bausch, S., & Han, L. (2006, October 11). US teens graduate from choosing IM buddy icons to creating elaborate social networking profiles, according to Nielsen//NetRatings. Retrieved February 21, 2007, from Nielson//NetRatings Web site: http://www.nielsen-netratings.com/pr/pr_061011.pdf

BBC (2006). BBC News. Country profile: China. Retrieved February 23, 2007 from: http://news.bbc.co.uk/1/hi/world/asia-pacific/country_profiles/1287798.stm

Brown, J.A. (1998). Media literacy perspectives. *Journal of Communication, Winter*, 44-57.

Chang, T-K. (2002). *China's window on the world*. Cresskill, N.J.: Hampton Press.

China First Media Service (2004). Some trends. Retrieved July 25, 2005 from: http:// www.chinafirstmedia.com/data/proposal CFMS2004.engl.pdf.

China Internet Network Information Center (2006). Statistical survey report on the internet development in China (January, 2006). Retrieved October 30, 2006 from http://cnnic.com.cn.

Christ, W.G. & Potter, W.J. (1998). Media literacy, media education, and the academy. *Journal of Communication, 5-15*.

Danwei (2005). China Media Guide (last updated August 7, 2005). Retrieved February 23, 2007 from http://www.danwei.org/China_Media_Guide.htm

Esarey, A. (2005). Cornering the market: State strategies for controlling China's commercial media. *Asian Perspective, 29*, 37-83.

Frechette, J. (2006). Cyber-censorship or cyber-literacy? Envisioning cyber-Learning through media education. In D. Buckingham & R. Willett (Eds.), *Digital Generations. Children, Young People and the New Media* (pp. 149-171). Mahwah, NJ: Lawrence Erlbaum.

Heiligmann, R. & Shield, V.R. (2005). Media literacy, visual syntax, and magazine advertisements: Conceptualizing the consumption of reading by media literate subjects. *Journal of Visual Literacy, 25*, 41-66.

Jing, X. (2006). Absorbing the culture shock. *Beijing Review, 49 (37)*, 23.

JupiterResearch Corporation (2006, January 30). JupiterResearch finds online consumers spend as much time online as in front of the TV. *Business Week*. Retrieved February 21, 2007 from: http://www.jupitermedia.com/corporate/releases/06.01.30newjupresearch.html

Lemish, D. (2007). *Children and television: A global perspective.* Malden, MA: Blackwell Publishing.

Livingstone, S. (2004). Media literacy and the challenge of new information and communication technologies. *The Communication Review, 7,* 3-14.

Livingstone, S. & Bober, M. (2006). Regulating the internet at home: Contrasting the perspectives of children and parents. In D. Buckingham & R. Willett (Eds.), *Digital Generations. Children, Young People and the New Media* (pp. 93-113). Mahwah, NJ: Lawrence Erlbaum.

Massey, B.L. & Luo, W. (2005). Chinese newspapers and market theories of web journalism. *Gazettte, 67,* 359-371.

Media literacy crucial in 21st century. (2004, October 4). *China Daily,* 3.

Messaris, P. (1998). Visual aspects of media literacy. *Journal of Communication, 48,* 70-80.

Metzger, M.J., Flanagan, A.J., & Zwarun, L. (2003). College student Web use, perceptions of information credibility, and verification behavior. *Computers & Education, 41,* 271-290.

National Center for Education Statistics (2003). *Computer and internet use by students in 2003.* Retrieved February 21, 2007, from: http://nces.ed.gov/pubs2006/2006065.pdf

Newspaper Association of America (2005). Targeting teens. Retrieved February 23, 2007 from http://www.naa.org/marketscope/TargetingTeensBrief.pdf

—. (2007). The Source: Newspapers by the Numbers. Retrieved February 22, 2007 from http://www.naa.org/thesource/

Nielsen Media Research (2007). Inside TV ratings. Retrieved February 22, 2007 from http://www.nielsenmedia.com

Nielsen//NetRatings (2006). *United States of America: Internet usage and broadband usage report.* Retrieved February 21, 2007, from Internet World Stats Web site: http://www.internetworldstats.com/am/us.htm

People's Daily Online (November 30, 2005). Harry Potter's "Goblet" conjures up 66.56 million yuan in China. Retrieved from: http://english.people.com.cn/200511/30/eng20051130_224505.html

Potter, W. J. (2004). Argument for the need for a cognitive theory of media literacy. *American Behavioral Scientist, 48,* 266-272.

Rideout, V.J., Vandewater, E.A., & Wartella, E.A. (2003, Fall). *Zero to six: Electronic media in the lives of toddlers and preschoolers.* Menlo Park, CA: Kaiser Family Foundation Report.

Sebag-Montefiore, P. (20, November, 2005). China's young escape into the web. *The Observer.* Retrieved from: http://observer.guardian.co.uk/international/story/0,6903,1646663,00.html

Subrahmanyam, K., Kraut, R., Greenfield, P., & Gross, E. (2001). New forms of electronic media. In D.G. Singer & J.L. Singer (Eds.), *Handbook of children and the media* (pp. 73-99). London: Sage Publications.

US Census Bureau (2006). Table 1112: Multimedia audiences—Summary 2005. US Census Bureau. Retrieved February 23, 2007 from: http://www.census.gov/prod/2006pubs/07statab/infocomm.pdf

Wall Street Journal Online (2006, May 24). *The Harris Poll: Poll shows more US adults are going online at home.* Retrieved February 21, 2007, from: http://online.wsj.com/public/article/SB114840389678260791-IREjYVgN_rGLee3_6Djin1jeJZc_20070523.html?mod=rss_free

Zhang, J. & Liu, Q. (2007). Beijing 2008 Olympic games: Letting the world discover the real China. *China Today, 56(2)*, 36-39.

CONTRIBUTORS

Daniel P. Auld is a doctoral student in the educational psychology program at Fordham University and Director of Technology Communications and Academic Support for Fordham University School of Law. Daniel's research interests are users' engagement in educational materials across media platforms.

Mark Blades is a Senior Lecturer in Developmental Psychology at the University of Sheffield. He has carried out research in children's eyewitness testimony, police interviews with children, children's environmental knowledge, and children's understanding of advertising. He has co-authored or co-edited several books on children's development including *Children's Source Monitoring* (Erlbaum, 2000), *The Cognition of Geographic Space* (Tauris, 2002), *Understanding Children's Development, 4th Edition* (Blackwell, 2003), *Advertising to Children on TV: Content, Content, Impact, and Regulation* (Erlbaum, 2004), and *Children and Their Environments: Learning, Using, and Designing Spaces* (Cambridge, 2005).

Fran C. Blumberg is an Associate Professor and coordinator of the educational psychology program at Fordham University. Her research interests concern the development of children's attention and attention strategies in the context of academic and non-academic learning situations. She has published and received funding for her research concerning children's attention and learning while playing video games and is a co-editor of *The Design of Instruction and Evaluation* (Erlbaum, 2004).

John A. Craven, III is an Associate Professor in the Department of Human Development and Learning at Dowling College. His research interests include science teacher education, non-formal learning environments, the nature of science, and science literacy. He teaches courses in science, environmental, and technology education.

Shalom M. Fisch is the president of MediaKidz Research & Consulting and former vice president of program research at Sesame Workshop. For over 20 years, he has used educational practice and empirical research to help create TV series, websites, magazines, and other media that both entertain and educate children.

Lauren Frankle is a doctoral student in the educational psychology program at Fordham University. Her research interests include the impact of media exposure on body image and associated eating behaviors in adolescent females.

Tracy Hogan is an Assistant Professor at Adelphi University where she teaches courses in adolescent development and science education. Her research interests include cognition and learning, educational media, and science literacy. She has published works in the fields of educational psychology and science education.

Li Yongna is a doctoral student in the Department of Psychology at the University at Albany, State University of New York. Her main research interest is visual attention. She has published articles on the visual search and attentional processing of compound stimuli.

Liz Nice is a Lecturer in journalism at the University of Sheffield after having been Deputy Editor of Britain's *Take a Break* and *More!* and editor-in-chief of two magazines for girls including *Bliss* and *Twist*. Liz continues to write freelance articles for a variety of magazines and newspapers.

Caroline J. Oates is a Lecturer in Marketing at the University of Sheffield Management School. Her main research interest is marketing to children. She has published several journal articles and co-authored a book in this area. She also is a member of the Centre for the Study of Childhood and Youth, at the University of Sheffield.

Sheryl F. Packman is a doctoral student in the educational psychology program at Fordham University. She is also a research intern at the College Board. She has co-authored articles and presentations concerning adults' learning while playing video games.

Min-Kyung Park is a doctoral student in the educational psychology program at Fordham University. Her research interests include the integration of technology in classrooms and the study of motivation.

Allison J. Schwartz is a completing her professional diploma in the school psychology program at Fordham University. Her research interests include children's responses to internet-based advertising.

Anbin Shi is Associate Professor of media and cultural studies in the School of Journalism and Communications at Tsinghua University. His research interests include media and cultural studies, intercultural communications, and Sino-US comparative journalism. His books include *Crisis Communication and Media Relation* and *A Comparative Approach to Redefining Chineseness in the Era of Globalization.*

Tom Tarnowsky has extensive experience as a photo-researcher and photo editor for feature and news publications, most notably, *Newsweek Magazine* and *The New Yorker.* He is currently completing a book chronicling the development of the water tunnel system in New York.

Bo Wang is an undergraduate psychology major in the School of Psychology at Beijing Normal University.

Nailene Chou Wiest is a visiting scholar at the Centre of Asian Studies at the University of Hong Kong. A journalist with 23 years of experience, she has worked for the Knight Ridder Newspapers, Reuters News Agency, and the Hong Kong-based English language newspaper, *South China Morning Po*st. She was also a Knight International Press Fellow from 2006-2007.

Jie Xu is a doctoral student at the College of Communication and Information Sciences at the University of Alabama. Her research interests include social marketing and international advertising.

Bin Yang is a graduate student and member of the State Key Lab of Cognitive Neuroscience and Learning at Beijing Normal University. His research interests concern visual attention.

Yichen Yao graduated from the Communication University of China, with a Masters degree in Mass Communication Study. Yichen has been involved in media analysis and survey practices for clients such as the China Center Television Station, CSM, and Liaoning Television Station. Yichen is currently a researcher for Millward Brown in Beijing, China.

Yinjiao Ye is a doctoral student at the College of Communication and Information Sciences at the University of Alabama. Her research focuses on health, communication, media entertainment, and international advertising.

Xue-min Zhang is an Associate Professor in the School of Psychology and Cognitive Neuroscience Institute at Beijing Normal University. His research interests include the study of visual perception and visual attention as well as the human-computer interface. He has published *Experimental Psychology: Theory, Method and Technology*.

Peng Zhou is a graduate student in the School of Psychology at Beijing Normal University. His research interests concern issues in clinical psychology.

Shuhua Zhou is an Associate Professor in the Department of Telecommunications and Film within the College of Communication & Information Sciences at the University of Alabama. His research focuses on the processing of mediated messages.

INDEX